CW01086692

COMMUNICATING WITH THE IBM PC SERIES

COMMUNICATING WITH THE IBM PC SERIES

Concepts, Hardware, Software, Networking

GILBERT HELD
4-Degree Consulting
Macon, Georgia, USA

John Wiley & Sons
Chichester · New York · Brisbane · Toronto · Singapore

Copyright © 1988 by John Wiley & Sons Ltd.

All rights reserved.

No part of this book may be reproduced by any means, or
transmitted, or translated into a machine language without the
written permission of the publisher.

Library of Congress Cataloging-in-Publication Data:
Held, Gilbert, 1943–
    Communicating with the IBM PC series.

    1. Local area networks (Computer networks)
2. IBM microcomputers.   I. Title.
TK5105.7.H438   1987   005.6′8   87–29595
ISBN 0 471 91667 6 (pbk.)

British Library Cataloguing in Publication Data:
Held, Gilbert
    Communicating with the IBM PC series:
    concepts, hardware
    software, networking
    1. Data transmission systems   2. IBM
    personal computer
    I. Title
    004.6′028′54165   TK5105

    ISBN 0 471 91667 6

Typeset by Photo·Graphics, Honiton, Devon
Printed in Great Britain by St Edmundsbury Press Ltd.
Bury St Edmunds, Suffolk

Contents

Preface

The purpose of this book as the title implies is fourfold: to explain the fundamental concepts associated with data communications, examine the communications hardware and software features that enable members of the IBM PC Series and compatible personal computers to communicate in a variety of ways and, using the preceding information as a foundation, to explore the various networking strategies associated with integrating personal computer communications requirements into data communications networks.

Since the variety of personal computer users requiring communications can range from individuals to members of Fortune 500 corporations, I have purposely written this book in a modular fashion. By this concept, although each chapter builds upon a previous chapter, one may read each chapter as a separate entity if one so desires. Thus, an individual with limited or no knowledge of data communications might begin his or her reading with Chapter 1, while persons with a previous background in communications might wish to read one or more chapters of particular interest to them.

To assist readers in their communications hardware, software and information utility selection process, I have included several lists of features one should consider as well as an explanation of such features. In addition, I have included numerous examples illustrating the operational utilization of software programs and information utility services that can be used as a guide by the reader for selecting a product or service most appropriate to his or her particular requirement. Since data communications services is one of the most rapidly evolving technological areas, I have purposely avoided directly comparing the features and services of information utilities, packet networks and electronic mail vendors with one another. Instead, after explaining the utilization and operation of one or more systems in each category, I have included a list of vendors in each category as well as their addresses to provide readers with a mechanism to obtain product guides and other relevant information they may require.

Communications is truly a mechanism to obtain a 'window to the world'. In view of this, the author encourages readers with limited exposure to communications to consider purchasing the introductory packages of several vendors that typically permit five hours of on-line usage for a minimal charge. Such introductory packages represent a low-cost mechanism for readers to obtain an understanding of the utilization of information utilities, the use of packet networks and electronic mail systems. For persons with communications experience, it is hoped that the detailed description of hardware, software and networking strategies will permit those readers to make more effective decisions regarding their individual or corporate communications.

Gilbert Held
Macon, GA

Acknowledgements

To write a book requires a tremendous effort, of which the author, although having the primary responsibility, is but one of numerous persons in the link between the initial concept and the book you are now reading.

First, I would like to thank the hardware and software vendors that were gracious enough to provide me with evaluation copies of their products, which I always managed to return prior to the end of the evaluation period, although this was difficult to do. While I would like to individually thank each organization, the responses to my requests so exceeded my expectations that rather than devote several pages to acknowledging their efforts I would like to issue a 'collective thank you', since the reader will become familiar with their products as he or she reads this book. In addition, I would like to express my appreciation to Auerbach Publishers and *Data Communications* magazine for permission to use extracts from a series of articles I previously authored covering intelligent modems and communications software.

As an old-fashioned writer I have not been able to break the habit of using a pen and pad which provides me with a mechanism to easily draw schematics and review each chapter several times, usually adding more material each time via a cryptic insertion process and forward and backward references, and somehow it all always gets proofed and typed correctly. Thus, once again I am indebted to Carol Ferrell for her fine effort in converting my notes and drawings into a manuscript.

Last but not least I must thank my family for their understanding during the evenings and weekends I closed the door to my study and wrote this book.

CHAPTER ONE

Introduction

Although the IBM Personal Computer was introduced during the summer of 1981, its effect upon users requiring desktop computational capability is probably as pronounced as the effect of the telephone and duplicating machine upon the typical office worker. In only a few short years, the IBM PC became a *de facto* personal computer standard to which over 50 hardware vendors measure their products' compatibility. Today it is difficult to find a business, education institution or government agency that does not have a large and growing base of IBM PCs or compatible devices.

The variety of applications for which the members of the IBM PC family and compatible computers can be used is limited only by one's imagination and the physical constraints of one's system. By introducing a series of personal computer products to include the original PC, the PC XT, the Portable Personal Computer, the Personal Computer Advanced Technology, which is referred to as the PCAT, the PC Convertible and the PS/2 series, IBM has provided personal computing systems to satisfy the requirements of users in the home and in business, as well as the executive on the go. While word processing and electronic spreadsheet programs are by far the primary software applications utilized with personal computers, no less important is the computer's ability to transfer and receive information via the process known as data communications. In fact, the variety of personal computer applications that are dependent upon a data-communications capability is so pervasive that in a few years time it will be hard to imagine any personal computer being sold without this capability included as a standard feature.

In this chapter, we will explore the rationale for obtaining a communications capability for one's personal computer by investigating a few of the many applications that are dependent upon this capability. While these applications are but a small example of the diverse scope by which data communications extends one's computational and processing power, they illustrate the fact that this capability, in effect, opens a 'window to the world' for the personal computer user.

Information utilities

A modern phenomenon of the personal computing age, information utilities can best be described as vendors that have constructed elaborate databases of information as well as developed a diversity of functions that can be accessed via data communications. Today such vendors as CompuServe, The Source and Dow Jones, to name but a few information utilities, provide the capability for subscribers to retrieve information as diverse as encyclopedia data from keyword searches to the latest financial information. Access to these information utilities is as simple as dialing a telephone number and entering one's user identification and password, resulting in the growth in their subscriber base to several million persons.

Bulletin boards

In early 1978, the first electronic bulletin board was established in Chicago. Known as the Computerized Bulletin Board System, this electronic bulletin board was designed to promote the exchange of information and software among members of the Chicago Area Computer Hobbyists Exchange Club. Since then, the number of electronic bulletin board systems has proliferated in proportion to the growth in the installed base of personal computers, with well over 1000 systems currently providing access to personal computer users via the direct dial telephone network. Today personal computer users can access general purpose and specialized bulletin boards to transmit and receive messages, obtain news about club meetings, new software reviews and similar subjects; buy and sell all types of goods in addition to computer hardware and software; and exchange programs by uploading their files into the bulletin board system and downloading programs from the bulletin board into their system. Specialized bulletin board areas of interest run the gamut from public domain software exchange to computer games and dating services.

Accessing the corporate mainframe

While the primary purpose for obtaining a personal computer resides in its computational capability, it can also be used to replace a conventional terminal connected to the corporate mainframe. In doing so, the personal computer user can obtain access to the corporate database as well as retain the ability to communicate with information utilities and bulletin boards by the appropriate selection of hardware and software. Although at first glance the replacement of a terminal by a personal computer may appear to be a simple process, in actuality this task can be a complex selection of the appropriate hardware and software based upon the structure of one's existing data communications network and the requirement to interface one's personal computer in an economical and efficient manner. As an example of this complexity, consider an organization that desires to utilize a member of the IBM PC Series as an IBM 3278 terminal. A few of the networking options available for consideration to connect the personal computer to the mainframe include the use of a protocol converter and emulation software on the personal computer; the use of specialized software on both the personal computer and the mainframe; the installation of a hardware board into the system unit of the personal computer to obtain a coaxial connection from the personal computer to a control unit, which in turn is connected to a mainframe; the use of a value-added carrier which performs protocol conversion via software and the interconnection of a personal computer to a local area network where the network has a gateway to the mainframe.

In this book, each of the previously mentioned networking techniques as well as other methods that can be employed to interconnect personal computers, personal computers and minicomputers and personal computers and mainframe computers will be covered. The examples illustrating these networking techniques were developed to provide the reader with a firm indication of the advantages and disadvantages associated with each networking strategy and should serve as a practical guide for integrating personal computer communications requirements into existing and planned corporate networks.

Local area networking

As a mechanism for moving information between devices located on the same premises, local area networks can play a key role in the total telecommunications requirements of organizations that have multiple personal computers. Such networks permit businesses and educational institutions as well as other organizations to easily transfer data between personal computers. In addition, some local area networks provide the capability to integrate voice, facsimile and video information with data on a common cable system while other local area networks provide the additional capability of linking different types of personal computers and large mainframes throughout a building or a campus.

By providing a common data-transport mechanism, local area networks permit personal computer users to share the use of peripheral devices to include letter-quality printers and large-capacity fixed disks. In such situations, multiple copies of application programs may become unnecessary as a personal computer user may be able to download a particular program he or she wishes to use into his or her computer from a central repository on the network. In addition, such features as electronic messaging between users becomes possible, which can be used to enhance the productivity of most office workers.

4

Electronic mail

While local area networks may provide a mechanism for the transfer of electronic messages between users on the net, such transfers are obviously localized to the network. For the traveling executive, company personnel at distributed locations, or individuals who wish to communicate with each other through the facilities of a third party that acts as a message relay service, an alternative means of messaging is required. This alternative mechanism will most likely consist of the facilities of one or more of the numerous electronic mail services that have commenced operation during the early 1980s. Subscribers to these services can perform a variety of tasks to include sending messages to the electronic mailboxes of other subscribers, sending mailgrams and interfacing to the worldwide Telex system.

Summary

The five application areas previously discussed represent some of the major communications-related uses of personal computers and form a firm basis for obtaining a communications capability for one's personal computer. Prior to discussing each of these data-communications-based applications in detail we will first focus our attention upon fundamental communications concepts and the hardware characteristics of the IBM PC product series as well as the various aspects of communications devices and software programs one must consider. This information is designed to provide the reader with a foundation of knowledge concerning the hardware and software required to enable personal computers to communicate as well as the concepts to enable the reader to understand the various methods by which personal computers can be linked into a communications network and the advantages, disadvantages, constraints and economics associated with these methods.

Each of the following chapters in this book was written as a separate entity, permitting readers to skim over or skip chapters whose contents they may be familiar with. Thus, as an example, a reader with a basic understanding of communications concepts might wish to skim through Chapter 2. Although this 'chapter modularity' was incorporated in this book to accommodate persons with a fundamental knowledge of communications, readers with limited exposure to data communications can also take advantage of its structure by reading chapters in the order of interest once Chapter 2 is read.

CHAPTER TWO

Fundamental Concepts

To transmit information between two locations it is necessary to have a transmitter, a receiver, and a transmission medium which provides a path between the transmitter and the receiver. In addition to transmitting signals, a transmitter must be capable of translating information from a form created by humans or machines into a signal suitable for transmission over the transmission medium. The transmission medium provides a path to convey the information to the receiver without introducing a prohibitive amount of signal distortion that could change the meaning of the transmitted signal. The receiver then converts the signal from its transmitted form into a form intelligible to humans or machines.

While the transmission of data may appear to be a simple process, many factors govern the success or failure of a communications session. In addition, the performance and economics associated with the use of an IBM Personal Computer in a data-communications environment can vary considerably, depending upon numerous variables. Such variables can include the type of communications hardware and software used with one's personal computer, the transmission medium employed and the method by which the personal computer is connected to other network devices that may be required to integrate the computer into an existing network. In this chapter, we will review the fundamental concepts associated with data communications. This will provide us with a background in data-communication concepts which will build a foundation for examining the various options one can consider in a networking environment which will be presented later in this book. Since a PC with appropriate hardware and software can function as a terminal connected to a mainframe computer, we will use these terms interchangeably throughout this chapter. In later chapters, we will discuss the PC hardware and software requirements necessary for these microcomputer-based systems to emulate or function as a specific type of terminal. In addition, unless a specific PC model is referenced we will use the term 'PC' to denote all members of the IBM PC series to include the original PC, the PC XT, the Portable PC, the PCAT, and the PS/2 family of computers.

2.1 LINE CONNECTIONS

Three basic types of line connections are available to connect personal computers to other computers: dedicated, switched and leased lines.

A dedicated line is similar to a leased line in that the personal computer is always connected to the device on the distant end, transmission always occurs on the same path, and, if required, the line can be easily tuned to increase transmission performance. The key difference between a dedicated and a leased line is that a dedicated line refers to a transmission medium internal to a user's facility, where the customer has the right of way for cable laying, whereas a leased line provides an interconnection between separate facilities. The term 'facility' is usually employed to denote a building, office, or industrial plant. Dedicated lines are also referenced as direct connect lines and normally link a personal computer, terminal or business machine on a direct path through the facility to another personal computer, terminal or computer located at that facility. The dedicated line can be a wire conductor installed by the employees of a company or by the computer manufacturer's personnel, or it can be a local line installed by the telephone company. Normally, the only cost associated with a dedicated line in addition to its installation cost is the cost of the cable required to connect the devices that are to communicate with one another.

A leased line is commonly called a private line and is obtained from a communications company to provide a transmission medium between two facilities which could be in separate buildings in one city or in distant cities. In addition to a one-time installation charge, the communications carrier normally bills the user on a monthly basis for the leased line, with the cost of the line usually based upon the distance between the locations connected by the line.

A switched line, often referred to as a dial-up line, permits contact with all parties having access to the public switched telephone network (PSTN). If the operator of a personal computer wants access to another computer, he or she dials the telephone number associated with a telephone line which, in turn, is connected to the other computer. In using switched or dial-up transmission, telephone company switching centers establish a connection between the dialing party and the dialed party. After the connection is set up, the devices at each end of the line conduct their communications. When communications are completed, the switching centers disconnect the path that was established for the connection and restore all paths used so that they become available for other connections.

The cost of a call on the PSTN is based upon many factors to include the time of day when the call was made, the distance between called and calling parties, the duration of the call and whether or not operator assistance was required in placing the call. Direct-dial calls made from a residence or business telephone without operator assistance are billed at a lower rate than calls requiring operator assistance. In addition, most telephone companies have three categories of rates: 'weekday', 'evening' and 'night and weekend'. Calls made between 8 a.m. and 5 p.m. Monday through Friday are normally billed at a weekday rate, while calls between 5 p.m. and 11 p.m. on weekdays are usually billed at an evening rate, which reflects a discount of approximately 25% over the weekday rate. The last category, 'night and weekend', is applicable to calls made between 11 p.m. and 8 a.m. on weekdays as well as any time on weekends and holidays. Calls during this rate period are usually discounted 50% from the weekday rate.

Table 2.1 contains a sample PSTN Rate Table which is included for illustrative purpose but which should not be used by readers for determining the actual cost of a PSTN call. This is due to the fact that the cost of intrastate calls by state and interstate calls vary. In addition, the cost of using different communications carriers to place a call between similar locations will typically vary from vendor to vendor and readers should obtain a current rate schedule of the vendor they plan to use to determine or project the cost of PSTN facilities.

Cost, speed of transmission and degradation of transmission are the primary factors used in the selection process between leased and switched lines. As an example of the economics associated with comparing the cost of PSTN and leased-line usage, assume a personal computer located 50 miles from a mainframe has a requirement to communicate between 8 a.m. and 5 p.m. with the mainframe once each business day for a period of 30 minutes. Using the data in Table 2.1, each call would cost $0.31 \times 1 + 0.19 \times 29$ or $5.82. Assuming there are 22 working days each month, the monthly PSTN cost for communications between the PC and the mainframe would be 5.82×22 or $128.04. If the monthly cost of a leased line between the two locations was $250, it is obviously less expensive to use the PSTN for communications. Suppose the communications application lengthened in duration to 2 hours per day. Then, from Table 2.1, the cost per call would become $0.31 \times 1 + 0.19 \times 119$ or $22.92. Again assuming 22 workdays per month, the monthly PSTN charge would increase to $504.24, making the leased line more economical. Thus, if data communications requirements to a mainframe computer involve occasional random contact from a number

Table 2.1 Sample PSTN Rate Table (cost per minute in cents)

| | RATE CATEGORY | | | | | |
| Mileage between locations | Weekend | | Evening | | Night and weekend | |
	First min.	Each add' 1 minute	First min.	Each add' 1 minute	First min.	Each add' 1 minute
1–100	0.31	0.19	0.23	0.15	0.15	0.10
101–200	0.35	0.23	0.26	0.18	0.17	0.12
201–400	0.48	0.30	0.36	0.23	0.24	0.15

of personal computers and terminals at different locations and each call is of short duration, dial-up service is normally employed. If a large amount of transmission occurs between a personal computer and another computer, leased lines are usually installed between the two devices.

Since a leased line is fixed as to its routeing, it can be conditioned to reduce errors in transmission as well as permit ease in determining the location of error conditions since its routeing is known. Normally, switched circuits are used for transmission at speeds up to 9600 bits per second (bps); however, in certain situations data rates as high as 19 200 bps are achievable when transmission on the PSTN occurs through telephone company offices equipped with modern electronic switches.

Some of the limiting factors involved in determing the type of line to use for transmission between personal computers and other computers are listed in Table 2.2.

Table 2.2 Line Selection Guide

Line type	Distance between transmission points	Speed of transmission	Use for transmission
Dedicated (direct connect)	Local	Limited by conductor	Short or long duration
Switched (dial-up)	Limited by telephone access availability	Normally less than 9600 bps	Short-duration transmission
Leased (private)	Limited by telephone company availability	Limited by type of facility	Long-duration or many short-duration calls

2.2. TYPES OF SERVICE AND TRANSMISSION DEVICES

Digital devices which include terminals, mainframe computers, and personal computers transmit data as unipolar digital signals as indicated in Figure 2.1(a). When the distance between a personal computer and another computer is relatively short, the transmission of digital information between the two devices may be obtained by cabling the devices together. As the distance between the two devices increases, the pulses of the digital signals become distorted due to the resistance, inductance and capacitance of the cable used as a transmission medium. At a certain distance between the two devices the pulses of the digital data will distort, such that they are unrecognizable by the receiver as illustrated in Figure 2.1(b). To extend the transmission distance between devices specialized equipment must be employed, with the type of equipment used dependent upon the type of transmission medium employed.

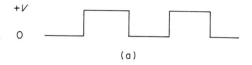

(a)

Figure 2.1(a) Digital Signaling

Digital devices to include terminals and computers transmit data as unipolar digital signals

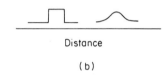

Distance

(b)

Figure 2.1(b) Digital Signal Distortion

As the distance between the transmitter and receiver increases digital signals become distorted due to the resistance, inductance and capacitance of the cable used as a transmission medium

Basically, one can transmit data in a digital or analog form. To transmit data long distances in digital form requires repeaters to be placed on the line at selected intervals to reconstruct the digital signals. The repeater is a device that essentially scans the line looking for the occurrence of a pulse and then regenerates the pulse into its original form. Thus, another name for the repeater is a data regenerator. As illustrated in Figure 2.2, a repeater extends the communications distance between terminal devices to include personal computers and mainframe computers or other business machines.

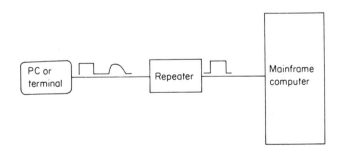

Figure 2.2 Transmitting Data in Digital Format

To transmit data long distances in digital format requires repeaters to be placed on the line to reconstruct the digital signals

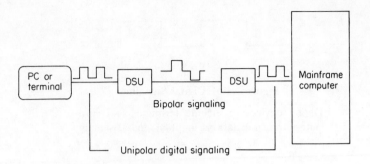

Figure 2.3 Transmitting Data on a Digital Network

To transmit data on a digital network, the unipolar digital signals
of terminal devices to include personal computers and mainframe
computers must be converted into a bipolar signal

Since unipolar signaling results in a d.c. voltage buildup when transmitting
over long distance, digital networks require unipolar signals to be converted
into a modified bipolar format for transmission on this type of network.
This requires the installation at each end of the circuit of a device known
as a digital service unit (DSU) in the United States and a network terminating
unit (NTU) in the United Kingdom. The utilization of DSUs for transmission
of data on a digital network is illustrated in Figure 2.3. Later in this chapter
we will examine digital facilities in more detail.

Modems

Since telephone lines were originally designed to carry analog or voice
signals, the digital signals transmitted from a terminal to another digital
device must be converted into a signal that is acceptable for transmission
by the telephone line. To effect transmission between distant points, a data
set or modem is used. A modem is a contraction of the compound term
'modulator–demodulator' and is an electronic device used to convert the
digital signals generated by computers and terminal devices into analog
tones for transmission over telephone network analog facilities. At the
receiving end, a similar device accepts the transmitted tones, reconverts
them to digital signals, and delivers these signals to the connected device.

Signal conversion performed by modems is illustrated in Figure 2.4. This
illustration shows the interrelationship of personal computers, mainframe
computers, and transmission lines when analog transmission service is used.
Both leased lines and switched lines employ analog service; therefore,
modems can be used for transmission of data over both types of analog line
connections. Although an analog transmission medium used to provide a

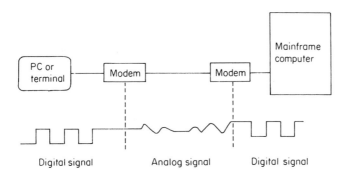

Figure 2.4 Signal Conversion Performed by Modems

A modem converts (modulates) the digital signal produced by a personal computer, terminal or business machine into an analog tone for transmission over an analog facility

transmission path between modems can be a direct-connect, leased, or switched line, modems are directly connected (hard wired) to direct-connect and leased lines, whereas they are interfaced to a switched facility. Thus, a terminal user can only communicate with the one distant location on a leased line, but can communicate with many devices when he or she has access to a switched line.

Acoustic couplers

Although acoustic couplers were popular with data terminal and personal computer users in the early 1980s, today only a small percentage of persons use them for communications. The acoustic coupler is a modem whose connection to the telephone line is obtained by acoustically coupling the telephone headset to the coupler. The primary advantage of the acoustic coupler is the fact that it requires no hard-wired connection to the switched telephone network, enabling terminals and personal computers to be portable with respect to their data transmission capability. Due to the growth in modular telephone jacks, modems that interface the switched telephone network via a plug, in effect, are portable devices. Since many hotels and older office buildings still have hard-wired telephones, the acoustic coupler permits terminal and personal computer users to communicate regardless of the method used to connect a telephone set to the telephone network. network.

The acoustic coupler converts the signals generated by a terminal or personal computer into a series of audible tones, which are then passed to the mouthpiece or transmitter of the telephone and in turn onto the switched telephone network. Information transmitted from the device at the other end of the data link is converted into audible tones at the earpiece of the telephone connected to the terminal's acoustic coupler. The coupler then converts those tones into the appropriate electrical signals recognized by the attached terminal. The interrelationship of terminal devices, acoustic couplers, modems and analog transmission media is illustrated in Figure 2.5. The reader should note that in the remainder of this book, a circle subdivided into four equal parts by two intersecting lines within the circle will be used as the symbol to denote the PSTN or switched telephone network.

Analog facilities

Several types of analog switched facilities are offered by communications carriers. Each type of facility has its own set of characteristics and rate structure. Normally, for extensive communications requirements, an analytic study is conducted to determine which type or types of service should be utilized to provide an optimum cost-effective service for the user. The common types of analog switched facilities are direct distance dialing, wide area telephone service and foreign exchange service.

Direct distance dialing (DDD) permits the user to dial directly any telephone connected to the public switched telephone network. The dialed telephone may be connected to another terminal device or mainframe computer. The charge for this service, in addition to installation costs, may be a fixed monthly fee if no long-distance calls are made, a message unit rate based upon the number and duration of local calls, or a fixed fee plus

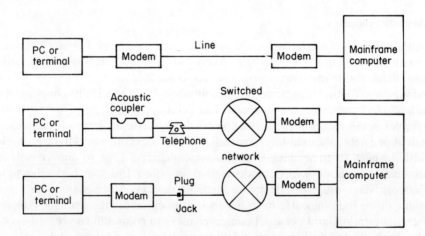

Figure 2.5 Interrelationship of Personal Computers, Terminals, Modems, Acoustic Couplers, Computers and Analog Transmission Media

When using modems on an analog transmission medium, the line can be a dedicated, leased, or switched facility. Terminal devices can use modems or acoustic couplers to transmit via the switched network

any long-distance charges incurred. Depending upon the time of day a long-distance call is initiated and its destination (intrastate or interstate), discounts from normal long-distance tolls are available for selected calls made without operator assistance as previously discussed in Section 2.1

WATS

Introduced by AT & T for interstate use in 1961, wide area telephone service (WATS) is now offered by several long-distance communications carriers. Its scope of coverage has been extended from the continental United States to Hawaii, Alaska, Puerto Rico, the U.S. Virgin Islands, Europe, as well as selected Pacific and Asian countries.

WATS may be obtained in two different forms, each designed for a particular type of communications requirement. Outward WATS is used when a specific location requires placing a large number of outgoing calls to geographically distributed locations. Inward WATS service provides the reverse capability, permitting a number of geographically distributed locations to communicate with a common facility. Calls on WATS are initiated in the same manner as a call placed on the PSTN. However, instead of being charged on an individual call basis, the user of WATS facilities pays a flat rate per hour based upon the number of communications hours per month occurring during weekday, evening and night/weekend time periods.

A voice-band trunk called an access line is provided to the WATS user. This line links the facility to a telephone company central office. Other than cost considerations and certain geographical calling restrictions which are a function of the service area of the WATS line, the user may place as many calls as desired on this trunk if the service is outward WATS or receive as many calls as desired if the service is inward. Inward WATS, the well-known '800' area code, permits remotely located personnel to call your facility toll free from the service area provided by the particular inward WATS-type of service selected. The charge for WATS is a function of the service area. This can be instrastate WATS, a group of states bordering the user's state where the user's main facility is located, a grouping of distant states, or international WATS which extends inbound 800 service to the United States from selected overseas locations.

Another service very similar to WATS is AT&T's 800 READYLINE[SM] service. This service is essentially similar to WATS; however, calls can originate or be directed to an existing telephone in place of the access line required for WATS service. Figure 2.6 illustrates the AT&T WATS service area 1 for the state of Georgia. If this service area is selected and a user in Georgia requires inward WATS service, he or she will pay for toll-free calls originating in the states surrounding Georgia–Florida, Alabama, Mississippi, Tennessee, Kentucky, South Carolina and North Carolina. Similarly, if outward WATS service is selected for service area 1, a person in Georgia connected to the WATS access line will be able to dial all telephones in the

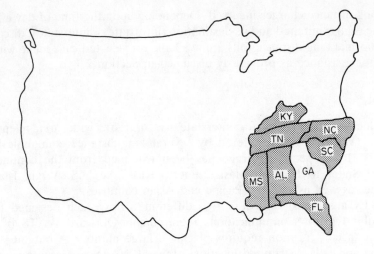

Figure 2.6 AT&T WATS Service Area 1 Access Line Located in Georgia

states previously mentioned. The states comprising a service area vary based upon the state in which the WATS access line is installed. Thus, the states in service area 1 when an access line is in New York would obviously differ from the states in a WATS service area 1 when the access line is in Georgia. Fortunately, AT&T publishes a comprehensive book which includes 50 maps of the United States, illustrating the composition of the service areas for each state. Similarly, a time-of-day rate schedule for each state based upon state service areas is also published by AT&T.

In general, since WATS is a service based upon volume usage, its cost per hour is less than the cost associated with the use of the PSTN for long-distance calls. Thus, one common application for the use of WATS facilities is to install one or more inward WATS access lines at a mainframe location and have terminal and personal computer users distributed over a wide geographical area use the inward WATS facilities to access the mainframe computer.

Since International 800 service enables employees and customers of US companies to call them toll free from foreign locations, this service may experience a considerable amount of data communications usage. This usage can be expected to include applications requiring access to such databases as hotel and travel reservation information as well as order entry and catalog sales data updating by persons traveling overseas with portable personal computers as well as by office personnel using terminals and personal computers in foreign countries who desire to access computational facilities and information utilities in the United States.

FX

Foreign exchange (FX) service may provide a method of transmission from a group of terminal devices remotely located from a central computer facility at less than the cost of direct distance dialing. An FX line can be viewed as a mixed analog switched and leased line. To use an FX line, a user dials a local number which is answered if the FX line is not in use. From the FX, the information is transmitted via a dedicated voice line to a permanent connection in the switching office of a communications carrier near the facility with which communication is desired. A line from the local switching office which terminates at the user's home office is included in the basic FX service. This is illustrated in Figure 2.7.

The use of an FX line permits the elimination of long-distance charges that would be incurred by users directly dialing the distant computer facility. Since only one person at a time may use the FX line, normally only groups of users whose usage can be scheduled are suitable for FX utilization. Figure 2.8 illustrates the possible connections between remotely located terminal devices and a central computer where transmission occurs over an analog facility.

The major difference between an FX line and a leased line is that any personal computer or terminal device dialing the FX line provides the second modem required for the transmission of data over the line; whereas a leased line used for data transmission normally has a fixed modem attached at both ends of the circuit.

Digital facilities

In addition to analog service, numerous digital service offerings have been implemented by communications carriers over the last decade. Using a

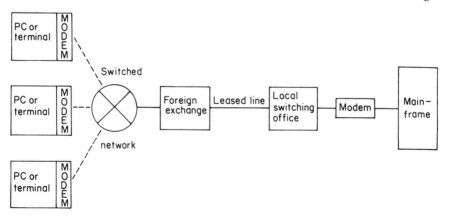

Figure 2.7 Foreign Exchange (FX) Service,

A foreign exchange line permits many terminal devices to use the facility on a scheduled or on a contention basis

16

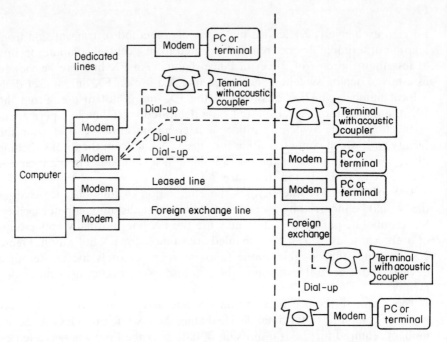

Figure 2.8 Terminal-to-Computer Connections via Analog Media

A mixture of dedicated, dial-up, leased lines, and foreign exchange lines can be employed to connect local and remote terminals to a central computer facility

digital service, data is transmitted from source to destination in digital form without the necessity of converting the signal into an analog form for transmission over analog facilities as is the case when modems or acoustic couplers are interfaced to analog facilities.

In the United States, AT&T offers several digital transmission facilities under the ACCUNET℠ Digital Service service mark. Dataphone® Digital Service was the charter member of the ACCUNET family and is deployed in 103 major metropolitan cities in the United States as well as having an interconnection to Canada's digital network. Dataphone Digital Service operates at synchronous data transfer rates of 2.4, 4.8, 9.6 and 56 kilobits per second (kbps), providing users of this service with dedicated, two-way simultaneous transmission capability. Another offering from AT&T, ACCUNET T1.5 Service is a high-capacity 1.544 megabit per second (mbps) terrestrial digital service which permits up to 24 voice-grade channels or a mixture of voice and data to be transmitted in digital form.

In Europe, a number of countries have established digital transmission facilities. One example of such offerings is British Telecom's KiloStream service. KiloStream provides synchronous data transmission at 2.4, 4.8, 9.6,

48 and 64 kbps and is very similar to AT&T's Dataphone Digital Service. Each KiloStream circuit is terminated by British Telecom with a Network Terminating Unit (NTU), which is the digital equivalent of the modem required on an analog circuit. In comparison, Dataphone Digital Service users can terminate their digital facilities with either a digital service unit or a channel service unit.

A digital service unit (DSU) provides a standard interface to a digital transmission service and handles such functions as signal translation, regeneration, reformatting and timing. The DSU is designed to operate at one of four speeds: 2.4, 4.8, 9.6 and 56 kbps. The transmitting portion of the DSU processes the customer's signal into bipolar pulses suitable for transmission over the digital facility. The receiving portion of the DSU is used both to extract timing information and to regenerate mark and space information from the received bipolar signal. The second interface arrangement for AT&T's Dataphone Digital Service is called a channel service unit (CSU) and is provided by the communication carrier to those customers who wish to perform the signal processing to and from the bipolar line, as well as to retime and regenerate the incoming line signals through the utilization of their own equipment.

As data is transmitted over digital facilities, the signal is regenerated by the communications carrier numerous times prior to its arrival at its destination. In general, digital service gives data communications users improved performance and reliability when compared to analog service, due to the nature of digital transmission and the design of digital networks. This improved performance and reliability is due to the fact that digital signals are regenerated, whereas analog signals are amplified with any distortion to the analog signal also being amplified.

Although digital service is offered in many locations, for those locations outside the serving area of a digital facility the user will have to employ analog devices as an extension in order to interface to the digital facility. The utilization of digital service via an analog extension is illustrated in Figure 2.9. As depicted in this illustration, if the closest city to the terminal located in city 2 that offers digital service is city 1, then to use digital service to communicate with the computer an analog extension must be installed between the terminal location and city 1. In such cases, the performance, reliability and possible cost advantages of using digital service may be completely dissipated. Digital service is available for both switched network and leased service. A leased digital line is similar to a leased analog line in that it is dedicated for full-time use to a particular user.

2.3 TRANSMISSION MODE

One method of characterizing lines, terminal devices, mainframe computers and modems is by their transmission or communications mode. The three classes of transmission modes are simplex, half-duplex and full-duplex.

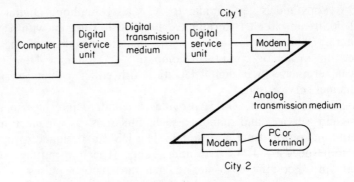

Figure 2.9 Analog Extension to Digital Service

Although data is transmitted in digital form from the computer
to city 1, it must be modulated by the modem at that location
for transmission over the analog extension

Simplex transmission is a transmission that occurs in one direction only, denying the receiver of information a means of responding to the transmission. A home AM radio that receives a signal transmitted from a radio station is an example of a simplex communications mode. In a data transmission environment, simplex transmission might be used to turn on or off specific devices at a certain time of the day or when a certain event occurs. An example of this is a computer-controlled environmental system in which a furnace is turned on or off depending upon the thermostat setting and the current temperature in various parts of a building. Normally, simplex transmission is not utilized where human–machine interaction is required due to the inability to turn the transmitter around so that the receiver can reply to the originator.

Half-duplex transmission permits transmission in either direction; however, transmission can occur in only one direction at a time. Half-duplex transmission is used in citizen band (CB) radio transmission where the operator can either transmit or receive but cannot perform both functions at the same time on the same channel. When the operator has completed a transmission, the other party must be advised that he or she is through transmitting and is ready to receive by saying the term 'over'. Then the other operator can begin transmission.

When data is transmitted over the telephone network, the transmitter and the receiver of the modem or acoustic coupler must be appropriately turned on and off as the direction of the transmission varies. Both simplex and half-duplex transmission require two wires to complete an electrical circuit. The top of Figure 2.10 illustrates a half-duplex modem interconnection while the lower portion of that illustration shows a typical sequence of events that might occur during the sign-on process to access a mainframe computer. In

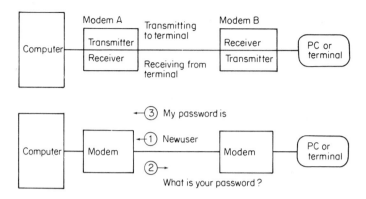

Figure 2.10 Half-Duplex Transmission

Top: Control signals from the mainframe computer and terminal operate the transmitter and receiver sections of the attached modems. When the transmitter of modem A is operating, the receiver of modem B operates; when the transmitter of modem B operates, the receiver of modem A operates. However, only one transmitter operates at any one time in the half-duplex mode of transmission. Bottom: During the sign-on sequence, transmission is turned around several times

the sign-on process, the user might first transmit the word 'NEWUSER' to inform the mainframe computer that a new user wishes to establish a connection. The computer responds by asking for the user's password, which is then furnished by the user. In the top portion of Figure 2.10, when data is transmitted from a mainframe computer to a terminal or personal computer, control signals are sent from the mainframe computer to modem A which turns on the modem A transmitter and causes the modem B receiver to respond.

When data is transmitted from the personal computer or terminal to the mainframe computer, the modem B receiver is disabled and its transmitter is turned on while the modem A transmitter is disabled and its receiver becomes active. The time necessary to effect these changes is called transmission turnaround time, and during this interval transmission is temporarily halted. Half-duplex transmission can occur on either a two-wire or four-wire circuit. The switched (PSTN) network is a two-wire circuit, whereas leased lines can be obtained as either two-wire or four-wire links. A four-wire circuit is essentially a pair of two-wire links which can be used for transmission in both directions simultaneously. This type of transmission is called the full-duplex mode.

Half-duplex communications can occur on either a two-wire or four-wire circuit. Although one would normally expect full-duplex transmission to be accomplished over a four-wire connection that provides two two-wire paths, full-duplex transmission can also occur on a two-wire connection. This is accomplished by the use of modems that subdivide the frequency bandwidth of the two-wire connection into two distinct channels, permitting simultaneous data flow in both directions on a two-wire circuit. This technique will be examined and explained in more detail in Chapter 3.

Full-duplex transmission is often used when large amounts of alternative traffic must be transmitted and received within a fixed time period. If two channels were used in our CB example, one for transmission and another for reception, two simultaneous transmissions could be effected. While full-duplex transmission provides more efficient throughput, this efficiency may be negated by the cost of software to obtain this capability and more complex equipment required by this mode of transmission. In Figure 2.11, the three types of transmission modes are illustrated, while Table 2.3 summarizes these modes.

The readers should note that the column CCITT in Table 2.3 refers to Consultive Committee on International Telephone and Telegraph. The CCITT operates as part of the International Telecommunications Union (ITU), which is a United Nations agency. Since CCITT modem standards are primarily followed in Europe, these standards may be of particular

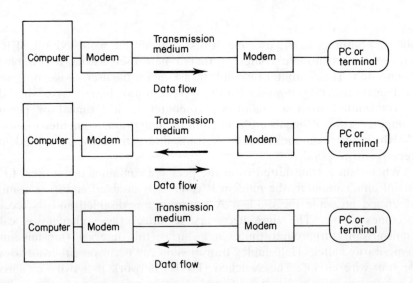

Figure 2.11 Transmission Modes

Top: Simplex transmission is in one direction only; transmission cannot reverse direction. Center: Half-duplex transmission permits transmission in both directions but only one way at a time. Bottom: Full-duplex transmission permits transmission in both directions simultaneously

Table 2.3 Transmission Mode Comparison

Symbol	ANSI	US Telecommuni-cations industry	CCITT	Historical physical line requirement
←	One-way only	Simplex		Two-wire
←⟶	Two-way alternate	Half-duplex (HDX)	Simplex	Two-wire
←⟶	Two-way simultaneous	Full-duplex (FDX)	Duplex	Four-wire

interest to persons in the United States that have to communicate with overseas locations or ship equipment purchased in the United States overseas. In Chapter 3, we will examine some of the more common CCITT modem standards to understand the compatibility problems that can occur between US and European manufactured modems.

PC/terminal and mainframe computer operations

When referring solely to personal computer and terminal operations, the terms 'half-duplex' and 'full-duplex operation' take on meanings different from the communications mode of the transmission medium. Vendors commonly use the term 'half-duplex' to denote that the PC or terminal device is in a local copy mode of operation. This means that each time a character is pressed on the keyboard it is printed or displayed on the local personal computer or terminal as well as transmitted. Thus, a terminal device operated in a half-duplex mode would have each character printed or displayed on its monitor as it is transmitted.

When one says a PC or terminal is in a full-duplex mode of operation this means that each character pressed on the keyboard is transmitted but not immediately displayed or printed. Here the device on the distant end of the transmission path must 'echo' the character back to the originator, which, upon receipt, displays or prints the character. Thus, a personal computer or terminal in a full-duplex mode of operation would only print or display the characters pressed on the keyboard after the character is echoed back by the device at the other end of the line. Figure 2.12 illustrates the terms 'full-' and 'half-duplex' as they apply to terminal devices. The reader should note that although most conventional terminals have a switch to control the duplex setting of the device, personal computer users normally obtain their duplex setting via the software program they are using. Thus, the term 'echo on' during the initialization of a communications software program would refer to the process of displaying each character on the user's screen as it is transmitted.

When we refer to half- and full-duplex with respect to mainframe computer systems we are normally referencing whether or not they echo received

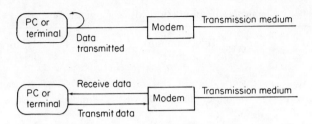

Figure 2.12 Terminal Operation Modes

Top: The term 'half-duplex terminal operation' implies
that data transmitted is also printed on the local
terminal. This is known as local copy. Bottom: The
term 'full-duplex terminal operation' implies that no
local copy is provided.

characters back to the originator. A half-duplex computer system does not echo characters back, while a full-duplex computer system echoes each character it receives.

When considering the operating mode of the terminal device, the transmission medium, and the operating mode of the mainframe computer on the distant end of the transmission path as an entity, three things could occur in response to each character one presses on a keyboard. Assuming a transmission medium is employed that can be used for either half- or full-duplex communications, a terminal device could print or display no character for each character transmitted, one character for each character transmitted, or two characters for each character transmitted. Here the resulting character printed or displayed would be dependent upon the operating mode of the terminal device and the host computer one is connected to, as indicated in Table 2.4.

To understand the character display column in Table 2.4, let us examine the two-character display result caused by the terminal device operating in a half-duplex mode while the mainframe computer operates in a full-duplex mode.

Table 2.4 Operating Mode and Character Display

| | Operating mode | |
Terminal device	Host computer	Character display
Half-duplex	Half-duplex	1 character
Half-duplex	Full-duplex	2 characters
Full-duplex	Half-duplex	No characters
Full-duplex	Full-duplex	1 character

When the PC or terminal is in a half-duplex mode it echoes each transmitted character onto its printer or display. At the other end of the communications path, if the mainframe computer is in a full-duplex mode of operation it will echo the received character back to the PC or terminal, causing a second copy of the transmitted character to be printed or displayed. Thus, two characters would appear on one's printer or display for each character one transmits. To alleviate this situation, one can change the transmission mode of one's terminal to full-duplex. This would normally be accomplished by turning 'echo' off during the initialization of one's communications software program if using a personal computer; or one would turn a switch to half-duplex if operating a conventional terminal.

2.4 TRANSMISSION TECHNIQUES

Data can be transmitted either synchronously or asynchronously. Asynchronous transmission is commonly referred to as a start–stop transmission where one character at a time is transmitted or received. Start and stop bits are used to separate characters and synchronize the receiver with the transmitter, thus providing a method of reducing the possibility that data becomes garbled. Most devices designed for human–machine interaction that are teletype-compatible transmit data asynchronously. By teletype-compatible, we reference terminals and personal computers that operate similar to the Teletype® terminal manufactured by Western Electric, a subsidiary of AT&T. Various versions of this popular terminal have been manufactured for over 30 years and an installed base of approximately one million such terminals is in operation worldwide. As characters are depressed on the device's keyboard they are transmitted to the computer, with idle time occurring between the transmission of characters. This is illustrated in the bottom part of Figure 2.13.

Asynchronous transmission

In asynchronous transmission, each character to be transmitted is encoded into a series of pulses. The transmission of the character is started by a start pulse equal in length to a code pulse. The encoded character (series of pulses) is followed by a stop pulse that may be equal to or longer than the code pulse, depending upon the transmission code used.

The start bit represents a transition from a mark to a space. Since in an idle condition when no data is transmitted the line is held in a marking condition, the start bit serves as an indicator to the receiving device that a character of data follows. Similarly, the stop bit causes the line to be placed back into its previous marking condition, signifying to the receiver that the data character is completed.

As illustrated in the top portion of Figure 2.13, the transmission of an 8-bit character requires either 10 or 11 bits, depending upon the length of the

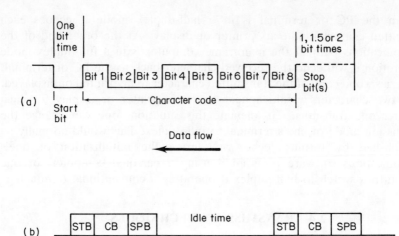

Figure 2.13 Asynchronous (Start-Stop) Transmission

(a) Transmission of one 8-bit character; (b) Transmission of many characters. STB = start bit; CB = character bits; SPB = stop bit(s); idle time is time between character transmission

stop bit. In the start–stop mode of transmission, transmission starts anew on each character and stops after each character. This is indicated in the lower portion of Figure 2.13. Since synchronization starts anew with each character, any timing discrepancy is cleared at the end of each character, and synchronization is maintained on a character-by-character basis. Asynchronous transmission normally is used for transmission at speeds up to 9600 bps over the switched telephone network, while data rates up to 19 200 bps are possible over a direct-connect cable whose distance is limited to 50 feet as well as conditioned leased lines.

The term asynchronous TTY- or TTY-compatible refers to the asynchronous start–stop protocol employed originally by Teletype terminals and is the protocol where data is transmitted on a line-by-line basis between a terminal device and a mainframe computer. In comparison, more modern terminals with cathode ray tube (CRT) displays are usually designed to transfer data on a full screen basis.

Personal computer users require only an asynchronous communications adapter and a software program that transmits and receives data on a line-by-line basis to connect to a mainframe that supports asynchronous TTY-compatible terminals. Here the software program that transmits and receives data on a line-by-line basis is normally referred to as a TTY emulator program and is the most common type of communications program written for use with personal computers.

Figure 2.14 Synchronous Transmission

In synchronous transmission, one or more syn characters are transmitted to establish clocking prior to the transmission of data

Synchronous transmission

A second type of transmission involves sending a grouping of characters in a continuous bit stream. This type of transmission is referred to as synchronous or bit-stream synchronization. In the synchronous mode of transmission, modems located at each end of the transmission medium normally provide a timing signal or clock which is used to establish the data transmission rate and enable the devices attached to the modems to identify the appropriate characters as they are being transmitted or received. In some instances, timing may be provided by the terminal device itself or a communication component, such as a multiplexer or front-end processor channel. No matter what timing source is used, prior to beginning the transmission of data the transmitting and receiving devices must establish synchronization among themselves. In order to keep the receiving clock in step with the transmitting clock for the duration of a stream of bits that may represent a large number of consecutive characters, the transmission of the data is preceded by the transmission of one or more special characters. These special synchronization or 'syn' characters are at the same code level (number of bits per character) as the coded information to be transmitted. However, they have a unique configuration of 0 and 1 bits which are interpreted as the syn character. Once a group of syn characters is transmitted, the receiver recognizes and synchronizes itself onto a stream of those syn characters.

After synchronization is achieved, then actual data transmission can proceed. Synchronous transmission is illustrated in Figure 2.14. In synchronous transmission, characters are grouped or blocked into groups of characters, requiring a buffer or memory area so that characters can be grouped together. In addition to having a buffer area, more complex circuitry is required for synchronous transmission since the receiving device must remain in phase with the transmitter for the duration of the transmitted block of information. Synchronous transmission is normally used for data transmission rates in excess of 2000 bps. The major characteristics of asynchronous and synchronous transmission are denoted in Table 2.5.

Table 2.5 Transmission Technique Characteristics

Asynchronous

1. Each character is prefixed by a start bit and followed by one or more stop bits.

2. Idle time (period of inactivity) can exist between transmitted characters.

3. Bits within a character are transmitted at prescribed time intervals.

4. Timing is established independently in the computer and terminal.

5. Transmission speeds normally do not exceed 9600 bps over switched facilities and 19 200 bps over dedicated links and leased lines.

Synchronous
1. Syn characters prefix transmitted data.

2. Syn characters are transmitted between blocks of data to maintain line synchronization.

3. No gaps exist between characters.

4. Timing is established and maintained by the transmitting and receiving modems, the terminal, or other devices.

5. Terminals must have buffers.

6. Transmission speeds normally are in excess of 2000 bps.

2.5 TYPES OF TRANSMISSION

The two types of data transmission one can consider are serial and parallel. For serial transmission the bits which comprise a character are transmitted in sequence over one line, whereas in parallel transmission characters are transmitted serially but the bits that represent the character are transmitted in parallel. If a character consists of eight bits, then parallel transmission requires a minimum of eight lines. Additional lines may be necessary for control signals or for the transmission of a parity bit. Although parallel transmission is used extensively in computer-to-peripheral unit transmission, it is not normally employed other than in dedicated data transmission usage due to the cost of the extra circuits required.

A typical use of parallel transmission is the in-plant connection of badge readers and similar devices to a computer in that facility. Parallel transmission may also reduce the cost of terminal circuitry since the terminal does not have to convert the internal character representation to a serial data stream for transmission. However, the cost of the transmission medium and interface will increase due to the additional number of conductors required. Since the total character can be transmitted at the same moment in time using parallel transmission, higher data-transfer rates can be obtained than possible with serial transmission facilities. For this reason, most local facility

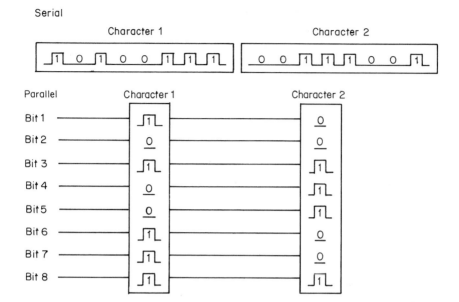

Figure 2.15 Types of Data Transmission

In serial transmission, the bits that comprise the character to be transmitted are sent in sequence over one line. In parallel transmission, the characters are transmitted serially but the bits that represent the character are transmitted in parallel

communications between computers and their peripheral devices are accomplished using parallel transmission. In comparison, communications between personal computers and other computers normally occurs serially since this requires only one line to interconnect two devices that need to communicate with one another. Figure 2.15 illustrates serial and parallel transmission.

2.6 LINE STRUCTURE

The geographical distribution of personal computers and terminal devices and the distance between each device and the device it transmits to are important parameters that must be considered in developing a network configuration. The method used to interconnect personal computers and terminals to mainframe computers or to other devices is known as line structure and results in a computer's network configuration. The two types of line structure used in networks are point-to-point and multipoint, the latter also commonly referred to as multidrop lines. Communications lines that connect only two points are point-to-point lines. An example of this line structure is depicted at the top of Figure 2.16. As illustrated, each

28

personal computer or terminal transmits and receives data to and from a computer via an individual connection that links a specific PC or terminal to the computer. The point-to-point connection can utilize a dedicated circuit, a leased line, or can be obtained via a connection initiated over the switched (dial-up) telephone network.

When two or more terminal locations share portions of a common line, the line is a multipoint or multidrop line. Although no two devices on such a line can transmit data at the same time, two or more devices may receive a message at the same time. The number of devices receiving such a message is dependent upon the addresses assigned to the message recipients. In some systems a 'broadcast' address permits all devices connected to the same

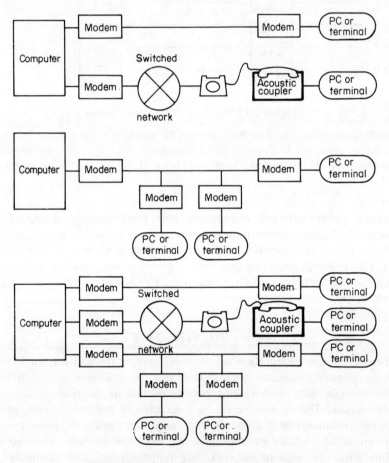

Figure 2.16 Line Structures in Networks

Top: Point-to-point line structure. Center: Multipoint (multidrop) line structure. Bottom: Mixed network line structure

multidrop line to receive a message at the same time. When multidrop lines are employed, overall line costs may be reduced since common portions of the line are shared for use by all devices connected to that line.To prevent data transmitted from one device from interfering with data transmitted from another device, a line discipline or control must be established for such a link.

This discipline controls transmission so no two devices transmit data at the same time. A multidrop line structure is depicted in the second portion of Figure 2.16. For a multidrop line linking n devices to a mainframe computer $n + 1$ modems are required, one for each device as well as one located at the computer facility.

Both point-to-point and multipoint lines may be intermixed in developing a network, and transmission can be either in the full- or half-duplex mode. This mixed line structure is shown in the lower portion of Figure 2.16.

2.7 LINE DISCIPLINE

When several devices share the use of a common, multipoint communications line, only one device may transmit at any one time; however, one or more devices may receive information simultaneously. To prevent two or more devices from transmitting at the same time, a technique known as poll-and-select is utilized as the method of line discipline for multidrop lines. To utilize poll-and-select, each device on the line must have a unique address of one or more characters as well as circuitry to recognize a message sent from the computer to that address. When the computer polls a line, in effect it asks each device in a predefined sequence if it has data to transmit. If the device has no data to transmit, it informs the computer of this fact and the computer continues its polling sequence until it encounters a device on the line that has data to send. Then the computer acts on that data transfer.

As the computer polls each device, the other devices on the line must wait until they are polled before they can be serviced. Conversely, transmission of data from the computer to each device on a multidrop line is accomplished by the computer selecting the device address to which that data is to be transferred, informing the device that data is to be transferred to it, and then transmitting data to the selected device. Polling and selecting can be used to service both asynchronous or synchronous operating terminal devices connected to independent multidrop lines. Due to the control overhead of polling and selecting, synchronous high-speed devices are normally serviced in this type of environment. By the use of signals and procedures, polling and selecting line control insures the orderly and efficient utilization of multidrop lines. An example of a computer polling the second personal computer or terminal on a multipoint line and then receiving data from that device is shown at the top of Figure 2.17. At the bottom of that illustration, the computer first selects the third device on the line and then transfers a block of data to that device.

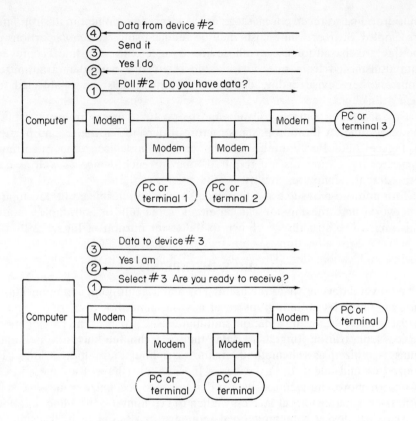

Figure 2.17 Poll-and-select Line Discipline

Poll-and-select is a line discipline which permits several devices to use a common line facility in an orderly manner

When PCs and terminals transmit data on a point-to-point line to a computer or another terminal, the transmission of that data occurs at the discretion of the terminal operator. This method of line control is known as non-poll-and-select or freewheeling transmission.

2.8 TRANSMISSION RATE

Many factors can affect the transmission rate at which data is transferred. The types of modem or acoustic coupler used as well as the line discipline and the type of communications adapter installed in one's personal computer all play governing roles that affect transmission rates; however, the transmission medium itself is an important factor in determining transmission rates.

Data transmission services offered by communications carriers such as AT&T and MCI are based on their available plant facilities. Depending upon personal computer and mainframe computer locations, two types of transmission services may be available. The first type of service, analog transmission, is most readily available and can be employed on switched or leased telephone lines. Digital transmission is available only in most large cities, and analog extensions are required to connect to this service from nondigital service locations as previously illustrated in Figure 2.9. Within each type of service several grades of transmission are available for consideration.

In general, analog service offers the user three grades of transmission: narrowband, voiceband, and wideband. The data-transmission rates achievable on each of these grades of service is dependent upon the bandwidth and electrical properties of each type of circuit offered within each grade of service. Basically, transmission speed is a function of the bandwidth of the communications line: The greater the bandwidth, the higher the possible speed of transmission.

Narrowband facilities are obtained by the carrier subdividing a voiceband circuit or by grouping a number of transmissions from different users onto a single portion of a circuit by time. Transmission rates obtained on narrowband facilities range between 45 and 300 bps. Teletype terminals that connect to message-switching systems are the primary example of the use of narrowband facilities.

While narrowband facilities have a bandwidth in the range of 200–400 Hz, voiceband facilities have a bandwidth in the range of 3000 Hz. Data-transmission speeds obtainable on voiceband facilities are differentiated by the type of voiceband facility utilized – switched dial-up transmission or transmission via a leased line. For transmission over the switched telephone network, maximum data transmission is normally under or up to 9600 bps, with data rates up to 100 percent higher obtainable when transmission occurs through modern electronic switches instead of the older, electromechanical switches still used in many telephone offices. Since leased lines can be conditioned, a speed of 9600–19 200 bps is frequently obtainable on such lines. Although low data speeds can be transmitted on both narrowband and voiceband circuits, one should not confuse the two since a low data speed on a voice circuit is transmission at a rate far less than the maximum permitted by that type of circuit, whereas, a low rate on a narrowband is at or near the maximum transmission rate permitted by that type of circuit.

Facilities which have a higher bandwidth than voice band are termed wideband or groupband facilities since they provide a wider bandwidth through the grouping of a number of voiceband circuits. Wideband facilities are available only on leased lines and permit transmission rates in excess of 19 200 bps. Transmission rates on wideband facilities vary with the offerings of communications carriers. Speeds normally available include 19.2, 40.8, 50, 230.4 and 1.544 mbps. Because the data rates on such lines normally exceed the serial data rate obtainable with a personal computer communications adapter, PCs are very rarely connected to wideband facilities.

For direct-connect circuits, transmission rates are a function of the distance between the personal computer and the mainframe computer as well as the gage of the conductor used and the type of communications adapter installed in the PC.

In the area of digital service, several offerings are currently available for user consideration. Digital data service is offered by AT&T as DATA-PHONE® digital service (DDS). It provides inter-state, full-duplex, point-to-point, and multipoint leased line as well as synchronous digital transmission at speeds of 2400, 4800, 9600 and 56 000 bps. It also provides data transmission at 1.544 mbps between the servicing areas of many digital cities.

A new high-speed AT&T digital switched communications service offers full-duplex, synchronous transmission over a common digital network at a transmission rate of 56 000 bps. In early 1988, two companies were marketing adapter boards designed to enable IBM PC and compatible computers to communicate over this digital facility. When equipped with such adapter boards, PCs can be used as terminals for high-speed data communications, desktop video conferencing or as a gateway to a local area network. Table 2.6 lists the main analog and digital facilities, the range of transmission speeds over those facilities, and the general use of such facilities.

2.9 TRANSMISSION CODES

Data within a computer is structured according to the architecture of the computer. The internal representation of data in a computer is seldom suitable for transmission to devices other than the peripheral units attached to the computer. In most cases, to effect data transmission, internal computer data must be redesigned or translated into a suitable transmission code. This transmission code creates a correspondence between the bit encoding of data for transmission or internal device representation and printed symbols. The end result of the translation is usually dictated by the character code used by the remote device the PC is attempting to access. Frequently available codes include Baudot, which is a 5-level (5 bits per character) code; binary-coded decimal (BCD), which is a 6-level code; American Standard Code for Information Interchange (ASCII), which is normally a 7-level code; and the extended binary-coded decimal interchange code (EBCDIC), which is an 8-level code.

In addition to information being encoded into a certain number of bits based upon the transmission code used, the unique configuration of those bits to represent certain control characters can be considered as a code that can be used to effect line discipline. These control characters may be used to indicate the acknowledgment of the receipt of a block of data without errors (ACK), the start of a message (SOH), or the end of a message

Table 2.6 Common Transmission Facilities

Facility	Transmission speed	Use
Analog		
Narrowband	45–300 bps	Message switching
Voiceband		
Switched	9600–19 200 bps	Time sharing; information utility access; remote job entry
Leased	Up to 19 200 bps	File transfer operation
Wideband	Over 19 200 bps	Mainframe computer-to-computer; remote job entry; tape-to-tape transmission; high-speed terminal to high-speed terminal
Digital		
Leased line	2.4, 4.8, 9.6, 56 and 1544 kbps	Remote job entry; mainframe computer-to-computer; high-speed facsimile
Switched	56 kbps	PC or terminal-to-PC or terminal; computer-to-computer; high-speed terminal to computer

(EXT), with the number of permissible control characters standardized according to the code employed. With the growth of data transmission between personal computers, a large amount of processing can be avoided by transferring the data in the format used by the computer for internal processing. Such transmission is known as binary-mode transmission, transparent data transfer, code-independent transmission, or native-mode transmission.

Morse code

One of the most commonly known codes, the Morse code, is not practical for utilization in a computer communications environment. This code consists of a series of dots and dashes, which, while easy for the human ear to decode, are of unequal length and not practical for data transmission implementation. In addition, since each character in the Morse code is not prefixed with a start bit and terminated with a stop bit, it was initially not possible to construct a machine to automatically translate received Morse transmissions into their appropriate characters.

Baudot code

The Baudot code which is a 5-level (5 bits per character) code was the first code to provide a mechanism for encoding characters by an equal number of bits, in this case, five. The 5-level Baudot code was devised by Emil Baudot to permit teletypewriters to operate faster and more accurately than relays used to transmit information via telegraph. Since the number of different characters which can be derived from a code having two different (binary) states is 2^m, where m is the number of positions in the code, the 5-level Baudot code permits 32 unique character-bit combinations. Although 32 characters could be represented normally with such a code, the necessity of transmitting digits, letters of the alphabet, and punctuation marks made it necessary to devise a mechanism to extend the capacity of the code to include additional character representations. The extension mechanism was accomplished by the use of two 'shift' characters: 'letters shift' and 'figures shift'. The transmission of a shift character informs the receiver that the characters which follow the shift character should be interpreted as characters from a symbol and numeric set or from the alphabetic set of characters.

The 5-level Baudot code is illustrated in Table 2.7 for one particular terminal pallet arrangement. A transmission of all 1s in bit positions 1–5 indicates a letter shift, and the characters following the transmission of that character are interpreted as letters. Similarly, the transmission of 1s in bit positions 1, 2, 4, and 5 indicates a figures shift, and the following characters are interpreted as numerals or symbols based upon their code structure. Although the Baudot code is quite old in comparison to the age of personal computers, it is the transmission code used by the Telex network which is employed in the business community to send messages through the world.

BCD code

The development of computer systems required the implementation of coding systems to convert alphanumeric characters into binary notation and the binary notation of computers into alphanumeric characters. The BCD system was one of the earliest codes used to convert data to a computer-acceptable form. This coding technique permits decimal numeric information to be represented by four binary bits and permits an alphanumeric character set to be represented through the use of 6 bits of information. This code is illustrated in Table 2.8. An advantage of this code is that two decimal digits can be stored in an 8-bit computer word and manipulated with appropriate computer instructions. Although only 36 characters are shown for illustrative purposes, a BCD code is capable of containing a set of 2^6 or 64 different characters.

In addition to transmitting letters, numerals, and punctuation marks, a considerable number of control characters may be required to promote line discipline. These control characters may be used to switch on and off devices

Table 2.7 Five-level Baudot Code

Letters	Figures	Bit selection 1	2	3	4	5
Characters						
A	—	1	1			
B	?	1			1	1
C	:		1	1	1	
D	$	1			1	.
E	3	1				
F	!	1		1	1	
G	&		1		1	1
H				1		1
I	8		1	1		
J	'	1	1		1	
K	(	1	1	1	1	
L	)		1			1
M	.			1	1	1
N	,			1	1	
O	9				1	1
P	0		1	1		1
Q	1	1	1	1		1
R	4		1		1	
S		1		1		
T	5				1	
U	7	1	1	1		
V	;		1	1	1	1
W	2	1	1			1
X	/	1		1	1	1
Y	6	1		1		1
Z	"	1				1
Functions						
Carriage return	<				1	
Line feed	=		1			
Space				1		
Letters shift		1	1	1	1	1
Figures shift		1	1		1	1

which are connected to the communications line, control the actual transmission of data, manipulate message formats, and perform additional functions. Thus, an extended character set is usually required for data communications. One such character set is the EBCDIC code. The extended binary decimal interchange code (EBCDIC) is an extension of the BCD system and uses 8 bits for character representation. This code permits 2^8 or 256 unique characters to be represented, although currently a lesser number is assigned meanings. This code is primarily used for transmission by byte-oriented computers, where a byte is a grouping of eight consecutive binary digits operated on as a unit by the computer. The use of this code by

36

Table 2.8 Binary-coded Decimal
System

b_6	b_5	b_4	b_3	b_2	b_1	Character
0	0	0	0	0	1	A
0	0	0	0	1	0	B
0	0	0	0	1	1	C
0	0	0	1	0	0	D
0	0	0	1	0	1	E
0	0	0	1	1	0	F
0	0	0	1	1	1	G
0	0	1	0	0	0	H
0	0	1	0	0	1	I
0	1	0	0	0	1	J
0	1	0	0	1	0	K
0	1	0	0	1	1	L
0	1	0	1	0	0	M
0	1	0	1	0	1	N
0	1	0	1	1	0	O
0	1	0	1	1	1	P
0	1	1	0	0	0	Q
0	1	1	0	0	1	R
1	0	0	0	1	0	S
1	0	0	0	1	1	T
1	0	0	1	0	0	U
1	0	0	1	0	1	V
1	0	0	1	1	0	W
1	0	0	1	1	1	X
1	0	1	0	0	0	Y
1	0	1	0	0	1	Z
1	1	0	0	0	0	0
1	1	0	0	0	1	1
1	1	0	0	1	0	2
1	1	0	0	1	1	3
1	1	0	1	0	0	4
1	1	0	1	0	1	5
1	1	0	1	1	0	6
1	1	0	1	1	1	7
1	1	1	0	0	0	8
1	1	1	0	0	1	9

computers may obviate the necessity of the computer performing code conversion if personal computers or terminals accessing an EBCDIC computer operate with the same character set. Several subsets of EBCDIC exist that have been tailored for use with certain devices. As an example, IBM 3270 type terminal products would not use a paper feed and its character representation is omitted in the EBCDIC character subset used to operate that type of device, as indicated in Table 2.9.

Table 2.9 EBCDIC Code Implemented for the IBM 3270 Information Display System

Bits 4567	Hex 1	00	00	00	00	01	01	01	01	10	10	10	10	11	11	11	11	Hex0
	Bits 2,3	00	01	10	11	00	01	10	11	00	01	10	11	00	01	10	11	
		0	1	2	3	4	5	6	7	8	9	A	B	C	D	E	F	
0000	0	NUL	DLE			SP	&	–										0
0001	1	SOH	SBA					/		a	j			A	J			1
0010	2	STX	EUA		SYN					b	k	s		B	K	S		2
0011	3	ETX	IC							c	l	t		C	L	T		3
0100	4						.			d	m	u		D	M	U		4
0101	5	PT	NL						.	e	n	v		E	N	V		5
0110	6			ETB						f	o	w		F	O	W		6
0111	7			EBC	EOT					g	p	x		G	P	X		7
1000	8									h	q	y		H	Q	Y		8
	9		EM							i	r	z		I	R	Z		9
1010	A					¢	!			:								
1011	B					.	$	,	#									
1100	C		DUP		RA	<	•	%	@									
1101	D		SF	ENQ	NAK	(	)	_	'									
1110	E		FM			+	;	>	-									
1111	F		ITB		SUB	|	¬	?	··									

ASCII code

As a result of the proliferation of data transmission codes, several attempts to develop standardized codes for data transmission have occurred. One such code is the American Standard Code for Information Interchange (ASCII). This 7-level code is based upon a 7-bit code developed by the International Standards Organization (ISO) and permits 128 possible combinations or character assignments to include 96 graphic characters that are printable or displayable and 32 control characters to include device control and information transfer control characters.

Table 2.10 lists the ASCII character set while Table 2.11 lists the ASCII control characters by position and their meaning. A more detailed explanation of these control characters is contained in the section covering protocols in this chapter.

Code conversion

A frequent problem in data communications is that of code conversion. Consider what must be done to enable a mainframe computer with an

Table 2.10 The ASCII Character Set

This coded character set is to be used for the general interchange of information processing systems, communications systems, and associated equipment

b_7					0	0	0	0	1	1	1	1
b_6					0	0	1	1	0	0	1	1
b_5					0	1	0	1	0	1	0	1
b_4	b_3	b_2	b_1	Column / Row	0	1	2	3	4	5	6	7
0	0	0	0	0	NUL	DLE	SP	0	@	P	\	p
0	0	0	1	1	SOH	DC1	!	1	A	Q	a	q
0	0	1	0	2	STX	DC2	"	2	B	R	b	r
0	0	1	1	3	ETX	DC3	#	3	C	S	c	s
0	1	0	0	4	EOT	DC4	$	4	D	T	d	t
0	1	0	1	5	ENQ	NAK	%	5	E	U	e	u
0	1	1	0	6	ACK	SYN	&	6	F	V	f	v
0	1	1	1	7	BEL	ETB	'	7	G	W	g	w
1	0	0	0	8	BS	CAN	(	8	H	X	h	x
1	0	0	1	9	HT	EM	)	9	I	Y	i	y
1	0	1	0	10	LF	SUB	*	:	J	Z	j	z
1	0	1	1	11	VT	ESC	+	;	K	[	k	{
1	1	0	0	12	FF	FS	,	<	L	\	l	|
1	1	0	1	13	CR	GS	–	=	M	]	m	}
1	1	1	0	14	SO	RS	.	>	N	^	n	~
1	1	1	1	15	SI	US	/	?	O	—	o	DEL

Note: b_7 is the higher-order bit and b_1 is the low-order bit as indicated by the following example for coding the letter C.

b_7	b_6	b_5	b_4	b_3	b_2	b_1
1	0	0	0	0	1	1

EBCDIC character set to transmit and receive information from a terminal or personal computer with an ASCII character set. When the PC or terminal transmits a character, that character is encoded according to the ASCII character code. Upon receipt of that character, the mainframe computer must convert the bits of information of the ASCII character into an equivalent EBCDIC character. Conversely, when data is to be transmitted to the personal computer or terminal, it must be converted from EBCDIC to ASCII so the PC or terminal will be able to decode and act according to the information in the character that the terminal or PC is built to interpret.

Normally, ASCII to EBCDIC code conversion is implemented when an IBM PC is required to operate as a 3270 type terminal. This type of terminal is typically connected to an IBM or IBM compatible mainframe computer and the terminal's replacement by an IBM PC requires the PC's ASCII coded data to be translated into EBCDIC. There are many ways to obtain this conversion to include emulation boards that are inserted into the system

Table 2.11 ASCII Control Characters

Column/row	Control character	Mnemonic and meaning	
0/0	ˆ@	NUL	Null (CC)
0/1	–A	SOH	Start of Heading (CC)
0/2	–B	STX	Start of Text (CC)
0/3	–C	ETX	End of Text (CC)
0/4	–D	EOT	End of Transmission (CC)
0/5	–E	ENQ	Enquiry (CC)
0/6	–F	ACK	Acknowledge (CC)
0/7	–G	BEL	Bell
0/8	–H	BS	Backspace (FE)
0/9	–I	HT	Horizontal Tabulation (FE)
0/10	–J	LF	Line Feed (FE)
0/11	–K	VT	Vertical Tabulation (FE)
0/12	–L	FF	Form Feed (FE)
0/13	–M	CR	Carriage Return (FE)
0/14	–N	SO	Shift Out
0/15	–O	SI	Shift In
1/0	–P	DLE	Data Link Escape (CC)
1/1	–Q	DC1	Device Control 1
1/2	–R	DC2	Device Control 2
1/3	–S	DC3	Device Control 3
1/4	–T	DC4	Device Control 4
1/5	–U	NAK	Negative Acknowledge (CC)
1/6	–V	SYN	Synchronous Idle (CC)
1/7	–W	ETB	End of Transmission Block (CC)
1/8	–X	CAN	Cancel
1/9	–Y	EM	End of Medium
1/10	–Z	SUB	Substitute
1/11	–[	ESC	Escape
1/12	–/	FS	File Separator (IS)
1/13	–]	GS	Group Separator (IS)
1/14	– –	RS	Record Separator (IS)
1/15	ˆ–	US	Unit Separator (IS)
7/15		DEL	Delete

(CC) Communications control; (FE) Format effector; (IS) Information separator

unit of a PC and protocol converters that are connected between the PC and the mainframe computer. In our examination of networking strategies later in this book, we will explore these and other methods that enable the PC to communicate with mainframe computers that transmit data coded in EBCDIC.

Table 2.12 lists the ASCII and EBCDIC code character values for the 10 digits for comparison purposes. In examining the difference between ASCII and EBCDIC coded digits the reader will note that each EBCDIC coded digit has a value precisely HEX C0 (decimal 192) higher than its ASCII equivalent. Although this might appear to make code conversion a simple

Table 2.12 ASCII and EBCDIC Digits
Comparison

ASCII			EBCDIC	
Dec	Oct	Hex	Hex	Digit
048	060	30	F0	0
049	061	31	F1	1
050	062	32	F2	2
051	063	33	F3	3
052	064	34	F4	4
053	065	35	F5	5
054	066	36	F6	6
055	067	37	F7	7
056	070	38	F8	8
057	071	39	F9	9

process of adding or subtracting a fixed quantity depending upon which way the code conversion takes place, in reality many of the same ASCII and EBCDIC coded characters differ by varying quantities. As an example, the slash (/) character is Hex 2F in ASCII and Hex 61 in EBCDIC, a difference of Hex 92 (decimal 146). In comparison, other characters, such as the carriage return and form feed, have the same coded value in ASCII and EBCDIC, while other characters are displaced by different amounts in these two codes. For this reason code conversion is typically performed as a table lookup process, with two buffer areas used to convert between codes in each of the two conversion directions. Thus, one buffer area might have the ASCII character set in hex order in one field of a two-field buffer area, with the equivalent EBCDIC hex values in a second field in the buffer area. Then, upon receipt of an ASCII character its hex value is obtained and matched to the equivalent value in the first field of the buffer area, with the value of the second field containing the equivalent EBCDIC hex value, which is then extracted to perform the code conversion.

Members of the IBM PC Series and compatible computers use a modified ASCII character set which is represented as an 8-level code. The first 128 characters in the character set, ASCII values 0–127, correspond to the ASCII character set listed in Table 2.10 while the next 128 characters can be viewed as an extension of that character set since they require an 8-bit representation.

Caution is advised when transferring IBM Personal Computer files since characters with ASCII values greater than 127 will be received in error when they are transmitted using 7 data bits. This is because the ASCII values of these characters will be truncated to values in the range 0–127 when transmitted with 7 bits from their actual range of 0–255. To prevent this problem from occurring, one can initialize one's communications software for 8-bit data transfer, but the receiving device must also be capable of supporting 8-bit ASCII data.

Although conventional ASCII files can be transmitted in a 7-bit format, many word-processing and computer programs contain text graphics represented by ASCII characters whose values exceed 127. In addition, EXE and COM files which are produced by assemblers and compilers contain binary data that must also be transmitted in 8-bit ASCII to be accurately received. While most communications programs can transmit 7- or 8-bit ASCII data, many programs may not be able to transmit binary files accurately. This is due to the fact that communications programs that use the control Z character (ASCII SUB) to identify the end of a file transfer misinterpret a group of 8 bits in the EXE or COM file being transmitted when they have the same 8-bit format as a control Z, and upon detection prematurely close the file. To avoid this situation, one should obtain a communications software program that transfers files by blocks of bits or converts the data into a hexadecimal or octal ASCII equivalent prior to transmission if this type of data transfers will be required.

2.10 ERROR DETECTION AND CORRECTION

As a signal propagates down a transmission medium, several factors can cause it to be received in error to include the transmission medium employed and impairments caused by nature and machinery.

The transmission medium has a certain level of resistance to current flow, and this causes signals to be attenuated. In addition, inductance and capacitance distort the transmitted signals and there is a degree of leakage which is the loss in a transmission line due to current flowing across, through insulators, or changes in the magnetic field. Transmission impairments result from numerous sources. First, Gaussian or white noise is always present as it is the noise level that exists due to the thermal motions of electrons in a circuit. Next, impulse can occur from line hits due to atmospheric static or from poor contacts in a telephone system.

Asynchronous transmission

In asynchronous transmission the most common form of error control is the use of a single bit, known as a parity bit, for the detection of errors. Due to the proliferation of personal computer communications, more sophisticated error-detection methods have been developed which resemble the methods employed with synchronous transmission.

Character parity checking, which is also known as vertical redundancy checking (VRC), requires an extra bit to be added to each character in order to make the total quantity of 1s in the character either odd or even, depending upon whether one is employing odd parity checking or even parity checking. When odd parity checking is employed, the parity bit is set to 1 if the number of 1s in the character's data bits is even, and to 0 if the number of 1s in the character's data bits is odd. When even parity checking is used, the parity bit is set to 0 if the number of 1s in the character's data bits is even, and to 1 if the number of 1s in the character's data bits is odd.

Two additional terms used to reference parity settings are mark and space. When the parity bit is set to a mark condition the parity bit is always 1 while space parity results in the parity bit always set to 0.

For an example of parity checking, let us examine the ASCII character R whose bit composition is 1010010. Since there are three 1 bits in the character R, a 0 bit is added as parity bit if odd parity checking is used or a 1 bit is added if even parity checking is employed. Thus, the ASCII character R would appear as follows:

|data bits| ⊢ parity bit

10100100   odd parity check

10100101   even parity check

Although parity checking is a simple mechanism to investigate if a single bit error has occurred, it can fail when multiple bit errors occur. This can be visualized by returning to the ASCII R character example and examining the effect of two bits erroneously being transformed as indicated in Table 2.13. Here the ASCII R character has three set bits, and a one-bit error could transform the number of set bits to four. Even if parity checking is employed, the received set parity bit results in the character containing five set bits, which is obviously an error since even parity checking is employed. Now suppose two bits are transformed in error as indicated in the lower portion of Table 2.13. This results in the reception of a character containing six set bits, which appears to be correct under even parity checking. Thus, two bit errors in this situation are not detected by a parity-error detection technique.

In addition to the potential of undetected errors, parity checking has several additional limitations. First, when the PC is used as an interactive terminal the response to parity errors varies according to the type of mainframe with which one is communicating. Certain mainframes issue a

Table 2.13 Character Parity Cannot Detect an Even Number
of Bit Errors

ASCII character R	1 0 1 0 0 1 0
Adding an even parity bit	1 0 1 0 0 1 0 1
	1
1 bit in error	1 0̸ 1 0 0 1 0 1
	1 1
2 bits in error	1 0̸ 1 0̸ 0 1 0 1

'retransmit' message upon detection of a parity error. Some mainframes transmit a character that appears as a 'fuzzy box' on one's screen in response to detecting a parity error, while other mainframes completely ignore parity errors.

When transmitting data asynchronously on a personal computer, most communications programs permit the user to set parity to odd, even, off, space, or mark. Off or no parity is used if the system with which one is communicating does not check the parity bit for transmission errors. No parity is used when one is transmitting 8-bit EBCDIC or extended 8-bit ASCII coded data, such as that available on the IBM PC and similar personal computers. Mark parity means that the parity bit is set to 1, while space parity means that the parity bit is set to 0.

In the asynchronous communications world two common sets of parameters are used by most bulletin boards, information utilities and supported by mainframe computers. The first set consists of 7 data bits and 1 stop bit with even parity checking employed, while the second set consists of 8 data bits and 1 stop bit using no parity checking. Table 2.14 compares the communications parameter settings of three popular information utilities.

Although visual identification of parity errors in an interactive environment is possible, what happens when one wishes to transfer a large file over the switched telephone network? For a typical call over the switched telephone network the probability of a random bit error occurring is approximately 1 in 100 000 bits at a data transmission rate of 1200 bps. If one desired to upload or download a 1000-line program containing an average of 40 characters per line, a total of 320 000 data bits would have to be transmitted. During the 4.4 minutes required to transfer this file one can expect 3.2 bit errors to occur, probably resulting in several program lines being received incorrectly if the errors occur randomly. In such situations one would prefer an alternative to visual inspection. Thus, a more efficient error-detection and -correction method is needed for large data transfers.

Block checking

In this method, data is grouped into blocks for transmission. A checksum character is generated and appended to the transmitted block and the

Table 2.14 Communication Parameter Settings

Parameter	Information Utility		
	CompuServe	Dow Jones	The Source
Data rate (bps)	300/1200	300/1200	300/1200
Data bits	7/8	8	8
Parity	even/none	none	none
Stop bits	1	1	1
Duplex	full	full	full

checksum is also calculated at the receiver, using the same algorithm. If the checksums match, the data block is considered to be received correctly. If the checksums do not match, the block is considered to be in error and the receiving station will request the transmitting station to retransmit the block.

One of the most popular asynchronous block checking methods is included in the XMODEM protocol, which is extensively used in personal computer communications. This protocol blocks groups of asynchronous characters together for transmission and computes a checksum which is appended to the end of the block. The checksum is obtained by first summing the ASCII value of each data character in the block and dividing that sum by 255. Then, the quotient is discarded and the remainder is appended to the block as the checksum. Thus, mathematically, the XMODEM checksum can be represented as:

$$\text{CHECKSUM} = R \left[\frac{\sum_{1}^{128} \text{ASCII value of character}}{255} \right]$$

where R is the remainder of the division process.

When data is transmitted using the XMODEM protocol, the receiving device at the other end of the link performs the same operation upon the block being received. This 'internally' generated checksum is compared to the transmitted checksum. If the two checksums match, the block is considered to have been received error free. If the two checksums do not match, the block is considered to be in error and the receiving device then requests the transmitting device to resend the block. Figure 2.18 illustrates the XMODEM protocol block format. The start of header is the ASCII SOH character whose bit composition is 00000001, while the 1s complement of the block number is obtained by subtracting the block number from 255. The block number and its complement are contained at the beginning of each block to reduce the possibility of a line hit at the beginning of the transmission of a block causing the block to be retransmitted. The XMODEM protocol will be examined in more detail in the protocol section of this chapter.

Although the XMODEM protocol significantly reduces the probability of an undetected transmission error occurring in comparison to simple parity

Start of head	Block number	1's complement block number	128 data characters	Checksum

Figure 2.18 XMODEM Protocol Block Format

checking, it is far from foolproof. As an example of the limitations of XMODEM error detection capability, consider a block consisting of all 1s. The ASCII value of the character representing the 1 digit is 49, resulting in the total summed ASCII value of 128 characters in the block becoming 6272. When divided by 255, the quotient is 24 and the remainder of 152 is transmitted as the the checksum.

Suppose during the transmission of the XMODEM block two line hits occur, causing one character to be changed from 0 1 1 0 0 0 1 to 0 1 1 0 0 0 0, while a second character is changed from 0 1 1 0 0 0 1 to 0 1 1 0 0 1 0. In this situation one of the ASCII 1 characters is converted into an ASCII 0 (ASCII value of 48) while a second ASCII 1 is converted into an ASCII 2 (ASCII value of 50). Then, during the checksum-generation process at the receiving device the total ASCII value of all characters in the block containing two errors is $48 + 50 + 49 \times 126$ or 6272. When the sum is divided by 255 the remainder of 152 matches the remainder transmitted as the checksum and the block is considered to have been received error free. In spite of being far from foolproof, the XMODEM error-detection mechanism is in wide use and can detect approximately 97 percent of randomly occurring transmission errors.

Synchronous transmission

The majority of error detection schemes employed in synchronous transmission involve geometric codes or cyclic code.

Geometric codes attack the deficiency of parity by extending it to two dimensions. This involves forming a parity bit on each individual character as well as on all the characters in the block. Figure 2.19 illustrates the use of block parity checking for a block of 10 data characters. As indicated, this block parity character is also known as the longitudinal redundancy check (LRC) character. Geometric codes are similar to the XMODEM error-detection technique in the fact that they are also far from foolproof. As an example of this, suppose a transmission impairment of two bits duration occurred at bit positions 3 and 4 when characters 7 and 9 in Figure 2.19 were transmitted. Here the two 1s in those bit positions might be replaced by two 0s. In this situation, each character parity bit as well as the block parity character would fail to detect the errors.

A transmission system using a geometric code for error detection has a slightly better capability to detect errors than the method used in the XMODEM protocol and is hundreds of times better than simple parity checking. While block parity checking substantially reduces the probability of an undetected error in comparison to simple parity checking on a character-by-character basis, other techniques can be used to further decrease the possibility of undetected errors. Among these techniques is the use of cyclic or polynomial code.

When a cyclic or polynomial code error-detection scheme is employed the message block is treated as a data polynomial $D(x)$, which is divided by a

Character	1	1 0 1 1 0 1 1 0
	2	0 1 0 0 1 0 1 0
	3	0 1 1 0 1 0 0 0
	4	1 0 0 1 0 0 1 0
	5	0 1 1 1 1 0 1 0
	6	1 0 1 0 0 0 0 1
	7	0 1 0 1 1 1 0 1
	8	0 1 1 1 0 0 1 1
	9	1 0 0 0 1 1 0 0
		0 1 1 0 1 0 1 1

Block parity
character (LRC)   1 1 1 0 1 0 0 0

Figure 2.19 VRC/LRC Geometric Code (Odd Parity Checking)

predefined generating polynomial $G(x)$, resulting in a quotient polynomial $Q(x)$ and a remainder polynomial $R(x)$, such that:

$$D(x)/G(x) = Q(x) + R(x)$$

The remainder of the division process is known as the cyclic redundancy check (CRC) and is normally 16 bits in length or two 8-bit bytes. The CRC checking method is used in synchronous transmission similar to the manner in which the CHECKSUM is employed in the XMODEM protocol previously discussed. That is, the CRC is appended to the block of data to be transmitted. The receiving device uses the same predefined generating polynomial to generate its own CRC based upon the received message block, and then compares the internally generated CRC with the transmitted CRC. If the two match, the receiver transmits a positive acknowledgement (ACK) communications control character to the transmitting device, which not only informs the distant device that the data was received correctly but also serves to inform the device that if additional blocks of data remain to be transmitted the next block can be sent. If an error has occurred, the internally generated CRC will not match the transmitted CRC and the receiver will transmit a negative acknowledgement (NAK) communications control character which informs the transmitting device to retransmit the block previously sent.

Table 2.15 lists three generating polynomials in common use today. The CRC-16 is based upon the American National Standards Institute and is commonly used in the United States. The CCITT CRC is commonly used in transmissions in Europe while the CRC-12 is used with 6-level transmission codes and has been basically superseded by the 16-bit polynomials. The column labeled polynomial in Table 2.15 actually indicates the set bits of

Table 2.15 Common Generating Polynomials

Standard	Polynomial
CRC-16(ANSI)	$X^{16} + X^{15} + X^5 + 1$
CRC (CCITT)	$X^{16} + X^{12} + X^5 + 1$
CRC-12	$X^{12} + X^{11} + X^3 + 1$

the 16-bit or 12-bit polynomial. Thus, the CRC-16 polynomial has a bit composition of 1 1 0 0 0 0 0 0 0 0 0 1 0 0 0 1.

2.11 PROTOCOLS

Two types of protocol should be considered in a data communications environment: terminal protocols and data link protocols.

The data link protocol defines the control characteristics of the network and is a set of conventions which govern the transmission of data and control information. A terminal or a personal computer can have a predefined control character or set of control characters which are unique to the terminal and are not interpreted by the line protocol. This internal protocol can include such control characters as the bell, line feed, and carriage return for conventional teletype terminals; blink and cursor positioning characters for a display terminal; and form control characters for a line printer.

For experimenting with members of the IBM PC Series and compatible computers, readers can execute the one-line BASIC program

    10 PRINT CHR$(X)"DEMO"

substituting different ASCII values for the value of X to see the effect of different PC terminal control characters. As an example, using the value 7 for X, the IBM PC will beep prior to displaying the message DEMO, since ASCII 7 is interpreted by the PC as a request to beep the speaker. Using the value 9 for X will cause the message DEMO to be printed commencing in position 9, since ASCII 9 is a tab character which causes the cursor to move on the screen 8 character positions to the right. Another example of a terminal control character is ASCII 11, which is the home character. Using the value of 11 for X will cause the message DEMO to be printed in the upper left-hand corner of the screen since the cursor is first placed at that location by the home character.

Although poll and select is normally thought of as a type of line discipline or control, it is also a data link protocol. In general, the data link protocol enables the exchange of information according to an order or sequence by establishing a series of rules for the interpretation of control signals which will govern the exchange of information. The control signals govern the execution of a number of tasks which are essential in controlling the exchange of information via a communications facility. Some of these information control tasks are listed in Table 2.16.

Table 2.16 Information Control Tasks

Connection establishment	Transmission sequence
Connection verification	Data sequence
Connection disengagement	Error control procedures

Although all of the tasks listed in Table 2.16 are important, not all are required for the transmission of data since the series of tasks required is a function of the total data-communications environment. As an example, a single terminal or personal computer connected directly to a mainframe or another terminal device by a leased line normally does not require the establishment and verification of the connection. However, several devices connected to a mainframe computer on a multidrop or multipoint line require the verification of the identification of each terminal device on the line to insure that data transmitted from the computer is received by the proper device. Similarly, when a device's session is completed, this fact must be recognized so that the mainframe computer's resources can be made available to other users. Thus, connection disengagement on devices other than those connected on a point-to-point leased line permits a port on the front-end processor to become available to service other users.

Another important task is the transmission sequence which is used to establish the precedence and order of transmission, to include both data and control information. As an example, this task defines the rules for when devices on a multipoint circuit may transmit and receive information. In addition to the transmission of information following a sequence, the data itself may be sequenced. Data sequencing is normally employed in synchronous transmission where a long block is broken into smaller blocks for transmission, the size of the blocks being a function of the personal computer's or terminal's buffer area and the error-control procedure employed. By dividing a block into smaller blocks for transmission, the amount of data that must be retransmitted, in the event that an error in transmission is detected, is reduced.

Although error-checking techniques currently employed are more efficient when short blocks of information are transmitted, the efficiency of transmission correspondingly decreases since an acknowledgement (negative or positive) is returned to the device transmitting after each block is received and checked. For communications between mainframe computers and either remote job-entry terminals or personal computers operating as remote job-entry devices, blocks of up to several thousand characters are typically used. However, block lengths from 80 to 512 characters are the most common sizes. Although some protocols specify block length, most protocols permit the user to set the size of the block.

Pertaining to error control procedures, the most commonly employed method to correct transmitted errors is to inform the transmitting device simply to retransmit a block. This procedure requires coordination between the sending and receiving devices, with the receiving device continuously informing the sending device of the status of each previously transmitted block. If the block previously transmitted contained no detected errors, the receiver transmits a positive acknowledgement and the sender transmits the next block. If the receiver detects an error, it transmits a negative acknowledgement and discards the block containing an error. The transmitting station then retransmits the previously sent block. Depending upon the protocol employed, a number of retransmissions may be attempted. However, if a default limit is reached due to a bad circuit or other problems, then the mainframe computer or terminal device acting as the master station may terminate the session, and the terminal operator will have to re-establish the connection.

COMMUNICATIONS CONTROL CHARACTERS

Prior to examining several protocols in more detail, let us first review the communications control characters in the ASCII character set. These characters were previously listed in Table 2.11 with the two-character designator CC following their meaning and will be reviewed in the order of their appearance in the referenced table.

NUL

As its name implies, the Null character is a non-printable time delay or filler character. This character is primarily used for communicating with printing devices that require a defined period of time after each carriage return in which to reposition the printhead to the beginning of the next line. Many mainframe computers and bulletin boards operating on personal computers prompt users to 'Enter the numbers of nulls'; this is a mechanism to permit both conventional terminals, personal computers, and personal computers with a variety of printers to use the system without obtaining garbled output.

SOH

The Start of Heading (SOH) is a communications control character used in several character-oriented protocols to define the beginning of a message heading data block. In synchronous transmission on a multipoint or multidrop line structure, the SOH is followed by an address which is checked by all devices on the common line to ascertain if they are the recipient of the data. In asynchronous transmission, the SOH character can be used to signal the beginning of a filename during multiple file transfers, permitting the transfer to occur without treating each file transfer as a separate communications session. Since asynchronous communications typically involves point-to-point communications, no address is required after the

SOH character; however, both devices must have the same communications software program that permits multiple file transfers in this manner.

STX

The Start of Text (STX) character signifies the end of heading data and the beginning of the actual information contained within the block. This communications control character is used in the bisynchronous protocol that will be examined later in this chapter.

ETX

The End of Text (ETX) character is used to inform the receiver that all the information within the block has been transmitted. This character is also used to denote the beginning of the block check characters appended to a transmission block as an error-detection mechanism. This communications control character is primarily used in the bisynchronous protocol.

EOT

The End of Transmission (EOT) character defines the end of transmission of all data associated with a message transmitted to a device. If transmission occurs on a multidrop circuit the EOT also informs other devices on the line to check later transmissions for the occurrence of messages that could be addressed to them. In the XMODEM protocol the EOT is used to indicate the end of a file-transfer operation.

ENQ

The Enquiry (ENQ) communications control character is used in the bisynchronous protocol to request a response or status from the other station on a point-to-point line or to a specifically addressed station on a multidrop line. In response to the ENQ character, the receiving station may respond with the number of the last block of data it successfully received. In a multidrop environment, the mainframe computer polls each device on the line by addressing the ENQ to one particular station at a time. Each station responds to the poll positively or negatively, depending upon whether or not they have information to send to the mainframe computer at that point in time.

ACK and DLE

The Acknowledgement (ACK) character is used to verify that a block of data was received correctly. After the receiver computes its own internal checksum or cyclic code and compares it to the one appended to the transmitted block, it transmits the ACK character if the two checksums match. In the XMODEM protocol the ACK character is used to inform the transmitter that the next block of data can be transmitted. In the bisynchronous protocol the Data Link Escape (DLE) character is normally used in conjunction with the 0 and 1 characters in place of the ACK character. Alternating DLE0 and DLE1 as positive acknowledgement to each correctly received block of data eliminates the potential of a lost or garbled acknowledgement resulting in the loss of data.

NAK

The Negative Acknowledgement (NAK) communications control character is transmitted by a receiving device to request the transmitting device to retransmit the previously sent data block. This character is transmitted when the receiver's internally generated checksum or cyclic code does not match the one transmitted, indicating that a transmission error has occurred. In the XMODEM protocol this character is used to inform the transmitting device that the receiver is ready to commence a file-transfer operation as well as to inform the transmitter of any blocks of data received in error.

SYN

The Synchronous Idle (SYN) character is employed in the bisynchronous protocol to maintain line synchronization between the transmitter and receiver during periods when no data is transmitted on the line. When a series of SYN characters is interrupted, this indicates to the receiver that a block of data is being transmitted.

ETB

The End of Transmission Block (ETB) character is used in the bisynchronous protocol in place of an ETX character when data is transmitted in multiple blocks. This character then indicates the end of a particular block of transmitted data.

Bisynchronous transmission

Among currently used protocols, one of the most frequently used for synchronous transmission is International Business Machines' BISYNC (binary synchronous communications) protocol. This particular protocol is actually a set of very similar protocols which provide rules which effect the synchronous transmission of binary-coded data. Although there are numerous versions of the bisynchronous protocol in existence, three versions account for the vast majority of devices operating in a bisynchronous environment. These three versions of the bisynchronous protocol are known as 2780,

3780, and 3270. The 2780 and 3780 bisynchronous protocols are used for remote job-entry communications into a mainframe computer, the major difference between these versions being the fact that the 3780 version performs space compression while the 2780 version does not incorporate this feature. In comparison to the 2780 and 3780 protocols, which are designed for point-to-point communications, the 3270 protocol is designed for operation with devices connected to a mainframe on a multidrop circuit or devices connected to a cluster controller which, in turn, is connected to the mainframe. Thus, 3270 is a poll-and-select software protocol.

An IBM PC or compatible computer can obtain a bisynchronous communications capability through the installation of a bisynchronous communications adapter card into the PC's system unit. This card is designed to operate in conjunction with a bisynchronous communications software program which with the adapter card enables the PC to operate as an IBM 2780 or 3780 workstation or as an IBM 3270 type of interactive terminal.

The bisynchronous transmission protocol can be used in a variety of transmission codes on many types of medium- to high-speed equipment. Some of the constraints of this protocol are that it is limited to half-duplex transmission and that it requires the acknowledgement of the receipt of every block of data transmitted. A large number of protocols have been developed due to the success of the BISYNC protocol. Some of these protocols are bit-oriented, whereas BISYNC is a character-oriented protocol; and some permit full-duplex transmission, whereas BISYNC is limited to half-duplex transmission.

Most bisynchronous protocols support several data codes to include ASCII and EBCDIC. Error control is obtained by using a two-dimensional parity check (LRC/VRC) when transmission is in ASCII. When transmission is in EBCDIC the CRC-16 polynomial is used to generate a block check character.

Figure 2.20 illustrates the generalized bisynchronous block structure. The start of message control code is normally the STX communications control character. The end of message control code can be either the ETX, ETB, or the EOT character; the actual character, however, depends upon whether the block is one of many blocks, the end of the transmission block, or the end of the transmission session.

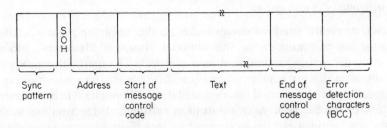

Figure 2.20 Generalized BSC Block Structure

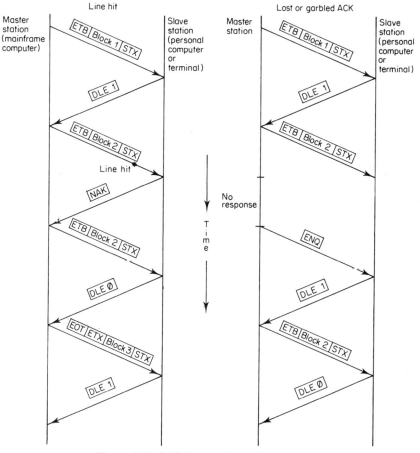

Figure 2.21 BSC Error Control Methods

Figure 2.21 illustrates the error-control mechanism employed in a bisynchronous protocol to handle the situation where a line hit occurs during transmission or if an acknowledgement to a previously transmitted data block becomes lost or garbled.

In the example on the left portion of Figure 2.21, a line hit occurs during the transmission of the second block of data from the mainframe computer to a terminal or a personal computer. Note that although Figure 2.21 is an abbreviated illustration of the actual bisynchronous block structure and does not show the actual block check characters in each block, in actuality they are contained in each block. Thus, the line hit which occurs during the transmission of the second block results in an internally generated BCC different from the BCC that was transmitted with the second block. This causes the terminal device to transmit an NAK to the mainframe, which results in the retransmission of the second block.

In the example on the right part of Figure 2.21, let us assume that the terminal received block 2 and sent an acknowledgement which was lost or garbled.

When a predefined timeout period has elapsed, the master station transmits an ENQ communications control character to check the status of the terminal. Upon receipt of the ENQ, the terminal transmits the alternating acknowledgement, currently DLE1; however, the mainframe was expecting DLE0. Thus, the mainframe is informed by this that block 2 was never acknowledged and as a result retransmits that block.

XMODEM protocol

The XMODEM protocol originally designed by Ward Christensen has been implemented into many asynchronous personal computer communications software programs and a large number of bulletin boards. Figure 2.22 illustrates the use of the XMODEM protocol for a file transfer consisting of two blocks of data. As illustrated, under the XMODEM protocol the receiving device transmits a Negative Acknowledgement (NAK) character to signal the transmitter that it is ready to receive data. In response to the NAK the transmitter sends a Start of Header (SOH) communications control character followed by two characters that represent the block number and the 1s complement of the block number. Here the ones complement is obtained by subtracting the block number from 255. Next a 128 character data block is transmitted which in turn is followed by the checksum character. As previously discussed, the checksum is computed by first adding the ASCII values of each of the characters in the 128-character block and dividing the sum by 255. Next, the quotient is disregarded and the remainder is retained as the checksum.

If the data blocks are damaged during transmission, the receiver can detect the occurrence of an error in one of three ways. If the Start of Header is damaged, it is undetected by the receiver and the data block is negatively acknowledged. If either the block count or the ones complement field are damaged, they will not be the ones complement of each other. Finally, the receiver computes its own checksum and compares it to the transmitted checksum. If the checksums do not match this is also an indicator that the transmitted block was received in error. If the two checksums do not match or the SOH was missing or the block count and its complement field are not the ones complement of each other, the block is considered to have been received in error. Then the receiving station transmits an NAK character which serves as a request to the transmitting station to retransmit the previously transmitted block.

As illustrated in Figure 2.22, a line hit occurring during the transmission of the second block resulted in the receiver transmitting an NAK and the transmitting device resending the second block. Suppose more line hits occur, thus effecting the retransmission of the second block. Under the

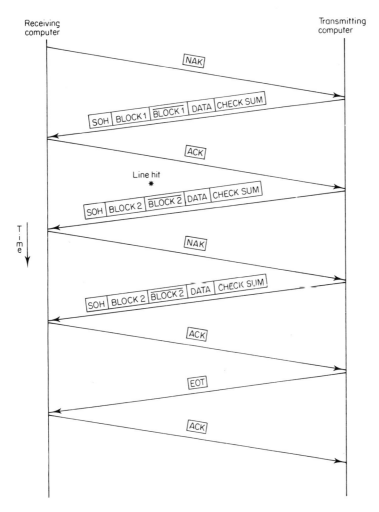

Figure 2.22 XMODEM Protocol File Transfer Operation

XMODEM protocol the retransmission process is repeated until the block is correctly received or until nine additional retransmission attempts occur. If due to a thunderstorm or other disturbance line noise is a problem, after ten attempts to retransmit a block the file transfer process is aborted. This requires a manual operator intervention to restart the file transfer at the beginning and is one of the major deficiencies of the XMODEM protocol.

In comparison, the Blocked Asynchronous Transmission communications program (BLAST) marketed by Communications Research Group in Baton Rouge, LA, is a more sophisticated commercial protocol which permits files to be retransmitted at the point from which the previous transmission terminated. In addition, this program employs a full-duplex protocol in comparison to the half-duplex XMODEM protocol, permitting transmission of data to be normally accomplished in less time since the acknowledgement to the preceding block can be transmitted at the same time the transmitting station is sending the next data block. BLAST is very similar to a full-duplex synchronous data link protocol since a number of blocks can be outstanding and unacknowledged at any point in time. This obviously adds to one's transmission efficiency in comparison to the XMODEM protocol, since under that protocol block n can only be transmitted after block $n-1$ is acknowledged. The reader will find additional information concerning the utilization of the BLAST program in Chapter 4.

In spite of the limitations of the XMODEM protocol, it is one of the most popular protocols employed by personal computer users for asynchronous data transfer due to several factors. First, the XMODEM protocol is in the public domain, which means it is readily available at no cost for software developers to incorporate into their communications programs. Secondly, the algorithm employed to generate the checksum is easy to implement using a higher-level language such as BASIC or Pascal. In comparison, a CRC-16 block check character is normally generated using assembly language. In addition, the simplistic nature of the protocol is also easy to implement in BASIC or Pascal, which enables many personal computer users to write their own routines to transfer files to and from bulletin boards using this protocol. Since the XMODEM protocol requires only a 256-character communications receiver buffer, it can be easily incorporated into communications software that will operate on personal computer systems with limited memory, such as the early systems that were produced with 64K or less RAM.

Several variations of the original XMODEM protocol have been introduced into the public domain. These modified XMODEM protocols incorporate a true CRC block check character error-detection scheme in place of the checksum character, resulting in a much higher level of error-detection capability.

Kermit

Kermit was developed at Columbia University in New York City primarily as a mechanism for downloading files from mainframes to microcomputers. Since its original development this protocol has evolved into a comprehensive communications system which can be employed for transferring data between most types of intelligent devices. Although the name might imply some type of acronym, in actuality, this protocol was named after Kermit the Frog, the star of the well-known Muppet television show.

Kermit is a half-duplex communications protocol which transfers data in variable sized packets, with a maximum packet size of 96 characters.

Packets are transmitted in alternate directions since each packet must be acknowledged in a manner similar to the XMODEM protocol.

In comparison to the XMODEM protocol which permits 7- and 8-level ASCII as well as binary data transfers in their original data composition, all Kermit transmissions occur in seven-level ASCII. The reason for this restriction is the fact that Kermit was originally designed to support file transfers to seven-level ASCII mainframes. Binary file transfers are supported by the protocol prefixing each byte whose eighth bit is set by the ampersand (&) character. In addition, all characters transmitted to include seven-level ASCII must be printable, resulting in Kermit transforming each ASCII control character with the pound (#) character. This transformation is accomplished through the complementation of the seventh bit of the control character. Thus, 64 modulo 64 is added or subtracted from each control character encountered in the input data stream. When an 8-bit byte is encountered whose low-order seven bits represent a control character, Kermit appends a double prefix to the character. Thus, the byte 100 000 001 would be transmitted as &#A.

Although character prefixing adds a considerable amount of overhead to the protocol, Kermit includes a run-length compression facility which may partially reduce the extra overhead associated with control character and binary data transmission. Here, the tilde (~) character is used as a prefix character to indicate run-length compression. The character following the tilde is a repeat count, while the third character in the sequence is the character to be repeated. Thus, the sequence ~XA is used to indicate a series of 88 As, since the value of X is 1011000 binary or decimal 88. Through the use of run-length compression the requirement to transmit printable characters results in an approximate 25 percent overhead increase in comparison to the XMODEM protocol for users transmitting binary files. If ASCII data is transmitted, Kermit's efficiency can range from more efficient to less efficient in comparison to the XMODEM protocol, with the number of control characters in the file to be transferred and the susceptibility of the data of run-length compression the governing factors in comparing the two protocols. Figure 2.23 illustrates the format of a Kermit packet. The Header field is the ASCII Start of Header (SOH) character. The Length field is a single character whose value ranges between 0 and 94. This one character field defines the packet length in characters less two, since it indicates the number of characters to include the checksum that follow this field.

Header	Length	Sequence	Type	Data	Check

Figure 2.23 The Kermit Packet Format

The Sequence field is another one-character field whose value varies between 0 and 63. The value of this field wraps around to 0 after each group of 64 packets is transmitted.

The Type field is a single printable character which defines the activity the packet initiates. Packet types include D (data), Y (acknowledgement), N (negative acknowledgement), B (end of transmission or break), F (file header), Z (end of file) and E (error).

The information contents of the packet are included in the Data field. As previously mentioned, control characters and binary data are prefixed prior to their placement in this field.

The Check field can be one, two or three characters in length depending upon which error-detection method is used, since the protocol supports three options. A single character is used when a checksum method is used for error detection. When this occurs, the checksum is formed by the addition of the ASCII values of all characters after the Header character through the last data character and the low-order 7 bits are then used as the checksum. The other two error-detection methods supported by Kermit include a two-character checksum and a three-character 16-bit CRC. The two-character checksum is formed similar to the one-character checksum; however, the low-order 12 bits of the arithmetic sum are used and broken into two 7-bit printable characters. The 16-bit CRC is formed using the CCITT standard polynomial, with the high-order 4 bits going into the first character while the middle 6 and low-order 6 bits are placed into the second and third characters, respectively.

By providing the capability to transfer both the filename and contents of files, Kermit provides a more comprehensive capability for file transfers than XMODEM. In addition, Kermit permits multiple files to be transferred in comparison to XMODEM, which requires the user to initiate file transfers on an individual basis.

Bit-oriented line control protocols

Computer vendors have implemented a number of bit-oriented line control procedures that are based upon the International Standards Organization (ISO) procedure known as High Level Data Link Control (HDLC). Various names for line control procedures similar to HDLC include IBM's Synchronous Data Link Control (SDLC) and Burroughs' Data Link Control (BDLC).

The advantages of bit-oriented protocols are threefold. First, their full-duplex capability supports the simultaneous transmission of data in two directions, resulting in a higher throughput than is obtainable in BISYNC. Secondly, bit-oriented protocols are naturally transparent to data, enabling the transmission of pure binary data without requiring special sequences of control characters to enable and disable a transparency transmission mode of operation as required with BISYNC. Lastly, most bit-oriented protocols permit multiple blocks of data to be transmitted. Then, if an error affects a particular block only that block has to be retransmitted.

SDLC link structure

Under the SDLC transmission protocol one station on the line is given the primary status to control the data link and supervise the flow of data on the link. All other stations on the link are secondary stations and respond to commands issued by the primary station.

The vehicle for transporting messages on an SDLC link is called a frame and is illustrated in the top portion of Figure 2.24.

The SDLC frame contains six fields, wherein two fields serve as frame delimiters and are known as the SDLC flag. The SDLC flag has the unique bit combination of 01111110, which defines the beginning and end of the frame. To protect the flag and assure transparency the transmission device will insert a 0 bit any time after a sequence of five 1 bits occurs to prevent data from being mistaken as a flag. This technique is known as zero insertion. The receiver will always delete a 0 after receiving five 1s to insure data integrity.

The address field is an 8-bit pattern that identifies the secondary station involved in the data transfer while the control field can be either 8 or 16 bits in length. This field identifies the type of frame transmitted as either an information frame or a command/response frame. The information field can be any length and is treated as pure binary information, while the frame-check sequence contains a 16-bit value generated using a cyclic redundancy check (CRC) algorithm.

Control field formats

The 8-bit control field formats are illustrated in the lower part of Figure 2.24. N(S) and N(R) are the send and receive sequence counts. They are maintained by each station for Information (I-frames) sent and received by that station. Each station increments its N(S) count by one each time it sends a new frame. The N(R) count indicates the expected number of the next frame to be received.

Using an 8-bit control field, the N(S)/N(R) count ranges from 0 to 7. Using a 16-bit control field the count can range from 0 to 127. The P/F bit is a poll/final bit. It is used as a poll by the primary (set to 1) to obtain a response from a secondary station. It is set to 1 as a final bit by a secondary station to indicate the last frame of a sequence of frames.

The supervisory command/response frame is used in SDLC to control the flow of data on the line. Figure 2.25 illustrates the composition of the supervisory control field: supervisory frames (S-frames) contain an N(R) count and are used to acknowledge I-frames, request retransmission of I-

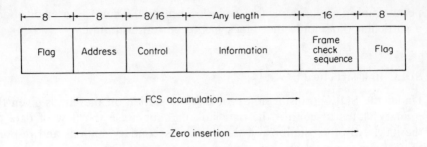

HDLC flag is Ø1111111Ø which is used to delimit an HDLC frame. To protect the flag and assure transparency the transmitter will insert a zero bit after a fifth 1 bit to prevent data from being mistaken as a flag. The receiver always deletes a zero after receiving five 1s.

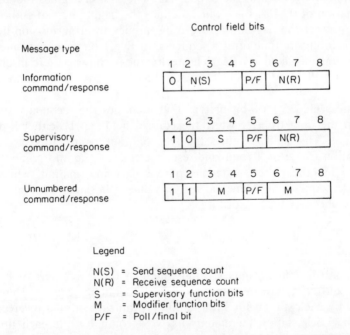

Figure 2.24 SDLC Frame and Control Field Formats

frames, request temporary suspension of I-frames, and perform similar functions.

To illustrate the advantages of SDLC over BISYNC transmission, consider the full-duplex data transfer illustrated in Figure 2.26. For each frame transmitted, this figure shows the type of frame, N(S), N(R), and Poll/Final (P/F) bit status.

In the transmission sequence illustrated in the left portion of Figure 2.26 the primary station has transmitted five frames, numbered zero through

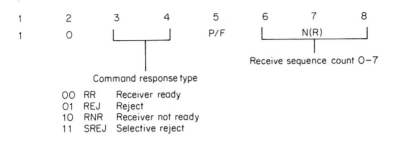

1	2	3	4	5	6	7	8
1	O			P/F		N(R)	

Command response type

00	RR	Receiver ready
01	REJ	Reject
10	RNR	Receiver not ready
11	SREJ	Selective reject

Receive sequence count 0–7

Figure 2.25 Supervisory Control Field

The composition of bits 3 and 4 in the control field defines the command response

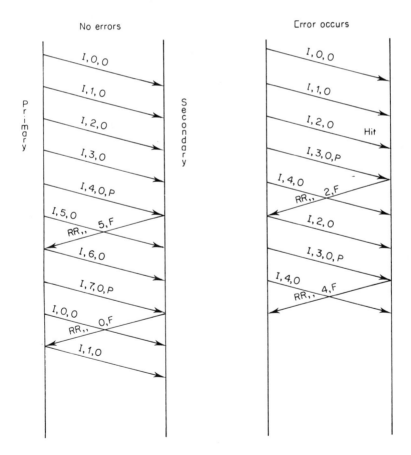

Figure 2.26 SDLC Full-Duplex Data Transfer Format: Type, N(S), N(R), P/F

four, when its poll bit is set in frame four. This poll bit is interpreted by the secondary station as a request for it to transmit its status and it responds by transmitting a Receiver Ready (RR) response, indicating that it expects to receive frame 5 next. This serves as an indicator to the primary station that frames 0–4 were received correctly. The secondary station sets its poll/ final bit as a final bit to indicate to the primary station that its transmission is completed.

Note that since full-duplex transmission is permissible under SDLC, the primary station continues to transmit information (I) frames while the secondary station is responding to the primary's polls. If an 8-bit control field is used, the maximum frame number that can be outstanding is limited to seven since 3 bit positions are used for N(S) frame numbering. Thus, after frame number 7 is transmitted, the primary station then begins frame numbering again at N(S) equal to zero. Notice that when the primary station sets its poll bit when transmitting frame 7 the secondary station responds, indicating that it expects to receive frame 0. This indicates to the primary station that frames 5–7 were received correctly, since the previous secondary response acknowledged frames 0–4.

In the transmission sequence indicated in the right of Figure 2.26, let us assume a line hit occurs during the transmission of frame 2. Note that in comparison to BISYNC, under SDLC the transmitting station does not have to wait for an acknowledgement of the previously transmitted data block; and it can continue to transmit frames until the maximum number of frames outstanding is reached; or it can issue a poll to the secondary station to query the status of its previously transmitted frames while it continues to transmit frames up until the maximum number of outstanding frames is reached.

Thus, the primary station polled the secondary in frame 3 and then sent frame 4 while it waited for the secondary's response. When the secondary's response was received, it indicated that the next frame the secondary expected to receive N(R) was 2. This informed the primary station that all frames after frame 1 would have to be retransmitted. Thus, after transmitting frame 4 the primary station then retransmitted frames 2 and 3 prior to retransmitting frame 4.

It should be noted that if selective rejection is implemented, the secondary could have issued a Selective Reject (SREJ) of frame 2. Then, upon its receipt, the primary station would retransmit frame 2 and have then continued its transmission with frame 5. Although selective rejection can considerably increase the throughput of SDLC, even without its use this protocol will provide the user with a considerable throughput increase in comparison to BISYNC.

2.12 THE DTE/DCE INTERFACE

In the world of data communications, equipment to include personal computers, terminals and computer ports is referred to as Data Terminal

Equipment or DTEs. In comparison, modems and other communications devices are referred to as Data Communications Equipment or DCEs. The physical, electrical, and logical rules for the exchange of data between DTEs and DCEs are specified by an interface standard; the most commonly used is the EIA RS-232-C standard which is very similar to the CCITT V.24 standard used in Europe and other locations outside of North America. The term EIA refers to the Electronic Industries Association, which is a national body that represents a large percentage of the manufacturers in the US electronics industry. The EIA's work in the area of standards has become widely recognized and many of its standards were adopted by other standard bodies. RS-232-C is a recommended standard (RS) published by the EIA in 1969, with the number 232 referencing the identification number of one particular communications standard and the suffix C designating the latest revision to that standard.

Since the RS-232-C standard defines the interfacing between DTEs and DCEs in the United States, this standard governs as an example the interconnection of terminal devices to stand-alone modems. The RS-232-C standard applies to serial data transfers between a DTE and DCE in the range from 0 to 20000 bits per second. Although the standard also limits the cable length between the DTE and DCE to 50 feet, since the pulse width of digital data is inversely proportional to the data rate, one can normally exceed this 50-foot limitation at lower data rates as wider pulses are less susceptible to distortion than narrower pulses. When a cable length in excess of 50 feet is required, it is highly recommended that low-capacitance shielded cable be used and tested prior to going on-line, to ensure that the signal quality is acceptable.

Another part of the RS-232-C standard specifies the cable heads that serve as connectors to the DTEs and DCEs. Here the connector is known as a DB-25 connector and each end of the cable is equipped with this male connector that is designed to be inserted into the DB-25 female connectors normally built into modems. Figure 2.27 illustrates the RS-232-C interface between a PC and a stand-alone modem. In actuality, the female connector on the PC is located on the communications adapter board which is installed

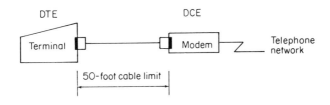

Figure 2.27 The RS-232-C Physical Interface

Standard cables are typically 6, 10, or 12 feet in length with male connectors on each end

in the system unit of the PC. If an internal modem is installed within the PC, there is no requirement for cabling between the PC's communications adapter board and modem since an internal modem includes both the communications adapter and modem on one card. In such situations, a telephone cable is used to connect the PC's internal modem card directly to the telephone network.

The reader will find additional information concerning the installation and operation of internal and external modems in Chapter 3.

Figure 2.28 illustrates the 25-pin female connector located on the asynchronous communications adapter when the adapter is installed inside the system unit of an IBM PC. Note that the 25 holes in the connector are designed to be mated to a male connector which attaches to a cable that can have up to 25 individual conductors. The signals on each of these conductors will be covered next in this chapter.

RS-232 signal characteristics

The RS-232-C interface specifies 25 interchange circuits or conductors that govern the data flow between the DTE and DCE. Although one can purchase a 25-conductor cable, normally fewer conductors are required. For asynchronous transmission, normally 9–12 conductors are required, while synchronous transmission typically requires 12–16 conductors, with the number of conductors required a function of the operational characteristics of the modem to be connected. The signal on each of these conductors occurs based upon a predefined voltage transition occurring as illustrated in Figure 2.29.

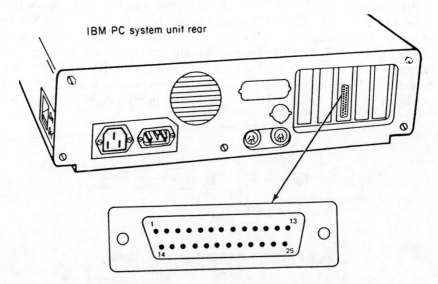

Figure 2.28 Asynchronous Communications Adapter Connector

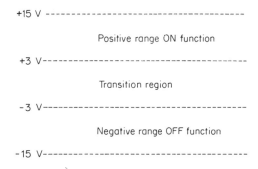

Figure 2.29 Interchange Circuit Voltage Ranges

A signal is considered to be ON when the voltage (V) on the interchange circuit is between $+3$ V and $+15$ V. In comparison, a voltage between -3 V and -15 V causes the interchange circuit to be placed in the OFF condition. The voltage range from $+3$ V to -3 V is a transition region that has no effect upon the condition of the circuit. Table 1.15 provides a comparison between the interchange circuit voltage, its binary state, signal condition and function.

Since the physical implementation of the RS-232-C standard is based upon the conductors used to interface a DTE to a DCE, we will examine the functions of each of the interchange circuits. Prior to discussing these circuits, an explanation of RS-232 terminology is warranted since there are three ways one can refer to the circuits in this interface.

The most commonly used method to refer to the RS-232 circuits is by specifying the number of the pin in the connector which the circuit uses.

A second method used to refer to the RS-232 circuit is by their two- or three-letter designation used by the standard to label its circuits. The first letter in the designator is used to group the circuits into one of six circuit categories as indicated by the second column, labeled 'Interchange Circuit' in Figure 2.30. As an example of the use of this method, the two ground circuits have the letter A as the first letter in the circuit designator and the signal ground circuit is called 'AB', since it is the second circuit in the 'A'

Table 2.17 Interchange Circuit Comparison

| | Interchange circuit voltage | |
	Negative	Positive
Binary state	1	0
Signal condition	Mark	Space
Function	OFF	ON

PIN NUMBER	Interchange Circuit	CCITT Equivalent	Description	Gnd	Data From DCE	Data To DCE	Control From DCE	Control To DCE	Timing From DCE	Timing To DCE
1	AA	101	Protective ground	X						
7	AB	102	Signal ground common return	X						
2	BA	103	Transmitted data			X				
3	BB	104	Received data		X					
4	CA	105	Request to send					X		
5	CB	106	Clear to send				X			
6	CC	107	Data set ready				X			
20	CD	108.2	Data terminal ready					X		
22	CE	125	Ring indicator				X			
8	CF	109	Received line signal detector				X			
21	CG	110	Signal quality detector				X			
23	CH	111	Data signal rate selector (DTE)					X		
23	CI	112	Data signal rate selector (DCE)				X			
24	DA	113	Transmitter signal element timing (DTE)							X
15	DB	114	Transmitter signal element timing (DCE)						X	
17	DD	115	Receiver signal element timing (DCE)						X	
14	SBA	118	Secondary transmitted data			X				
16	SBB	119	Secondary received data		X					
19	SCA	120	Secondary request to send					X		
13	SCB	121	Secondary clear to send				X			
12	SCF	122	Secondary Rec'd line signal detector				X			

Figure 2.30 RS-232-C/CCITT V.24 Interchange Circuits by Category

ground category. Since these designators are rather cryptic, they are not commonly used.

A third method used to describe the circuits is by describing the function of the circuit. Thus, pin 2, which is the transmit data circuit, can be easily referenced as transmit data. Many persons have created acronyms for the descriptions, which are easier to remember than the RS-232 pin number or interchange circuit designator. For example, transmit data is referred to as 'TD', which is easier to remember than any of the RS-232 designators previously discussed.

Although the list of circuits in Figure 2.30 may appear overwhelming at first glance, in most instances only a subset of the 25 conductors are employed. To better understand this interface standard, we will first examine those interchange circuits required to connect an asynchronously operated personal computer or terminal device to an asynchronous modem. Then we can expand upon our knowledge of these interchange circuits by examining the functions of the remaining circuits, to include those additional circuits that would be used to connect a synchronously operated PC or terminal to a synchronous modem.

Asynchronous operations

Figure 2.31 illustrates the signals that are required to connect an IBM PC asynchronous communications adapter to a particular type of low-speed asynchronous modem known as a 103A-type modem. Note that although a 25-conductor cable can be used to cable the terminal to the modem, only 9 conductors are actually required. Thus, a 9-conductor cable could be used

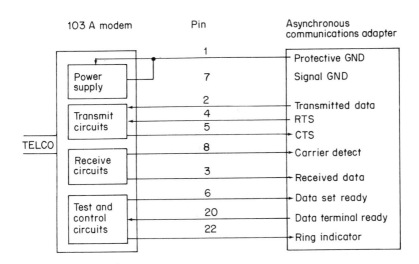

Figure 2.31 DTE–DCE Interface Example

to connect a 103-type modem to an asynchronously operated PC, which could result in a significant reduction in cable costs when one is cabling many DTEs to DCEs.

By reading the modem vendor's specification sheet one can easily determine the number of conductors required to cable DTEs to DCEs. Although most cables have straight-through conductors, in certain instances the conductor pins at one end of a cable may require reversal or two conductors may be connected onto a common pin. In fact, many times only one conductor will be used for both protective ground and signal ground, with the common conductor cabled to pins 1 and 7 at both ends of the cable. With this in mind, let us review the functions of the ten circuits illustrated in Figure 2.31.

Protective ground (GND, pin 1)

This interchange circuit is normally electrically bonded to the equipment's frame. In some instances, it can be further connected to external grounds as required by applicable regulations.

Signal ground (SG, pin 7)

This circuit must be included in all RS-232 interfaces as it establishes a ground reference for all other lines. The voltage on this circuit is set to 0 V to provide a reference for all other signals. Although the conductors for pins 1 and 7 can be independent of one another, typical practice is to 'strap' pin 7 to pin 1 at the modem. This is known as tying signal ground to frame ground.

Transmitted data (TD, pin 2)

The signals on this circuit are transmitted from the asynchronous communications adapter, hereafter referred to as the terminal device, to the modem. When no data is being transmitted the terminal device maintains this circuit in a marking or logical 1 condition. This is the circuit over which the actual serial bit stream of data flows from the terminal device to the modem, where it is modulated for transmission.

Request to send (RTS, pin 4)

The signal on this circuit is sent from the adapter to the modem to prepare the modem for transmission. Prior to actually sending data, the adapter must receive a Clear to Send signal from the modem on pin 5.

Clear to send (CTS, pin 5)

This interchange circuit is used by the modem to send a signal to the attached device, indicating that the modem is ready to transmit. By turning this circuit OFF, the modem informs the terminal device that it is not ready to recive data. The modem raises the CTS signal after the terminal device initiates a Request to Send (RTS) signal.

Carrier detect (CD, pin 8)

This circuit is commonly referred to as received line signal detector (RLSD), and a signal on it is used to indicate to the terminal device that the modem is receiving a carrier signal from a remote modem. The presence of this signal is also used to illuminate the carrier detect light emitting diode (LED) indicator on modems equipped with that display indicator. If this light indicator should go out during a communications session, it indicates that the session has terminated due to a loss of carrier and software that samples for this condition will display the message 'carrier lost' or a similar message to indicate this condition has occurred.

Receive data (RD, pin 3)

After data is demodulated by a modem, it is transferred to the attached terminal device over this interchange circuit. When the modem is not sending data to the terminal device, this circuit is held in the marking condition.

Dataset ready (DSR, pin 6)

Signals on this interchange circuit are used to indicate the status of the data set connected to the terminal. When this circuit is in the ON (logic 0) condition, it serves as a signal to the terminal that the modem is connected to the telephone line and is ready to transmit data. Since the RS-232 standard specifies that the DSR signal is ON when the modem is connected to the communications channel and not in any test condition, a modem using a self-testing feature or automatic dialing capability would pass this signal to the terminal device after the self-test is completed or after the telephone number of a remote location was successfully dialed.

Data terminal ready (DTR, pin 20)

This circuit is used to control the modem's connection to the telephone line. An ON condition on this circuit prepares the modem to be connected to the telephone line, after which the connection can be established by manual or automatic dialing. If the signal on this circuit is placed in an OFF condition, it causes the modem to drop any telephone connection in progress, providing a mechanism for the terminal device to control the line connection.

Ring indicator (RI, pin 22)

This interchange circuit indicates to the terminal device that a ringing signal is being received on the communications channel. This circuit is used by an auto-answer modem to 'wake-up' the attached terminal device. Since a telephone rings for 1 second and then pauses for 4 seconds prior to ringing again, this line becomes active for 1 second every 5 seconds when an incoming call occurs.

Synchronous operations

To communicate synchronously, an IBM PC must have a synchronous communications adapter installed in its system unit. Examples of currently available synchronous adapters include the IBM bisynchronous communications adapter and the IBM synchronous data link control (SDLC) communications adapter. One major difference between asynchronous and synchronous modems is the timing signals required for synchronous transmission.

Timing Signals

When a synchronous modem is used, it puts out a square wave on pin 15 at a frequency equal to the modem's bit rate. This timing signal serves as a clock from which the attached PC or terminal would synchronize its transmission of data onto pin 2 to the modem. Thus, pin 15 is referred to as transmit clock as well as its formal designator of Transmission Signal Element Timing (DCE), with DCE referencing the fact that the communications device supplies the timing.

Whenever a synchronous modem receives a signal from the telephone line it puts out a square wave on pin 17 to the attached terminal device at a frequency equal to the modem's bit rate, while the actual data is passed to the device on pin 3. Since pin 17 provides receiver clocking, it is known as 'receive clock' as well as its more formal designator of Receiver Signal Element Timing.

In certain cases a terminal device such as a computer port can provide timing signals to the DCE. In such situations the DTE will provide a clocking signal to the DCE on pin 24 while the formal designator of Transmitter Signal Element Timing (DTE) is used to reference this signal.

Intelligent operations

There are three interchange circuits that can be employed to change the operation of the attached communications device. One circuit can be used to first determine that a deterioration in the quality of a circuit has occurred, while the other two circuits can be employed to change the transmission rate to reflect the circuit quality.

Signal quality detector (CG, pin 21)

Signals on this circuit are transmitted from the modem to the attached terminal device whenever there is a high probability of an error in the received data due to the quality of the circuit falling below a predefined level. This circuit is maintained in an ON condition when the signal quality is acceptable and turned to an OFF condition when there is a high probability of an error.

Data signal rate selector (CH/CI, pin 23)

When an intelligent terminal device such as a personal computer or a mainframe computer port receives an OFF condition on pin 21 for a predefined period of time, it may be programmed to change the data rate of the attached modem, assuming that the modem is capable of operating at dual data rates. This can be accomplished by the terminal device providing an ON condition on pin 23 to select the higher data signaling rate or range of rates while an OFF condition would select the lower data signaling rate or range of rates. When the data terminal equipment selects the operating rate the signal on pin 23 flows from the DTE to the DCE and the circuit is known as circuit CH. If the data communications equipment is used to select the data rate of the terminal device, the signal on pin 23 flows from the DCE to the DTE and the circuit is known as circuit CI.

Secondary circuits

In certain instances a synchronous modem will be designed with the capability to transmit data on a secondary channel simultaneously with transmission occurring on the primary channel. In such cases the data rate of the secondary channel is normally a fraction of the data rate of the primary channel.

To control the data flow on the secondary channel the RS 232 standard employs five interchange circuits. Pins 14 and 16 are equivalent to the circuits on pins 2 and 3, except that they are used to transmit and receive data on the secondary channel. Similarly, pins 19, 13, and 12 perform the same functions as pins 4, 5, and 8 used for controlling the flow of information on the primary data channel.

2.13 POWER MEASUREMENTS

In referencing the operation of certain types of communications equipment, the measurement of power gains and losses is frequently expressed in terms of decibels (dB). When used to express a loss, a minus sign is placed before dB, while the absence of a minus sign or the presence of a plus sign is used to indicate a power gain.

Instead of telling one the actual amount of power, the decibel is used to describe the ratio of power in a circuit, describing the power output of a circuit to its input power. If there is less output power than input power, there is a dB loss. If there is more output power than input power, there is a dB gain.

Decibel gains and losses are computed using the formula:

Number of decibels $= 10 \log (P_1/P_2)$

where: P_1 is the larger power
P_2 is the smaller power

To illustrate the use of decibels, assume the input power to a transmission circuit is 1 milliwatt (mW) and its output is .5 mW. The power change on this circuit would become:

$$dB = 10 \log (1/0.5) = 10 \log 2$$

From a table of logarithms log 2 is 0.3010; thus the number of decibels is 3.01. Since the input power was greater than the output power, we have a power loss and the dB loss is then -3.01 dB.

From the preceding, it should be apparent that a loss of 3 dB represents a 50 percent power loss, while a gain of 3 dB represents a gain of twice as much power. Table 2.18 lists the relationship between a dB gain or loss and the ratio of power input to output on a circuit.

Table 2.18 Relationship between dB and Power

When you have this dB gain or loss	Larger power divided by smaller power is
1	1.2
2	1.6
3	2.0
4	2.5
5	3.2
6	4.0
7	5.0
8	6.4
9	8.0
10	10.0
20	100.0
30	1000.0
40	10 000.0

In telephone operations the reference level of power is 0.001 W (1 mW). This level was selected as it represents the average amount of power generated in the telephone transmitter during a voice conversation.

Thus, by using a 1 mW power level telephone company personnel have a reference level for comparing gains and losses in a circuit. For convenience, 1 mW of power is designated as being equal to 0 dB. To ensure that no one forgets that 1 mW is the reference level, the letter m is attached to the power level. Thus, 0 dB becomes 0 dBm. As a voice circuit is routed by the telephone company through amplifiers, the losses and gains are added algebraically. Thus, a -20 dBm loss on a circuit followed by a gain of $+12$ dBm due to an amplifier would result in a -8 dBm overall loss.

In addition to using a reference power level, telephone company personnel also use a standard frequency for testing voice circuits. In the United States a frequency of 1000 Hz (1 KHz) is used, resulting in a device that supplies 0 dBm of power to a circuit at a frequency of 1 kHz for line-testing purposes.

The null modem

No discussion of cabling would be complete without a description of a null modem, which is also referred to as a modem eliminator. A null modem is a special cable that is designed to eliminate the requirement for modems when interconnecting two collocated data terminal equipment devices. One example of this is a requirement to transfer data between two collocated personal computers that do not have modems. In this situation, the interconnection of the two PCs via a null modem cable would permit programs and data to be transferred between the personal computers.

Since DTEs transmit data on pin 2 and receive data on pin 3, one could never connect two such devices together with a conventional cable as the data transmitted from one device would never be received by the other. In order for two DTEs to communicate with one another, a connector on pin 2 of one device must be wired to connector pin 3 on the other device. Figure 2.32 illustrates an example of the wiring diagram of a null modem cable, showing how pins 2 and 3 are cross connected as well as the configuration of the control circuit pins on this type of cable.

Since a terminal device will raise or apply a positive voltage in the 9–12 V range to turn on a control signal, one can safely divide this voltage to provide up to three different signals without going below the signal threshold of 3 V previously illustrated in Figure 2.29. In examining Figure 2.32, we should note the following control signal interactions are caused by the pin cabling:

1. Data Terminal Ready (DTR, pin 20) raises Data Set Ready (DSR, pin 6) at the other end of the cable.
2. Request to Send (RTS, pin 4) raises Data Carrier Detect (CD, pin 8)

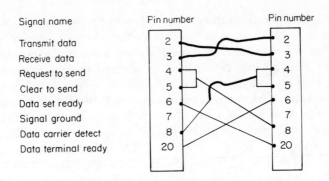

Signal name	Pin number		Pin number
Transmit data	2		2
Receive data	3		3
Request to send	4		4
Clear to send	5		5
Data set ready	6		6
Signal ground	7		7
Data carrier detect	8		8
Data terminal ready	20		20

Figure 2.32 Null Modem Cable

on the other end and signals Clear-to-Send (CTS, pin 5) at the original end of the cable.

3. Once the handshaking of control signals is completed, we can transmit data onto one end of the cable (TD, pin 2) which becomes receive data (RD, pin 3) at the other end.

The cable configuration illustrated in Figure 2.32 will work for most data terminal equipment interconnections; however, there are a few exceptions. The most common exception is when a terminal device is to be cabled to a port on a mainframe computer that operates as a 'ring-start' port. This means that the computer port must obtain a Ring Indicator (RI, pin 22) signal. In this situation, the null modem must be modified so that Data Set Ready (DSR, pin 6) is jumpered to Ring Indicator (RI, pin 22) at the other end of the cable to initiate a connect sequence to a 'ring-start' system.

Due to the omission of transmit and receive clocks, a null modem can be used only for asynchronous transmission. For synchronous transmission one must either drive a clocking device at one end of the cable or employ another technique. Here one would use a modem eliminator which differs from a null modem by providing a clocking signal to the interface.

Plugs and jacks

Data communications equipment is connected to telephone company facilities by a plug and jack arrangement as illustrated in Figure 2.33. Although the connection appears to be, and in fact is, simplistic, the number of connection arrangements and differences in the types of jacks offered by telephone companies usually ensures that the specification of an appropriate jack can be a complex task. Fortunately, most modems and other communications products include explicit instructions covering the type of jack the equipment must be connected to as well as providing the purchaser with information that must be furnished to the telephone company in order to legally connect the device to the telephone company line.

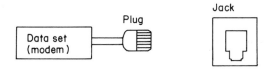

Figure 2.33 Connection to Telephone Company Facilities

Data communications equipment can be connected to telephone company facilities by plugging the device into a telephone company jack

Connecting arrangements

There are three connecting arrangements that can be used to connect data communications equipment to telephone facilities. The object of these arrangements is to ensure that the signal received at the telephone company central office does not exceed $-12\,$dBm.

Permissive arrangement

The permissive arrangement is used when one desires to connect a modem to an organization's switchboard, such as a private branch exchange (PBX). When a permissive arrangement is employed, the output signal from the modem is fixed at a maximum of $-9\,$dBm and the plug that is attached to the data set cable can be connected to three types of telephone company jacks as illustrated in Figure 2.34. The RJ11 jack can be obtained as a surface mounting (RJ11C) for desk sets or as a wall mounted (RJ11W) unit, while the RJ41S and RJ45S are available only for surface mounting.

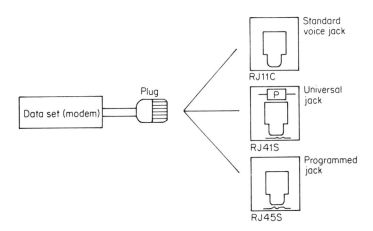

Figure 2.34 Permissive Arrangement Jack Options

Since permissive jacks use the same 6-pin capacity miniature jack used for standard voice telephone installations, this arrangement provides for good mobility of terminals and modems.

Fixed-loss loop arrangement

Under the fixed-loss loop arrangement the output signal from the modem is fixed at a maximum of -4 dBm and the line between the subscriber's location and the telephone company central office is set to 8 dB of attenutation by a pad located within the jack provided by the telephone company. As illustrated in Figure 2.35, the only jack that can be used under the fixed-loss loop arrangement is the RJ41S. This jack has a switch labeled FLL-PROG, which must be placed in the FLL position under this arrangement. Since the modem output is limited to -4 dBm, the 8 dB attenuation of the pad ensures that the transmitted signal reaches the telephone company office at -12 dBm. As the pad in the jack reduces the receiver signal-to-noise ratio by 8 dB, this type of arrangement is more susceptible to impulse noise and should be used only if one cannot use either of the two other arrangements.

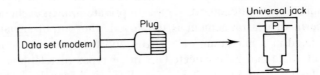

Figure 2.35 Fixed Loss Loop Arrangement

Programmable arrangement

Under the programmable arrangement configuration a level setting resistor inside the standard jack provided by the telephone company is used to set the transmit level within a range between 0 and -12 dBm. Since the line from the user is directly routed to the local telephone company central office at installation time, the telephone company will measure the loop loss and set the value of the resistor based upon the loss measurement. As the resistor automatically adjusts the transmitted output of the modem so the signal reaches the telephone company office at -12 dBm, the modem will always transmit at its maximum allowable level. As this is a different line interface in comparison to permissive or fixed-loss data sets, the data set must be designed to operate with the programmability feature of the jack.

Either the RJ41S universal jack or the RJ45S programmed jack can be used with the programmed arrangement as illustrated in Figure 2.36. The RJ41S jack is installed by the telephone company with both the resistor and pad for programmed and fixed-loss loop arrangements. By setting the switch to PROG, the programmed arrangement will be set. Since the RJ45S jack

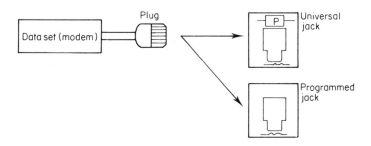

Figure 2.36 Programmed Arrangement Jack

can operate in either the permissive or programmed arrangement without a switch, it is usually preferred as it eliminates the possibility of an inadvertent switch reset.

Telephone options

A telephone set can be connected to one's data line and used for voice conversations, call origination, and call answering. As part of the ordering procedure you must specify a series of specific options that are listed in Table 2.19.

When the telephone set is optioned for 'telephone set controls the line', calls are originated or answered with the telephone by lifting the handset off the hook. When the 'data set controls the line' option is selected, calls can be automatically originated or answered by the data equipment without lifting the telephone handset. Obviously, PC owners who anticipate using an intelligent modem would select option A2.

Aural monitoring enables the telephone set to monitor call progress tones as well as voice answer back messages without requiring the user to switch from data to voice.

Users can select option B3 if aural monitoring is not required, while option B4 should be selected if it is required. Option C5 should be selected

Table 2.19 Telephone Ordering Options

Decision		Description
A	1	Telephone set controls line
	2	Data set controls line
B	3	No aural monitoring
	4	Aural monitoring provided
C	5	Touchtone dialing
	6	Rotary dialing
D	7	Switchhook indicator
	8	Mode indicator

if touchtone dialing is to be used, while option C6 should be specified for rotary dial telephones. Under option D7, the exclusion key will be bypassed, resulting in the lifting of the telephone handset causing the closure of the switchhook contact in the telephone. In comparison, option D8 results in the exclusion key contacts being wired in series with the switchhook contacts, indicating to the user whether he or she is in a voice or data mode.

Ordering the business line

Ordering a business line to transmit data over the switched telephone network currently requires one to provide the telephone company with four items of information. First, one must supply the telephone company with the Federal Communications Commission (FCC) registration number of the device to be connected to the switched telephone network. This 14-character number can be obtained from the vendor who must first register their device for operation on the switched network prior to making it available for use on that network.

Next, one must provide the ringer equivalence number of the data set to be connected to the switched network. This is a three-character number, such as 0.4A, and represents a unitless quotient formed in accordance with certain circuit parameters. This number is also provided by the equipment vendor. Finally, one must provide the jack numbers and arrangement to be used as well as the telephone options if you intend to use a handset.

2.14 THE ISO REFERENCE MODEL

The International Standards Organization (ISO) established a framework for standardizing communication systems called the Open System Interconnection (OSI) Reference Model. The OSI architecture defines seven layers of communication protocol with specific functions isolated to and associated with each layer. Each layer as illustrated in Figure 2.37 covers lower-layer processes, effectively isolating them from higher-layer functions. In this way, each layer performs a set of functions necessary to provide a set of services to the layer above it. Layer isolation permits the characteristics of a given layer to change without impacting the remainder of the model, provided that the supporting services remain the same.

At the lowest or most basic level, the physical layer (level 1) is a set of rules that specifies the electrical and physical connection between devices. This level specifies the cable connections and the electrical rules necessary to transfer data between devices. Typically, the physical link corresponds to established interface standards such as RS-232-C and includes hardware, such as modems and communications adapters as well as the software and/or control electronics which operate the hardware.

The next layer, which is known as the data link layer (level 2), denotes how a device gains access to the medium specified in the physical layer; it

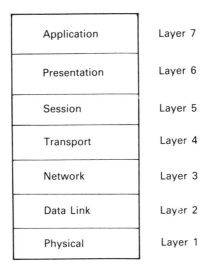

Figure 2.37 ISO Reference Model

also defines data formats to include the framing of data within transmitted messages, error-control procedures, and other link control activities. Data link control protocols such as binary synchronous communications (BSC) and high-level data link control (HDLC) reside in this layer.

The network layer (level 3) is responsible for arranging a logical connection between a source and destination on the network. This layer provides services associated with the movement of data through a network, to include addressing, routeing, switching, sequencing, and flow-control procedures. In a complex network the source and destination may not be directly connected by a single path, but instead require a path to be established that consists of many subpaths. Thus, routeing data through the network onto the correct paths is an important feature of this layer.

The transport layer (level 4) is responsible for guaranteeing that data is correctly received by the destination. Thus, the primary function of this layer is to control the communications session between network nodes once a path has been established by the network control layer. Error control, sequence checking, and other end-to-end data reliability factors are the primary concern of this layer.

The session layer (level 5) provides a set of rules for establishing and terminating data streams between nodes in a network. The services that this session layer can provide include establishing and terminating node connections, message flow control, dialogue control and end-to-end data control.

The presentation layer (level 6) services are concerned with data transformation, formatting, and syntax. One of the primary functions performed by the presentation layer is the conversion of transmitted data into a display format appropriate for a receiving device. Data encryption/decryption and compression and decompression are additional examples of the data transformation that could be handled by this layer.

Finally, the application layer (level 7) acts as a window through which the application gains access to all of the services provided by the model. Examples of functions at this level include file transfers, resource sharing and database access. While the first four layers are fairly well defined, the top three layers may vary considerably depending upon the network used. Figure 2.38 illustrates the OSI model in schematic format, showing the various levels of the model with respect to a terminal or personal computer accessing an application on a host computer system.

As data flows within an ISO network, each layer appends appropriate heading information to frames of information flowing within the network while removing the heading information added by a lower layer. Figure 2.39 illustrates the appending and removal of frame header information as data flows through a network constructed according to the ISO reference model. Since each higher level removes the header appended by a lower level, the frame traversing the network arrives in its original form at its destination.

As the reader will surmise from the previous illustrations, the ISO Reference Model is designed to simplify the construction of data networks. This simplification is due to the eventual standardization of methods and procedures to append appropriate heading information to frames flowing

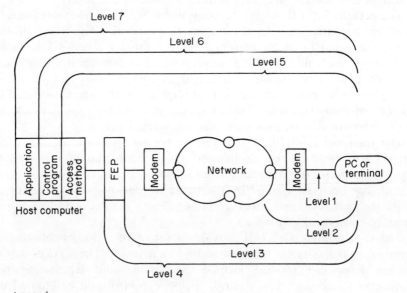

Legend

O   = network node
FEP = front-end processor

Figure 2.38 OSI Model Schematic

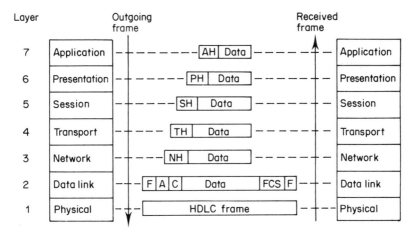

Figure 2.39 Data Flow Within an ISO Reference Model Network

through a network, permitting data to be routed to its appropriate destination following a uniform procedure.

2.15 NETWORK ARCHITECTURE AND SNA

To satisfy the requirements of cutomers for remote computing capability, mainframe computer manufacturers developed a variety of network architectures. Such architectures defined the interrelationship of a particular vendor's hardware and software products necessary to permit communications to flow through a network to the manufacturers' mainframe computer. IBM's System Network Architecture (SNA) is a very complex and sophisticated network architecture which defines the rules, procedures and structure of communications from the input/output statements of an application program to the screen display on a user's personal computer or terminal. SNA consists of protocols, formats and operational sequences which govern the flow of information within a data-communications network linking IBM mainframe computers, minicomputers, terminal controllers, communications controllers, personal computers and terminals.

SNA concepts

An SNA network consists of one or more domains, where a domain refers to all of the logical and physical components that are connected to and

82

controlled by one common point in the network. This common point of control is called the system services control point, which is commonly known by its abbreviation as the SSCP. There are three types of network-addressable units in an SNA network – SSCPs, physical units and logical units.

The SSCP resides in the communications access method operating in an IBM mainframe computer, such as virtual telecommunications access method (VTAM), operating in a System/360, System/370, 4300 series or 308X computer, or in the system control program of an IBM minicomputer, such as a System/34, System/36 or System/38. The SSCP contains the network's address tables, routeing tables and translation tables which it uses to establish connections between nodes in the network as well as to control the flow of information in an SNA network. Figure 2.40 illustrates single and multiple domain SNA networks.

Each network domain includes one or more nodes, with an SNA network node consisting of a grouping of networking components which provides it with a unique characteristic. Examples of SNA nodes include cluster controllers, communications controllers and terminal devices, with the address of each device in the network providing its unique characteristic in comparison to a similar device contained in the network.

Each node in an SNA network contains a physical unit (PU) which controls the other resources contained in the node. The PU is not a physical device as its name appears to suggest, but rather a set of SNA components which provide services used to control terminals, controllers, processors and data links in the network. In programmable devices, such as mainframe computers and communications controllers, the PU is normally implemented

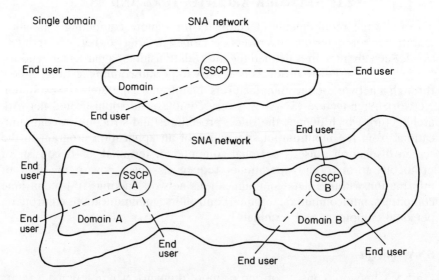

Figure 2.40 Single and Multiple Domain SNA Networks

in software. In less intelligent devices, such as cluster controllers and terminals, the PU is typically implemented in read only memory.

The third type of network-addressable unit in an SNA network is the logical unit, known by its abbreviation as the LU. The LU is the interface or point of access between the end-user and an SNA network. Through the LU an end-user gains access to network resources and transmits and receives data over the network. Each PU can have one or more LUs, with each LU having a distinct address.

As an example of the communications capability of SNA, consider an end-user with an IBM PC and an SDLC communications adapter who establishes a connection to an IBM mainframe computer. The IBM PC is a PU, with its display and printer considered to be LUs. After communication is established, the PC user could direct a file to his or her printer by establishing an LU-to-LU session between the mainframe and printer while using the PC as an interactive terminal running an application program as a second LU-to-LU session.

In Table 2.20, the reader will find a list of the five types of physical units in an SNA network and their corresponding SNA node type. In addition, this table contains representative examples of hardware devices that can operate as a specific type of PU. As indicated in Table 2.20, the different types of PUs form a hierarchy of hardware classifications. At the lowest level, PU Type 1 is a single terminal. PU Type 2 is a cluster controller which is used to connect many SNA devices onto a common communications circuit. PU Type 4 is a communications controller which is also known as a front-end processor. This device provides communications support for up to several hundred line terminations, where individual lines in turn can be connected to cluster controllers. At the top of the hardware hierarchy, PU Type 5 is a mainframe computer.

Figure 2.41 illustrates a two-domain SNA network. By establishing a physical connection between the communications controller in each domain and coding appropriate software for operation on each controller, cross-domain data flow becomes possible. When cross-domain data flow is established, terminal devices connected to one mainframe gain the capability to access applications operating on the other mainframe computer.

Table 2.20 SNA PU Summary

PU type	Node type	Representative hardware
PU Type 5	Mainframe	S/370, 43XX, 308X
PU Type 4	Communications controller	3705, 3725
PU Type 3	Not currently defined	N/A
PU Type 2	Cluster controller	3274, 3276
PU Type 1	Terminal	3180, PC with SNA adapter

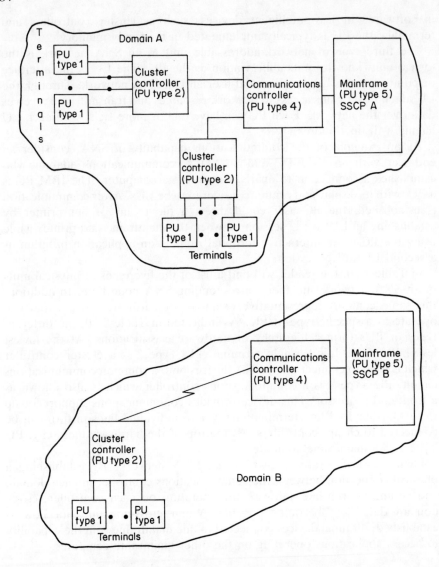

Figure 2.41 Two-Domain SNA Network

SNA was originally implemented as a networking architecture in which users establish sessions with application programs that operate on a mainframe computer within the network. Once a session is established, a network control program (NCP) operating on an IBM communications controller, which in turn is connected to the IBM mainframe, controls the information flow between the user and the applications program. With the growth in personal computing, many users no longer required access to a mainframe to obtain connectivity to another personal computer connected to the network. Thus, IBM modified SNA to permit peer-to-peer communications capability in which two devices on the network with appropriate hardware and software could communicate with one another without requiring access through a mainframe computer.

IBM's SNA is a layered protocol which provides six layers of control for every message that flows through the network. Figure 2.42 illustrates the six SNA layers and provides a comparison to the seven-layer ISO Reference Model.

In comparison to the ISO model which defines the physical level, in SNA the data link level is the lowest defined layer. This layer formats messages into SDLC frames for transmission across an SNA network and is responsible for the orderly and successful transmission of data. Although SDLC is the only data link protocol defined by SNA, some implementations of this architecture can support bisynchronous and asynchronous transmission.

Two of the major functions of the path control layer are routeing and flow control. Concerning routeing, since there can be many data links connected to a node, path control is responsible for insuring that data is correctly passed through intermediate nodes as it flows from source to destination. At the beginning of an SNA session, both sending and receiving nodes as well as all nodes between those nodes cooperate to select the most efficient route for the session. Since this route is established only for the duration of the session, it is known as a virtual route. To increase the efficiency of transmission in an SNA network, the path control layer at each node through which the virtual route is established has the ability to divide long messages into shorter segments for transmission by the data link layer.

SNA layers	ISO layers
Application	
NAU Services Manager	Presentation
Function Management Data services	Session
Transmission Control services	Transport
Path control	Network
Data link	Data link
Physical	

Figure 2.42 Comparing SNA to the ISO Reference Model

Similarly, path control may block short messages into larger data blocks for transmission by the data link layer.

Transmission control services layer functions include session level pacing, as well as encryption and decryption of data when so requested by a session. Here, pacing insures that a transmitting device does not send more data than a receiving device can accept during a given period of time. Thus, pacing can be viewed as similar to the flow control of data in a network.

The data flow control services layer handles the order of communications within a session for error control and flow control. Here, the order of communications is set by the layer controlling the transmission mode. Transmission modes available include full-duplex, which permits each device to transmit at any time, half-duplex flip-flop, in which devices can only transmit alternately, and half-duplex contention, in which one device is considered a master device and the slave cannot transmit until the master completes its transmission.

The function management data services layer performs the connection and disconnection of sessions as well as updating the network configuration and performing network management functions. At the highest layer in an SNA network, the network addressable unit (NAU) services manager is responsible for formatting of data from an application to match the display or printer that is communicating with the application. Other functions performed at this layer include the compression and decompression of data to increase the efficiency of transmission on an SNA network.

SNA developments

The most significant development to SNA can be considered the addition of new LU and PU subtypes to support what is known as advanced peer-to-peer communications (APPC). Previously, LU types used to define an LU-to-LU session were restricted to application-to-device and program-to-program sessions. LU1–LU4 and LU7 are application-to-device sessions as indicated in Table 2.21, whereas LU4 and LU6 are program-to-program sessions.

Table 2.21 SNA LU Session Types

LU Type	Session Type
LU1	Host application and a remote batch terminal
LU2	Host application and a 3270 display terminal
LU3	Host application and a 3270 printer
LU4	Host application and SNA word processor or between two terminals via mainframe
LU6	Between applications programs typically residing on different mainframe computers
LU6.2	Peer-to-peer
LU7	Host application and a 5250 terminal

The addition of LU6.2, which operates in conjunction with PU2.1 to support LU6.2 connections, permits devices supporting this new LU to transfer data to any other device also supporting this LU without first sending the data through a mainframe computer. As new software products are introduced to support LU6.2, a more dynamic flow of data through SNA networks will occur, with many data links to mainframes that were previously heavily utilized or saturated gaining capacity as sessions between devices permit data flow to bypass the mainframe.

CHAPTER THREE

PC and Communications Hardware

In this chapter, we will first examine the system unit which is the key to the functionality of most members of the IBM PC Series to include the PC, PC XT, Portable PC and PC AT. This examination will focus upon the adapter boards that can be added into one's system unit to obtain a communications capability. Next, we will examine the operation and utilization of two of the most common transmission devices used with personal computers, the acoustic coupler and modem.

3.1 THE SYSTEM UNIT

The system unit of each member of the IBM PC series is very similar in many respects. Once the cover of the system unit is removed, a series of expansion slots becomes visible in the upper left-hand portion of the unit. The functionality of one's PC, to include communications support, is then obtained by the installation of various adapter boards into these expansion slots.

The procedure required to remove the cover of the system unit of IBM PCs, PC XTs and PC ATs is very similar. Regardless of the personal computer model you have prior to disassembling any equipment you should first insure that the power switch of the system unit and any externally connected devices are in the OFF position. Then, you should unplug the system unit power cable from the wall outlet and disconnect any cables from the rear of the system unit that will interfere with the removal of the cover of the unit. As an example, if an IBM monochrome display is connected to your system unit, you will have to move the display prior to removing the system unit cover. To move the monochrome display you will have to disconnect the display's power cable which is connected to the system unit as well as the cable connector which attaches the display to the monochrome display and parallel printer adapter previously installed in your system unit.

Figure 3.1 illustrates the preliminary steps required to prepare for the removal of the system unit cover of an IBM PC. The reader should note that the keyboard connector should only be removed if the keyboard must be relocated more than 6 feet from the PC or PC XT to obtain space for

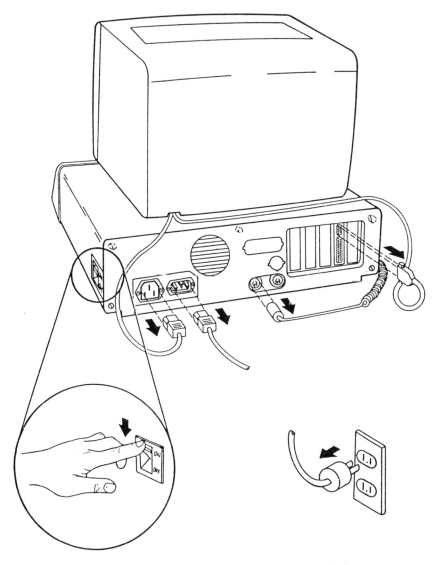

Figure 3.1 Preparing to Remove the System Unit Cover

Prior to removing the system unit cover, insure that all power cables are disconnected and the power switch is in the off position

the removal of the system unit cover. If you have a PC XT, its longer keyboard cable may permit you to easily relocate the keyboard without having to disconnect the keyboard connector from the system unit.

After you have positioned the system unit to allow access to its rear you can remove the cover mounting screws which fasten the cover to the system unit. Early versions of the IBM PC had their system unit cover fastened to the system unit by two screws, one located in each of the lower left- and right-hand corners on the rear of the system unit. PCs manufactured after mid-1982, as well as all PC XTs and PC ATs, have five cover-mounting screws fastening the cover to the system unit. As illustrated in Figure 3.2, these screws can be removed by using a flat-blade screwdriver, turning the screwdriver in a counterclockwise direction.

Once the screws holding the system unit cover are removed, the cover is also ready for removal.

If you have a PC or PC XT you should first slide the system unit cover away from the rear as illustrated in Figure 3.3. When the cover will go no further, tilt the cover up at approximately a 15 degree angle and lift it away from the base of the system unit. If you have a PC AT, you only have to slide the cover directly away from the rear as illustrated in Figure 3.3.

Figure 3.4 is a photograph of the interior of the system unit of an IBM PC. Note the upper left portion of the system unit contains five vacant system expansion slots. Into each of these expansion slots users can install a variety of adapter boards to include the asynchronous communications adapter, which is designed to operate with the 8-bit data bus of the Intel 8088 microprocessor that provides the computing power of the IBM PC.

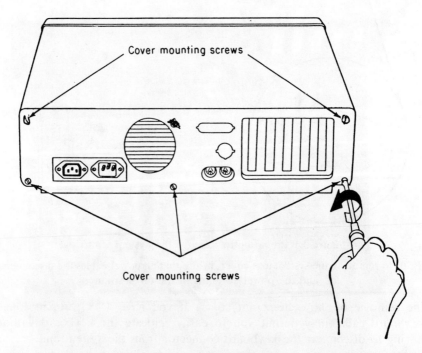

Figure 3.2 Unfastening the System Unit Cover

Turning the cover mounting screws counterclockwise will unfasten the cover of the system unit

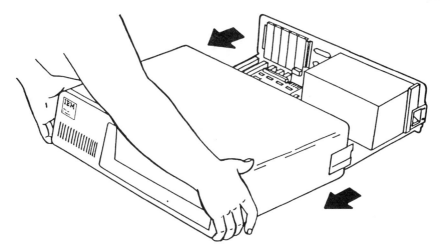

Figure 3.3 Removing the System Unit Cover

If you have a PC or PC XT, slide the cover away from the rear until it will go no further. Then, tilt the cover up at a 15 degree angle to remove it from the base of the system unit. If you have a PC AT, you only have to slide the cover away from the rear of the system unit.

Figure 3.4 Interior of IBM PC System Unit

Photograph courtesy of IBM Corporation.

Since the IBM PC XT and Portable Personal Computer (PPC) also use the 8088 microprocessor, adapters that work in the PC can be used in the PC XT and PPC. The IBM PC AT uses the Intel 80286 microprocessor which has a 16-bit data path, causing some adapter boards designed for use in the earlier marketed PCs 8-bit data path to be incompatible for use in the AT.

One major difference between the IBM PC and the PC XT and PC AT is the number of system expansion slots in their system unit. The PC has five system expansion slots while the PC XT and the PC AT each have eight system expansion slots. Since the PS/2 models 25 and 30 use an 8-bit bus, adapters designed for most PCs can be used in those computers. Unfortunately, the micro channel bus used in other members of the PS/2 series precludes the use of adapters designed for PCs in those computers.

Asynchronous communications adapter

Figure 3.5 is a photograph of the IBM Asynchronous Communications Adapter which, among other functions, converts the parallel data flow of 8 bits per byte inside the PC into a serial data stream for communications. Similarly, the adapter accepts a received serial data stream and converts 8

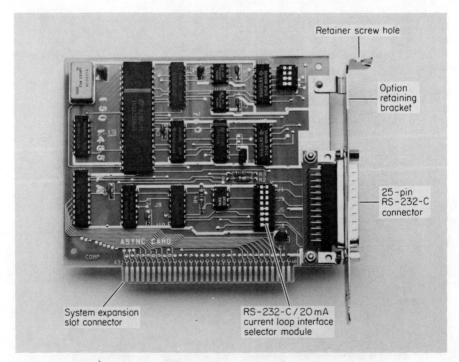

Figure 3.5 IBM Asynchronous Communications Adapter

Photograph courtesy of IBM Corporation

serially received bits into a parallel formed byte for internal processing by the personal computer.

In examining the IBM asynchronous communications adapter, there are several components of the adapter that warranted attention. Although almost everyone will use this adapter to obtain an RS-232-C interface, positioning the lower four pluggable modules on the RS-232-C/20 mA current loop interface selector module to the upper four positions will change the interface to a 20 mA current loop. This enables teletype type devices operating with a current loop interface to be connected to the PC or for the PC to be connected to a current-loop mainframe computer port via the PC's asynchronous communications adapter.

Prior to installing the asynchronous communications adapter or any other adapter in the system unit, you must first remove a system expansion slot over. Figure 3.6 illustrates the removal of a system expansion slot cover which occurs by turning the screw holding the cover in the counterclockwise direction. Since the screw holding the expansion slot cover will be used to fasten the adapter to the system unit you should save this screw.

To install the asynchronous communications adapter or any other adapter, you should hold it by the top corners of the card and press it firmly into the expansion slot that has previously had its expansion slot cover removed. Next, align the hole in the option-retaining bracket of the adapter card with

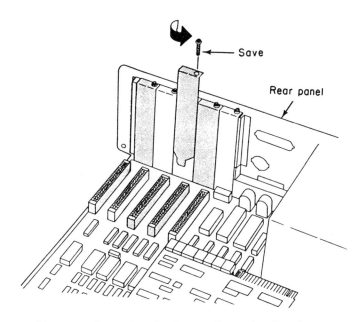

Figure 3.6 Removing the System Expansion Slot Cover

Turn the screw holding the system expansion slot cover in the counterclockwise direction

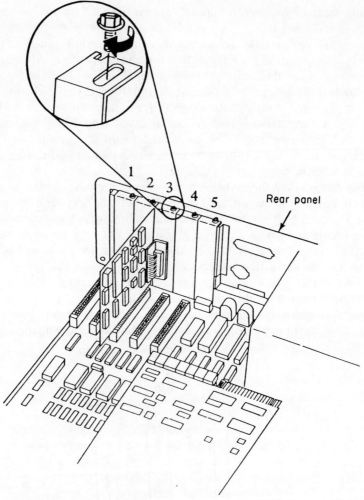

Figure 3.7 Fastening the Adapter to the System Unit

Use the screw which previously held the system expansion slot cover to fasten the adapter card to the system unit.

the hole in the rear panel of the system unit from which the screw previously holding the expansion slot cover was removed. Using the screw that previously held the expansion slot cover, insert it into the hole in the option-retaining bracket and turn it clockwise to fasten the adapter to the system unit. This process is illustrated in Figure 3.7. Assuming the asynchronous communications adapter was installed in system expansion slot 3 of an IBM PC, Figure 3.8 illustrates how the RS-232-C connector would appear at the rear of the system unit. This connector can then be cabled to a modem or a serial printer.

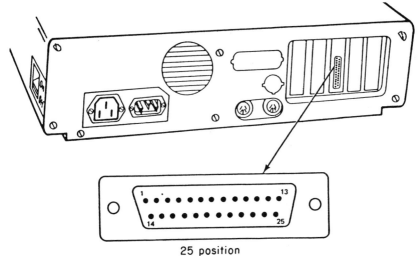

25 position

Figure 3.8 The RS-232 Connector

Serial/parallel adapter

For the PC AT, IBM markets a serial/parallel adapter whose serial interface provides asynchronous communications support. Both the asynchronous communications adapter and the serial/parallel adapter are similar in that they regulate the data transmission rate at a predetermined fixed rate between 75 and 9600 bps and support data rates of 75, 110, 150, 300, 600, 1200, 1800, 2400, 4800 and 9600 bps, which are selected by the program used to perform asynchronous communications.

Since by definition asynchronous communications is not continuous, each character must contain its own timing information in the form of start and stop bits. Both devices add a start bit to each character being transmitted and delete this bit from each received character. To inform the other end of the link of the termination of a character requires a stop bit to be appended to each transmitted character. Under program control, each adapter will add a stop bit 1, 1.5 or 2 bit times in length to the end of each transmitted character, where it will be removed by the adapter at the other end of the link. Normally, a stop bit 2 bit times in length is used at data rates of 110 bps or less, while a stop bit of 1 bit time in length is used with data rates of 300 bps and above. A stop bit of 1.5 bit intervals is normally used when a PC is used to emulate older types of terminals.

In addition to the previously discussed timing information, each adapter can be controlled by software to add a parity bit to each transmitted character. Through the addition of a parity bit, the total number of bits per character can be set to an even or odd count via program control. Doing so will enable the receiving adapter to check the received character for a parity error and, if detected, to signal the user through the communications software program that a transmission error has occurred.

Another function performed by each adapter card is the generation of a break signal which should not be confused with the break key on one's PC keyboard. Under program control, the adapter will generate a 20 millisecond marking condition which is recognized by many mainframe computers as a signal to interrupt or break the current activity being performed.

Although the maximum official data rate of each adapter is 9600 bps, both adapters have supported data rates up to 19 200 bps when connected to recently introduced high-speed asynchronous modems.

As the name implies, the IBM PC AT serial/parallel adapter includes a parallel port and a serial port on one adapter card. The rear of the adapter contains a 9-pin D-shell connector at the top of the card which is classified as an RS-232-C port. The serial port of the PC AT serial/parallel adapter card illustrating the numbering of the 9 pins is illustrated in the upper right of Figure 3.9. Table 3.1 lists the relationship between the pins on the 9-pin D-shell connector and the RS-232-C 25 pin connector equivalents.

Since modems and couplers normally have an RS-232-C interface, you cannot directly cable the 9-pin connector on the PC AT serial/parallel adapter card with a straight-through conductor cable to a modem or coupler. This is because as Table 3.1 indicates, pin #2 on the adapter must be routed to pin #3 on the 25-pin connector connected to a modem or coupler, pin #3 on the 9-pin connector must be routed to pin #3 on the 25-pin connector, and so on. To obtain compatibility with 25-pin connector devices, IBM and

Table 3.1 PC AT Serial/Parallel Adapter Serial Port Pin Assignment

9 Pin Connector Pin #	RS-232-C Circuit	25 Pin Connector Equivalent
1	Carrier Detect	8
2	Receive Data	3
3	Transmit Data	2
4	Data Terminal Ready	20
5	Signal Ground	7
6	Data Set Ready	6
7	Request to Send	
8	Clear to Send	5
9	Ring Indicator	22

other vendors market what is known as a serial adapter connector. This connector is actually a cable with a 25-pin connector attached to one end of the cable and a 9-pin connector attached to the other end of the cable. The conductors in the cable are wired to insure that the circuits from the pins on the 9-pin shell connector are routed to the appropriate pins on the 25-pin connector.

Communications port numbers

The basic input ouput system (BIOS) of members of the IBM PC Series is capable of supporting the operation of up to four communications ports. Unlike the asynchronous communications adapter which has the fixed address of communications port 1, the serial output port of the serial/parallel adapter card can be addressed as either communications port 1 or communications port 2. The lower portion of Figure 3.9 illustrates the appropriate positioning of the J1 jumper on the serial/parallel adapter card to address the serial output port.

If more than one adapter card containing a serial port is to be installed in the system unit of a PC, care must be taken to prevent an addressing conflict from occurring. If an addressing conflict occurs due to two or more adapter cards or ports on adapter cards having the same address, your computer will probably 'freeze' the first time you attempt to use one of the ports or two or more ports that have the same address. This will result in the loss of any data in memory and cause you to reboot the system. Addressing conflicts can be avoided by insuring that a different port address is assigned to each similar type port on additional adapter cards which are to be installed in your system unit.

To conserve expansion slots, many third-party vendors offer multifunction boards. These boards typically contain additional memory capacity as well as one or more serial and parallel ports and a clock/calendar. The serial

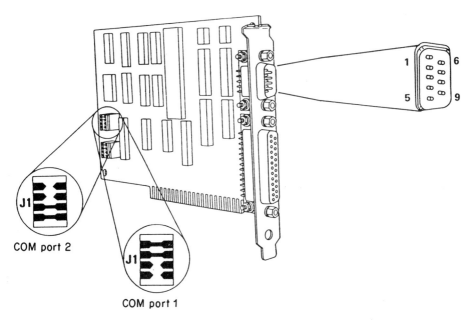

Figure 3.9 PC AT Serial/Parallel Adapter Card

98

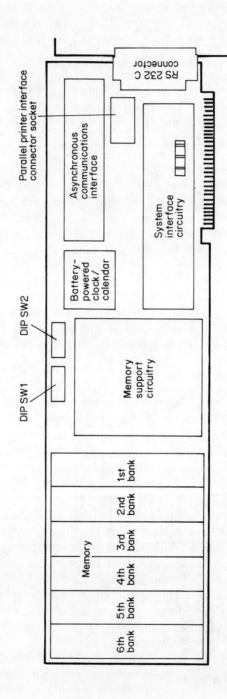

Figure 3.10 Quadram Corporation Quadboard

The serial port on this multifunction board can be configured to be addressed as 'COM1:' or 'COM2:' by setting the appropriate DIP switch elements on DIP switch 2

port on these multifunction boards is normally equivalent to a stand-alone asynchronous communications adapter or the serial interface on the serial/ parallel adapter and their use in place of an IBM adapter is normally transparent to the user.

Figure 3.10 illustrates a block diagram of the Quadram Corporation Quadboard. This adapter board permits you to expand the memory of your PC or PC XT system in increments of 64K bytes, adding up to 384K bytes of memory to your personal computer. In addition to memory, the adapter board contains a clock/calendar, parallel port and serial port. By configuring appropriate elements on DIP switch 2 (SW2) on the adapter, you can configure the serial port on the board to be addressed as device 'COM1:'or 'COM2:' or you can disable the use of the port. Thus, if you previously installed an IBM asynchronous communications adapter in your PC or PC XT whose device address is fixed as 'COM1:', you would set the DIP switch elements on the Quadboard to configure its serial port as 'COM2:' to avoid the occurrence of an addressing conflict.

Internal modem

Although called an internal modem, this device can actually be considered as a multifunction board as it combines the functions of a communications adapter and modem onto one adapter card. Since the cost of an internal modem is normally less than the cost of a separate communications adapter and a stand-alone external modem, many personal computer users prefer to install this device in their computer's system unit. In addition to economic savings of one device in comparison to two, an internal modem eliminates the cable required to connect the asynchronous communications adapter to a stand-alone modem which can add an additional $10 to $20 to one's communications cost. Another advantage of an internal modem in comparison to separate devices is the fact that it eliminates the footprint of a separate modem from one's desk. In certain situations, this fact by itself may be a governing factor for selecting an internal modem.

Figure 3.11 contains a photograph of Digital Communications Associates Fastlink ™ single-board modem. Note the edge connector on the left part of the photograph which is the bottom of the board. By installing the board into one of the system expansion slots in the PC, XT or PPC, one obtains both an asynchronous communications adapter and internal modem while only occupying one slot. This revolutionary modem is really four modems in one, capable of operating at industry standard data rates of 300, 1200 and 2400 bps as well as its proprietary data rate that can range in small increments of bps up to 19 200 bps.

Figure 3.12 contains a photograph of the Hayes Smartmodem 2400™ which is one of the most popular 'intelligent' modems marketed for use with personal computers. This stand-alone external modem is cabled to an asynchronous communications adapter installed in the system unit of a PC

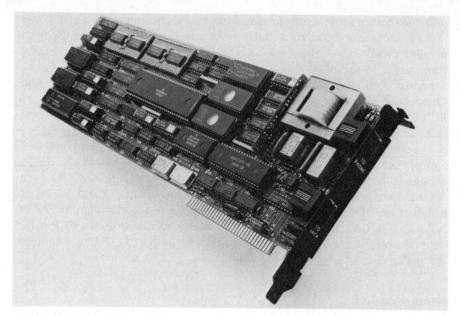

Figure 3.11 Digital Communications Associates Fastlink™ Single-board Modem

Photograph courtesy of Digital Communications Associates

and recognizes a set of commands to perform such functions as automatic dialing and automatic answering of calls. Due to the number of software programs written to be 'Hayes' compatible, most hardware vendors offering modems have designed their devices to recognize the Hayes command set.

Figure 3.12 Hayes Smartmodem 2400™

Reproduced by permission of Hayes Microcomputer Products, Inc

Table 3.2 Popular Communications Adapters

Adapter card	Functional capability
Asynchronous communications	Provides a serial RS-232 asynchronous communications capability
Serial/parallel	Provides both serial RS-232 and parallel ports on one adapter card
Bisychronous communications	Provides a bisynchronous communications capability
SDLC communications	Provides a synchronous data link control (SDLC) communications capability
PC network	Provides a communications interface to the broadband PC local area network
Token ring	Provides a communications interface to the token ring local area network
Twinax	Permits PCs to be connected to IBM System 34/36/38 minicomputers as a 5251-type terminal
X.25	Permits a PC to communicate directly to a mainframe computer via a public or private X.25 packet network

Today, the variety of communications equipment that can be installed or attached to the system unit of an IBM PC or compatible computer is staggering. Over 100 companies manufacture various types of communications adapter boards, acoustic couplers and modems that can be employed to provide a PC with a communications capability. Table 3.2 lists eight of the more popular adapter cards that can be installed in the system unit of a PC to obtain different types of communications capability. The first two adapters were previously discussed in this chapter; the remaining adapters will be covered later in this book.

3.2 ACOUSTIC COUPLERS

Unlike conventional modems which may require a permanent or semipermanent connection to a telephone line, an acoustic coupler is in essence a modem which permits data transmission through the utilization of the handset of an ordinary telephone. Similar in functioning to a modem, an acoustic coupler is a device which will accept a serial asynchronous data stream from a personal computer or a terminal device, modulate that data stream into the audio spectrum, and then transmit the audio tones over a switched or dial-up telephone connection.

Acoustic couplers are equipped with built-in cradles or fittings into which a conventional telephone headset is placed. Through the process of acoustic coupling, the modulated tones produced by the acoustic coupler are directly picked up by the attached telephone headset. Likewise, the audible tones transmitted over a telephone line are picked up by the telephone earpiece and demodulated by the acoustic coupler into a serial data stream which is acceptable to an attached personal computer or terminal. Acoustic couplers normally use two distinct frequencies to transmit information, while two other frequencies are employed for data reception. A frequency from each pair is used to create a mark tone which represents an encoded binary one from the digital data stream, while another pair of frequencies generates a space tone which represents a binary zero. This utilization of two pairs of frequencies permits full-duplex transmission to occur over the two-wire switched telephone network.

Since acoustic couplers enable any conventional telephone to be used for data-transmission purposes, the coupler does not have to be physically wired to the line and thus permits considerable flexibility in choosing a working area, which can be anywhere with a telephone handset and standard electrical outlet available.

Acoustic couplers are normally employed to permit portable computers and terminals to communicate with mainframe computers located at a data-processing facility. Since a large portion of low-speed modems at such facilities in the United States was originally furnished by the American Telegraph and Telephone Company (AT&T) and its operating companies prior to its breakup into independent organizations, most manufacturers of acoustic couplers have designed them to be compatible with low-speed 'Bell System' modems. Here the term 'Bell System' refers to the operating characteristics of modems that were manufactured by Western Electric for use by AT&T operating companies prior to those operating companies' becoming independent organizations.

In Europe, most acoustic couplers are designed to be compatible with CCITT recommendations that govern the operation of low-speed modems. To understand the differences between low-speed Bell System and CCITT modems, we will examine acoustic couplers that operate at data rates betwen 0 and 450 bps. In the United States, such couplers are compatibile with Bell System 103 and 113 type modems while in Europe such couplers are compatible with the CCITT V.21 recommendation.

Table 3.3 lists the operating frequencies of acoustic couplers designed to operate with Bell System 103/113 type modems and modems that follow the CCITT V.21 recommendation.

Basically, couplers like low-speed modems must operate in one of two modes – originate or answer. This operational mode should not be confused with a transmission mode of simplex, half-duplex, or full-duplex. What the operational mode refers to is the frequency assignments for transmitting marks and spaces. Thus, from Table 3.3, an acoustic coupler compatible with a Bell System 103/113 type modem would transmit a tone at 1270 Hz to represent a mark and a tone at 1070 Hz to represent a space when it is in the originate mode of operation. To communicate effectively, the device (modem or coupler) at the other end of the line must be in the answer mode of operation. If so, then it would receive a mark at 1270 Hz and a

Table 3.3 Acoustic Coupler Modem Compatibility

	(Operating frequencies in Hz) Bell System 103/113 Type		CCITT V.21	
	Originate	Answer	Originate	Answer
Transmit				
Mark	1270	2225	980	1650
Space	1070	2025	1180	1850
Receive				
Mark	2225	1270	1650	980
Space	2025	1070	1850	1180

space at 1070 Hz, ensuring that the tones transmitted by the originate-mode device would be heard by the receive-mode device. This explains why two personal computer or terminal operators, each with an originate-mode coupler, could not communicate with one another. This communications incompatibility results from the fact that one coupler would transmit a mark 1270 Hz, while the other coupler would be set to receive the mark at 2225 Hz. Thus, the second coupler would never hear the tone originated by the first coupler.

By convention, originate-mode couplers and modems are connected to terminals while answer-mode devices are connected to computer ports, since personal computers and terminals normally originate calls and mainframe computers typically answer such calls. Some couplers can be obtained with an originate/answer mode switch. By changing the position of the switch, one changes the coupler's operating-frequency assignments. Couplers with an originate/answer-mode switch should be obtained when there is a requirement to communicate between personal computers or terminals, or if one believes this requirement could materialize.

In Figure 3.13 the frequency assignments of couplers designed to be compatible with Bell System 103/113 type modems is graphically illustrated.

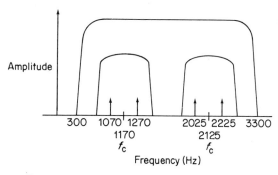

Figure 3.13 Bell System 103/113 Frequency Spectrum

Note that 1170 Hz and 2125 Hz are the channel center frequencies and two independent data channels are derived by frequency, permitting full-duplex transmission to occur over the two-wire public switched telephone network.

Returning to Table 3.3, note that the operating frequencies of Bell System 103/113 type modems are completely different from modems designed to operate according to the V.21 recommendation.

This frequency incompatibility explains why, as an example, a travelling American in Europe more likely than not will be unable to use his or her portable personal computer to communicate with either a public packet network or his or her company's mainframe computer located in Europe.

Although the majority of acoustic couplers on the market transmit and receive data at 300 bps, several vendors market devices that operate at 1200 bps. Such couplers are compatible with either Bell System 202 or 212A or CCITT V.22 modems and their method of modulation will be described in Section 3.3 of this chapter when modems are covered.

Operation

When a personal computer is attached to an acoustic coupler and the operator wishes to communicate, he or she merely dials the appropriate telephone access number and upon establishing the proper connection by hearing a high-pitched tone, places the telephone headset into the coupler. Although PC usage varies by their numerous applications, the prevalent utilization of acoustic couplers is in obtaining access to a mainframe computer or information utility when one is travelling. Typically, the PC user dials a telephone number assigned to a group of dial-in computer telephone access numbers that are interfaced to a rotary. The rotary enables users to dial the low telephone number of the group and it automatically 'steps' or bypasses currently busy numbers. Each telephone line is then connected to a modem on a permanent basis, and the modem in turn is connected to a mainframe computer port or channel. An automatic answering device in each modem automatically answers the incoming call and in effect establishes a connection from the user who dialed the number to the computer port, as shown in Figure 3.14.

A disadvantage associated with the use of acoustic couplers is a reduction of transmission rates when compared to rates which can be obtained by using modems. Due to the properties of carbon microphones in telephone headsets, the frequency band that can be passed is not as wide as the band modems can pass. Although typical data rates of acoustic couplers vary between 110 and 300 bps, some units manufactured permit transmission at 450, 600 and 1200 bps. Thus, acoustic couplers can be viewed as a low-cost alternative to a modem while increasing user transmission location flexibility.

Problems in usage

A possible cause of errors in the transmission of data can occur from ambient

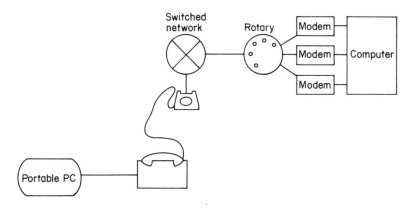

Figure 3.14 Network Access to a Mainframe Computer

After dialing the computer access number the terminal user places the telephone
headset into the cradle of the acoustic coupler

noise leaking into the acoustic coupler. To reduce the potential of this
problem occurring, one should try to move the coupler as far away from
the attached personal computer as possible to reduce noise levels. Similarly,
if the PC is not in use, one should remove the telephone from the coupler
since the continuous placement of the headset in the device can cause
crystallization of the speaker and receiver elements of the telephone to
occur which will act to reduce the level of signal strength. Another item
which may warrant user attention is the placement of a piece of cotton
inside the earpiece behind the receiver of the telephone. Although the
placement of cotton at this location is normally done by most telephone
companies, this should be checked, since the cotton keeps speaker and
receiver noise from interfering with each other and acts to prevent transmitted
data from interfering with received data.

An easily resolved problem is the placement of the telephone headset
into the coupler. On many occasions users have hastily placed the handset
only partially into the coupler, and this will act to reduce the level of signal
strength necessary for error-free transmission.

3.3 MODEMS

Today, despite the introduction of a number of all-digital transmission
facilities by several communications carriers, the analog telephone system
remains the primary facility utilized for data communications. Since personal
computers produce digital pulses, whereas telephone circuits are designed
to transmit analog signals which fall within the audio spectrum used in
human speech, a device to interface the digital data pulses of personal
computers with the analog tones carried on telephone circuits becomes
necessary when one wishes to transmit data over such circuits. Such a device
is called a modem, which derives its meaning from a contraction of the two

main functions of such a unit — modulation and demodulation. Although modem is the term most frequently used for such a device that performs modulation and demodulation, data set is another common term which is synonymous.

In its most basic form a modem consists of a power supply, a transmitter, and a receiver. The power supply provides the voltage necessary to operate the modem's circuitry. In the transmitter a modulator, amplifier, as well as filtering, waveshaping, and signal control circuitry convert digital direct current pulses; these pulses, originated by a computer or terminal, are converted into an analog, wave-shaped signal which can be transmitted over a telephone line. The receiver contains a demodulator and associated circuitry which reverse the process by converting the analog telephone signal back into a series of digital pulses that is acceptable to the computer or terminal device. This signal conversion is illustrated in Figure 3.15.

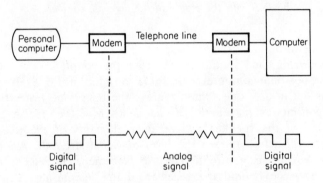

Figure 3.15 Signal Conversion Performed by Modems

A modem converts a digital signal to an analog tone (modulation) and reconverts the analog tone (demodulation) into its original digital signal

The modulation process

The modulation process alters the characteristics of a carrier signal. By itself, a carrier is a repeating signal that conveys no information. However, when the carrier is changed by the modulation process information is impressed upon the signal. For analog signals, the carrier is a sine wave, represented by:

$$a = A \sin(2\pi ft + \varphi)$$

where

a = instantaneous value of voltage at time t

A = maximum amplitude

$f =$ frequency

$\varphi =$ phase.

Thus, the carrier's characteristics that can be altered are the carrier's amplitude for amplitude modulation (AM), the carrier's frequency for frequency modulation (FM), and the carrier's phase angle for phase modulation (φM).

Amplitude modulation

The simplest method of employing amplitude modulation is to vary the magnitude of the signal from a zero level to represent a binary 0 to a fixed peak-to-peak voltage to represent a binary 1. Figure 3.16 illustrates the use of amplitude modulation to encode a digital data stream into an appropriate series of analog signals. Although pure amplitude modulation is normally used for very low data rates, it is also employed in conjunction with phase modulation to obtain a method of modulating high-speed digital data sources.

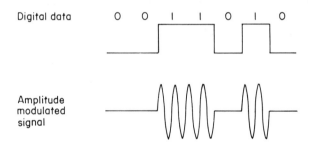

Figure 3.16 Amplitude Modulation

Frequency modulation

Frequency modulation refers to how frequently a signal repeats itself at a given amplitude. One of the earliest uses of frequency modulation was in the design of low-speed acoustic couplers and modems where the transmitter shifted from one frequency to another as the input digital data changed from a binary 1 to a binary 0 or from a 0 to a 1. This shifting in frequency is known as frequency-shift keying (FSK) and is primarily used by modems operating at data rates up to 300 bps in a full-duplex mode of operation and up to 1200 bps in a half-duplex mode of operation. Figure 3.17 illustrates frequency-shift (keying) frequency modulation.

Phase modulation

Phase modulation is the process of varying the carrier signal with respect to the origination of its cycle, as illustrated in Figure 3.18. Several forms of

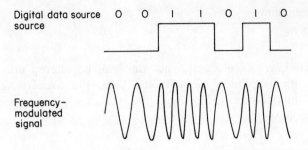

Digital data source   O   O   I   I   O   I   O
source

Frequency–
modulated
signal

Figure 3.17 Frequency Modulation

phase modulation are used in modems to include single- and multiple-bit phase-shift keying (PSK) and the combination of amplitude and multiple-bit, phase-shift keying.

In a single-bit, phase-shift keying, the transmitter simply shifts the phase of the signal to represent each bit entering the modem. Thus, a binary one might be represented by a 90° phase change while a zero bit could be represented by a 270° phase change. Due to the variance of phase between two phase values to represent binary 1s and 0s this technique is also known as two-phase modulation.

Prior to discussing multiple-bit, phase-shift keying we will examine the difference between the data rate and signaling speed and the basic parameters of a voice circuit. This will enable us to understand the rationale for the

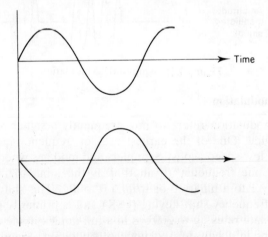

Time

Figure 3.18 Phase Modulation

Phase is the position of the wave form of a signal with respect to the origination of the carrier cycle In this illustration, the bottom wave is 180 degrees out of phase with a normal sine wave illustrated at the top.

utilization of multiple-bit, phase-shift keying, where two or more bits are grouped together and represented by one phase shift in a signal.

BPS vs Baud

Bits per second is the number of binary digits transferred per second and represents the data transmission rate of a device. Baud is the signaling rate of a device such as a modem. If the signal of the modem changes with respect to each bit entering the device, then 1 bps = 1 baud. Suppose our modem is constructed such that one signal change is used to represent two bits. Then the baud rate is one-half the bps rate.

When two bits are used to represent one baud, the encoding technique is known as dibit encoding. Similarly, the process of using three bits to represent one baud is known as tribit encoding and the bit rate is then one-third of the baud rate. Both dibit and tribit encoding are known as multilevel coding techniques and are commonly implemented using phase modulation.

Voice circuit parameters

Bandwidth is a measurement of the width of a range of requencies. A voice-grade telephone channel has a passband, which defines its slot in the frequency spectrum, which ranges from 300 to 3300 Hz. Thus, the bandwidth of a voice-grade telephone channel is 3300−300 or 3000 Hz.

As data enters a modem it is converted into a series of analog signals, with the signal change rate of the modem known as its baud rate. In 1928, Nyquist developed the relationship between the bandwidth and the baud rate on a circuit as:

$$B = 2W$$

where:

B = baud rate

W = bandwidth in Hz

For a voice-grade circuit with a bandwidth of 3000 Hz, this relationship means that data transmission can only be supported at baud rates lower than 6000 symbols or signaling elements per second, prior to one signal interfering with another and causing intersymbol interference.

Since any oscillating modulation technique immediately halves the signaling rates, this means that most modems are limited to operating at one-half of the Nyquist limit. Thus, in a single-bit, phase-shift keying modulation technique, where each bit entering the modem results in a phase shift, the maximum data rate obtainable is limited to approximately 3000 bps. In such a situation the bit rate equals the baud rate, since there is one signal change for each bit.

To overcome the Nyquist limit, engineers needed to design modems that first grouped a sequence of bits together, examined the composition of the bits, and then implemented a phase shift based upon the value of the grouped bits. This technique is known as multiple-bit, phase-shift keying or multilevel, phase-shift keying. Two-bit codes called dibits and three-bit codes known as tribits are formed and transmitted by a single phase shift from a group of 4 or 8 possible phase states.

Most modems operating at 600–4800 bps employ multilevel, phase-shift keying modulation. Some of the more commonly used phase patterns employed by modems using dibit and tribit encoding are listed in Table 3.4.

Table 3.4 Common Phase-angle Values used in Multilevel Phase-shift Keying

Bits transmitted	Possible phase-angle values (Degrees)		
00	0	45	90
01	90	135	0
10	180	225	270
11	270	315	180
000	0	22.5	45
001	45	67.5	0
010	90	112.5	90
011	135	157.5	135
100	180	202.5	180
101	225	247.5	225
110	270	292.5	270
111	315	337.5	315

Combined modulation techniques

Since the most practical method to overcome the Nyquist limit is obtained by placing additional bits into each signal change, modem designers have combined modulation techniques to obtain very high-speed data transmission over voice-grade circuits. One combined modulation technique commonly used involves both amplitude and phase modulation. This technique is known as quadrature amplitude modulation (QAM) and results in four bits being placed into each signal change, with the signal operating at 2400 (baud), causing the data rate to become 9600 bps.

The first implementation of QAM involved a combination of phase and amplitude modulation, in which 12 values of phase and 3 values of amplitude are employed to produce 16 possible signal states as illustrated in Figure 3.19. One of the earliest modems to use QAM in the United States was the Bell System 209, which modulated a 1650 Hz carrier at a 2400 baud rate

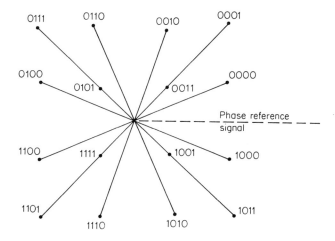

Figure 3.19 Quadrature Amplitude Modulation produces
Sixteen Signal States from a Combination of Twelve
Angles and Three Amplitude Levels

to effect data transmission at 9600 bps. Today, most 9600 bps modems manufactured adhere to the CCITT V.29 standard. The V.29 modem uses a carrier of 1700 Hz which is varied in both phase and amplitude, resulting in 16 combinations of 8 phase angles and 4 amplitudes. Under the V.29 standard, fallback data rates of 7200 and 4800 bps are specified.

In addition to combining two modulation techniques, QAM also differs from the previously discussed modulation methods by its use of two carrier signals. Figure 3.20 illustrates a simplified block diagram of a modem's transmitter employng QAM. The encoder operates upon four bits from the serial data stream and causes both an in-phase (IP) cosine carrier and a sine wave that serves as the quadrature component (QC) of the signal to be modulated. The IP and QC signals are then summoned and result in the transmitted signal being changed in both amplitude and phase, with each

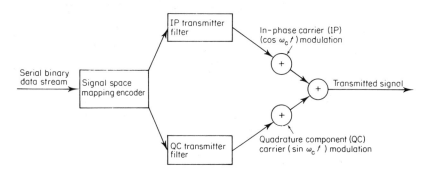

Figure 3.20 QAM Modem Transmitter

point placed at the *x–y* coordinates representing the modulation levels of the cosine and the sine carrier.

If one plots the signal points previously illustrated in Figure 3.19, which represent all of the data samples possible in that particular method of QAM, the series of points can be considered to be the signal structure of the modulation technique. Another popular term used to describe these points is known as the constellation pattern. By an examination of the constellation pattern of a modem, it becomes possible to predetermine its susceptibility to certain transmission impairments. As an example, phase jitter which causes signal points to rotate about the origin can result in one signal being misinterpreted for another, which would cause four bits to be received in error. Since there are 12 angles in the QAM method illustrated in Figure 3.19, the minimum rotation angle is 30°, which provides a reasonable immunity to phase jitter.

New techniques

By the late 1980s several vendors were offering modems that operated at data rates up to 19 200 bps over leased voice-grade circuits. Originally, modems that operated at 14 400 bps employed a quadrature amplitude-modulation technique, collecting data bits into a 6-bit symbol 2400 times per second, resulting in the transmission of a signal point selected from a 64-point signal constellation. The signal pattern of one vendor's 14 400 bps modem is illustrated in Figure 3.21. Note that this particular signal appears to form a hexagonal pattern, and according to the vendor was used since it provides a better performance level with respect to signal-to-noise (S/N) ratio and phase jitter than conventional rectangular grid signal structures.

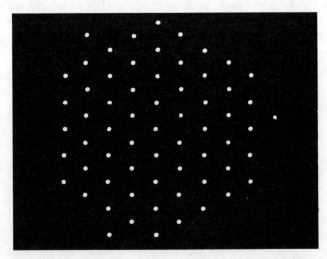

Figure 3.21 14400 BPS Hexagonal Signal Constellation Pattern

However, in spite of hexagonal packed-signal structures, it should be obvious that the distance between signal points for a 14 400 bps modem are closer than the resulting points from a 9600 bps modem. This means that a 14 400 bps conventional QAM modem is more susceptible to transmission impairments, and the overall data throughput under certain situations can be less than that obtainable with 9600 bps modems. Figure 3.22 illustrates the typical throughput variance of 9600 and 14 400 bps modems with respect to the ratio of noise to the strength of the signal (N/S) on the circuit. From this illustration, it should be apparent that 14 400 bps modems using conventional quadrature amplitude modulation should only be used on high quality circuits.

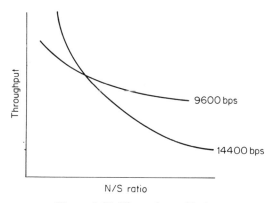

Figure 3.22 Throughput Variance

Under certain conditions the throughput obtained
by using 9600 bps modems can exceed the throughput
obtained when using 14 400 bps devices

Modems that transmit data at 16 000 bps are very similar to 14 400 bps devices, with the major difference in the baud rate. Thus, most 16 000 bps modems encode data into 6-bit symbols and transmit the signals 2667 times per second. This method also employs a total of 64 signal points; however, the baud rate is increased from 2400 to 2667 to obtain the higher data-transfer rate.

Trellis-coded modulation

Due to the susceptibility of conventional QAM modems to transmission impairments, a new generation of modems based on Trellis coded modulation (TCM) has been developed. Such modems tolerate more than twice as much noise power as conventional QAM modems, permitting 9600 to 14 400 bps transmission over the switched telephone network and reliable data transmission at speeds ranging from 14 400 to 19 200 bps over good-quality leased lines.

To understand how TCM provides a higher tolerance to noise and other line impairments to include phase jitter and distortion, let us consider what happens when a line impairment occurs when conventional QAM modems are used. Here the impairment causes the received signal point to be displaced from its appropriate location in the signal constellation. The receiver then selects the signal point in the constellation that is closest to what it received. Obviously, when line impairments are large enough to cause the received point to be closer to a single point that is different from the one transmitted an error occurs. To minimize the possibility of such errors, TCM employs an encoder that adds a redundant code bit to each symbol interval.

In actuality, at 14 400 bps the transmitter converts the serial data stream into 6-bit symbols and encodes two of the six bits employing a binary convulutional encoding scheme as illustrated in Figure 3.23. The encoder adds a code bit to the two input bits, forming three encoded bits in each symbol interval. As a result of this encoding operation, three encoded bits and four remaining data bits are then mapped into a signal point which is selected from a 128-point (2^7) signal constellation.

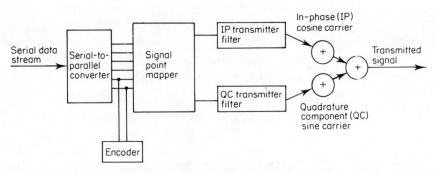

Figure 3.23 Trellis-coded Modulation

The redundancy introduced by the encoder results in only certain sequences of signal points being valid. Thus, if an impairment occurs which causes a signal point to be shifted, the receiver will then compare the observed point to all valid points and select the valid signal point closest to the observed signal. As a result of this technique, a TCM modem is only half as susceptible to as much noise power as a conventional QAM modem, and its utilization can reduce one's error rate by approximately three orders of magnitude.

Thus a conventional QAM modem which might require one of every ten data blocks to be retransmitted could be replaced by a TCM modem with the result that only one in every 10 000 data blocks might then be received in error.

Mode of transmission

If the transmitter or the receiver of the modem is such that the modem can send or receive data in one directly only, the modem will function as a simplex modem. If the operations of the transmitter and the receiver are combined so that the modem may transmit and receive data alternatively, the modem will function as a half-duplex modem. In the half-duplex mode of operation, the transmitter must be turned off at one location, and the transmitter of the modem at the other end of the line must be turned on before each change in transmission direction. The time interval required for this operation is referred to as turnaround time. If the transmitter and receiver operate simultaneously, the modem will function as a full-duplex modem. This simultaneous transmission in both directions can be accomplished either by splitting the telephone line's bandwidth into two channels on a two-wire circuit or by the utilization of two two-wire circuits, such as obtained on a four-wire leased line.

Transmission technique

Modems are designed for asynchronous or synchronous data transmission. Asynchronous transmission is also referred to as start-stop transmission and is usually employed when the time between character transmission occurs randomly. In asynchronous transmission, the character being transmitted is initialized by the character's start bit as a mark-to-space transition on the line and terminated by the character's stop bit which is converted to a 'space/marking' signal on the line. The digital pulses between the start and stop bits are the encoded bits which determine the type of character which was transmitted. Between the stop bit of one character and the start bit of the next character, the asynchronous modem places the line in the 'marking' condition. Upon receipt of the start bit of the next character the line is switched to a mark-to-space transition, and the modem at the other end of the line starts to sample the data. The marking and spacing conditions are audio tones produced by the modulator of the modem to denote the binary data levels. These tones are produced at predefined frequencies, and their transition between the two states as each bit of the character is transmitted defines the character. Asynchronous transmission is usually used at data rates up to 2400 bps, although some modems support data rates of 9600–19 200 bps.

Synchronous transmission permits more efficient line utilization since the bits of one character are immediately followed by the bits of the next character, with no start and stop bits required to delimit individual characters. In synchronous transmission, groups of characters are formed into data blocks, with the length of the block varying from a few characters to a thousand or more. Often, the block length is a function of the physical characteristics of the data to be transmitted. As an example, for the transmission of data that represents punched-card images, it may be convenient to transmit 80 characters of one card as a block, as there are that many characters if one constructs the card image from an 80-column card deck. In synchronous transmission, the individual bits of each of the characters within each block are identified based upon a transmitted timing signal which is usually provided by the modem and which places each bit into a unique time period. This timing or clock signal is transmitted simultaneously with the serial bit stream as shown in Figure 3.24.

Modem operations and compatibility

Many modem manufacturers describe their product offerings in terms of compatibility or equivalency with modems manufactured by Western Electric for the Bell System prior to its breakup into independent telephone companies or with the recommendations of the Consultative Committee for International Telephone and Telegraph (CCITT). The CCITT, which is part of the International Telecommunications Union based in Geneva, has developed a series of modem standards for recommended use. These recommendations are primarily adapted by the post, telephone and telegraph (PTT) organizations that operate the telephone networks of many countries outside the United States; however, due to the popularity of certain CCITT recommendations they have also been followed in designing certain modems for operation on communications facilities within the United States. The following examination of the operation and compatibility of the major types of Bell System and CCITT modems is based upon their operating rate.

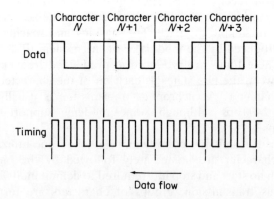

Figure 3.24 Synchronous Timing Signals

The timing signal is used to place the bits that form
each character into a unique time period

300 bps

Modems operating at 300 bps use a frequency-shift keying (FSK) modulation technique as previously described during the discussion of acoustic couplers in Section 2.2. In this technique the frequency of the carrier is alternated to one of two frequencies, one frequency representing a space or 0 bit while theother frequency represents a mark or a 1 bit. Table 3.5 lists the frequency assignments for Bell System 103/113 and CCITT V.21 modems which represent the two major types of modems that operate that at 300 bps.

Table 3.5 Frequency Assignments (Hz) for 300 bps Modems

Major modem types	Originate	Answer
Bell system	Mark 1270	2225
(103/113 type)	Space 1070	2025
CCITT V.21	Mark 980	1650
	Space 1180	1850

Bell System 103 and 113 series modems are designed so that one channel is assigned to the 1070–1270 Hz frequency band while the second channel is assigned to the 2025–2225 Hz frequency band. Modems that transmit in the 1070–1270 Hz band but receive in the 2025–2225 Hz band are designated as originate modems, while a modem which transmits the 2025–2225 Hz band but receives in the 1070–1270 Hz band is designated as an answer modem. When using such modems, their correct pairing is important, since two originate modems cannot communicate with each other. Bell System 113A modems are originate-only devices that should normally be used when calls are to be placed in one direction. This type of modem is mainly used to enable teletype-compatible terminals and personal computers to communicate with mainframe systems when the terminal or PC only originates calls. Bell System 113B modems are answer-only and are primarily used at computer sites where users dial in to establish communications. Since these modems are designed to transmit and receive on a single set of frequencies, their circuitry requirements are less than other modems and their costs are thus more economical.

Modems in the 103 series, which includes the 103A, E, F, G, and J modems, can transmit and receive in either the low or the high band. This ability to switch modes is denoted as 'originate and answer', in comparison to the Bell 113A which operates only in the originate mode and the Bell 113B which operates only in the answer mode.

As indicated in Table 3.5, modems operating in accordance with the CCITT V.21 recommendation employ a different set of frequencies for the transmission and reception of marks and spaces. Thus, Bell System 103/113 type modems and CCITT V.21 devices can never communicate with one another.

The two pairs of frequencies used by the modems listed in Table 3.5 permit the bandwidth of a communications channel to be split into two subchannels by frequency. This technique is illustrated in Figure 3.25 for Bell System 103/113 modems. Since each subchannel can permit data to be transmitted in a direction opposite that transmitted on the other subchannel, this technique permits full-duplex transmission to occur on the switched telephone network which is a two-wire circuit that normally can support only half-duplex transmission.

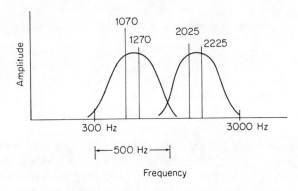

Figure 3.25 FSK Operation for 300 bps Modems

300–1800 bps

There are several Bell System and CCITT V series modems that operate in the range 300–1800 bps. Some of these modems such as the Bell System 212A and CCITT V.22 devices can operate at either of two speeds; and other modems such as the Bell System 202 and the CCITT V.23 only operate at one data rate. We will examine these modems in pairs, enabling their similarities and differences to be compared.

Bell system 212A and V.22 modems

The Bell System 212A modem permits either asynchronous or synchronous transmission over the public switched telephone network. The 212A contains a 103-type modem for asynchronous transmission at speeds up to 300 bps. At this data rate FSK modulation is employed, using the frequency assignments previously indicated in Table 3.5. At 1200 bps, dibit phase-shift keyed (DPSK) modulation is used which permits the modem to operate either asynchronously or synchronously. The phase-bit encoding of the 212A type modem is illustrated in Table 3.6.

Table 3.6 212A Type Modem
Phase-shift Encoding

Dibit	Phase shift (degrees)
00	90
01	0
10	180
11	270

One advantage in the use of this modem is that it permits the reception of transmission from terminal devices at two different transmission speeds. Before the operator initiates a call, he or she selects the operating speed at the originating set. The manner in which the operating speed is selected depends upon the type of 212A modem used. If the modem is what is now commonly referred to as a 'dumb' modem, the operator selects the higher operating speed by pressing a 'HS' (high-speed) button on the front panel of the modem. If the modem is an intelligent modem built to respond to software commands the operators can either use a communications program of send a series of commands through the serial port of the PC to the modem to set its operating speed. Due to the substantial use of intelligent modems with personal computers, these modems will be reviewed as a separate entity later in this chapter. When the call is made, the answering 212A modem automatically switches to that operating speed. During data transmission, both modems remain in the same speed mode until the call is terminated, when the answering 212A can be set to the other speed by a new call. The dual-speed 212A permits both terminals connected to Bell System 100 series data sets operating at up to 300 bps or terminal devices connected to other 212A modems operating at 1200 bps to share the use of one modem at a computer site and thus can reduce central computer site equipment requirements.

The V.22 standard is for modems that operate at 1200 bps on the PSTN or leased circuits and has a fallback data rate of 600 bps. The modulation technique employed is four-phase PSK at 1200 bps and two-phase PSK at 600 bps, with five possible operational modes specified for the modem at 1200 bps. Table 3.7 lists the V.22 modulation phase shifts with respect to the bit patterns entering the modem's transmitter. Modes 1 and 2 are for synchronous and asynchronous data transmission at 1200 bps respectively, while mode 3 is for synchronous transmission at 600 bps. Mode 4 is for asynchronous transmission at 600 bps while mode 5 represents an alternate phase change set for 1200 bps asynchronous transmission.

In comparing V.22 modems to the Bell System 212A devices it should be apparent that they are totally incompatible at the lower data rate, since both the operating speed and modulation techniques differ. At 1200 bps the

Table 3.7 V.22 Modulation Phase Shift vs. Bit Patterns

Dibit values (1200 bps)	Bit values (600 bps)	Phase change Modes 1, 2, 3, 4	Phase change Mode V
00	0	90	270
01	—	0	180
11	1	270	90
10	—	180	0

modulation techniques used by a V.22 modem in modes 1–4 are exactly the same as that used by a Bell System 212A device. Unfortunately, a Bell 212A modem answers a call sends a tone of 2225 Hz on the line that the originating modem is supposed to recognize. This frequency is used due to the construction of the switched telephone network in the United States and other parts of North America. Under V.22, the answering modem first sends a tone of 2100 Hz since this frequency is more compatible with the design of European switched telephone networks. Then, the V.22 modem sends a 2400 Hz tone that would not be any better except that the V.22 modem also sends a burst of data whose primary frequency is about 2250 Hz, which is close enough to the Bell standard of 2225 Hz that many Bell 212A type modems will respond. Thus, some Bell 212A modems can communicate with CCITT V.22 modems at 1200 bps while other 212 type modems may not be able to communicate with V.22 devices, with the ability to successfully communicate based upon the tolerance of the 212 type modem to recognize the V.22 modems data burst at 2250 Hz.

Bell System 202 series modems

Bell System 202 series modems are designed for speeds up to 1200 or 1800 bps. The 202C modem can operate on either the switched network or on leased lines, in the half-duplex mode on the former and the full-duplex mode on the latter. The 202C modem can operate half-duplex or full-duplex on leased lines. This series of modems uses frequency-shift keyed (FSK) modulation, and the frequency assignments are such that a mark is at 1200 Hz and a space at 2200 Hz. When either modem is used for transmission over a leased four-wire circuit in the full-duplex mode, modem control is identical to the 103 series modem in that both transmitters can be strapped on continuously, which alleviates the necessity of line turnarounds.

Since the 202 series modems do not have separate bands, on switched network utilization half-duplex operation is required. This means that both transmitters (one in each modem) must be alternately turned on and off to provide two-way communication.

The Bell 202 series modems have a 5 bps reverse channel for switched network use, which employs amplitude modulation for the transmission of

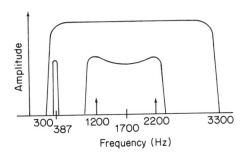

Figure 3.26 Bell System 202 Type Modem Channel Assignments

information. The channel assignments used by a Bell System 202 type modem are illustrated in Figure 3.26, where the 387 Hz signal represents the optional 5 bps AM reverse channel.

Due to the slowness of this reverse channel, it use is limited to status and control function transmission. Status information such as 'ready to receive data' or 'device out of paper' can be transmitted on this channel. Due to the slow transmission rate, error detection of received messages and an associated NAK and request for retransmission is normally accomplished on the primary channel since even with the turnaround time it can be completed at almost the same rate one obtains in using the reverse channel for that purpose. Non-Bell 202-equivalent modems produced by many manufacturers provide reverse channels of 75–150 bps, which can be utilized to enhance overall system performance. Reverse keyboard-entered data as well as error-detection information can be practically transmitted over such a channel.

While a data rate of up to 1800 bps can be obtained with the 202D modem, transmission at this speed requires that the leased line be conditioned for transmission by the telephone company. The 202S and 202T modems are additions to the 202 series and are designed for transmission at 1200 and 1800 bps over the switched network and leased lines, respectively. At speeds in excess of 1400 bps, the 202T requires line conditioning when interfaced to either two- or four-wire circuits, whereas for a two-wire circuit, conditioning is required at speeds in excess of 1200 bps when an optional reverse channel is used.

V.23 modems

The V.23 standard is for modems that transmit at 600 or 1200 bps over the PSTN. Both asynchronous and synchronous transmission are supported by using FSK modulation and an optional 75 bps backward or reverse channel can be used for error control. Figure 3.27 illustrates the channel assignments for a V.23 modem. In comparing Figure 3.27 with Figure 3.26, it is obvious that Bell System 202 and V.23 modems are incompatible with each other.

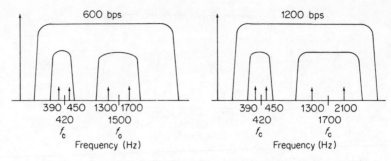

Figure 3.27 V.23 Channel Assignments

2400 bps

Examples of modems that operate at 2400 bps include the Bell System 201, CCITT V.26 series, and the V.22 bis modem. The Bell System 201 and CCITT V.26 series modems are designed for synchronous bits-serial transmission at a data rate of 2400 bps, while the V.22 bis standard governs 2400 bps asynchronous transmission.

Bell System 201 B/C

Current members of the 201 series include the 201B and 201C models. Both of these modems use dibit phase-shift keying modulation, with the phase shifts based upon the dibit values listed in Table 3.8.

The 201B modem is designed for half- or full-duplex synchronous transmission at 2400 bps over leased lines. In comparison, the 201C is designed for half-duplex, synchronous transmission over the PSTN. A more modern version of the 201C is AT&T's 2024A modem, which is compatible with the 201C.

Table 3.8 Bell System 201 B/C
Phase Shift vs. bit Pattern

Dibit values	Phase shift
00	2250
10	3150
11	450
10	1350

V.26 modem

The V.26 standard specifies the characteristics for a 2400 bps synchronous modem for use on a four-wire leased line. Modems operating according to the V.26 standard employ dibit phase-shift keying, using one of two

Table 3.9 V.26 Modulation Phase Shift vs. bit Pattern

Dibit values	Phase change	
	Pattern A	Pattern B
00	0	45
01	90	135
11	180	225
10	270	315

recommended coding schemes. The phase change based upon the dibit values for each of the V.26 coding schemes is listed in Table 3.9.

Two similar CCITT recommendations to V.26 are V.26 bis and V.26 ter. The V.26 bis recommendation defines a dual speed 2400/1200 bps modem for use on the PSTN. At 2400 bps the modulation and coding method is the same as the V.26 recommendation for pattern B listed in Table 3.9. At the reduced data rate of 1200 bps a two-phase shift modulation scheme is employed, with a binary zero represented by a 90° phase shift while a binary one is represented by a 270° phase shift. The V.26 bis recommendation also includes an optional reverse or backward channel that can be used for data transfer up to 75 bps. When employed, frequency-shift keying is used to obtain this channel capacity, with a mark or 1 bit represented by a 390 Hz signal and a space or 0 bit represented by a 450 Hz signal.

The V.26 ter recommendation uses the same phase shift scheme as the V.26 modem, but incorporates an echo-canceling technique that allows transmitted and received signals to occupy the same bandwidth. Thus, the V.26 ter modem is capable of operating in full-duplex at 2400 bps on the PSTN. Echo canceling will be described later in this chapter when the V.32 modem is discussed.

V.22 bis

The CCITT V.22 bis recommendation governs modems designed for asynchronous data transmission at 2400 bps over the PSTN, with a fallback rate of 1200 bps. Since V.22 bis defines operatons at 1200 bps to follow the V.22 format, communications capability with Bell System 212A type modems at that data rate may not always be possible due to the answer tone incompatibility usually encountered between modems following Bell System specifications and CCITT recommendations. In addition, V.22 bis modems manufactured in the United States are usually not compatible with such modems manufactured in Europe at fallback data rates. This is because V.22 bis modems manufactured in Europe follow the V.22 format, with fallback data rates of 1200 and 600 bps. At 1200 bps, the incompatibility between most European telephone networks (which are designed to accept only 2100 Hz answer tones) and the US telephone network (which usually accepts an answer tone between 2100 and 2225 Hz) may preclude communications between a US and a European manufactured V.22 bis modem at 1200 bps. At a lower fallback speed, the European modem will operate at 600 bps while the US V.22 bis modem operates at 300 bps, insuring incompatibility.

In spite of the previously mentioned problems, V.22 bis modems are becoming a *de facto* standard for use with personal computers communicating over the PSTN. This is due to several factors, to include the manufacture in the United States of V.22 bis modems that are Bell System 212A compatible, permitting PC users with such modems to be able to communicate with other PCs and mainframe computers connected to either 212A or 103/113 type modems. In addition, at 2400 bps, US V.22 bis modems can communicate with European V.22 bis, in effect, providing worldwide communications capability over the PSTN.

4800 bps

The Bell System 208 series and CCITT V.27 modems represent the most common types of modems designed for synchronous data transmission at 4800 bps. The Bell System 208 Series modems use a quadrature amplitude-modulation technique. The 208A modem is designed for either half-duplex or full-duplex operation at 4800 bps over leased lines. The 208B modem is designed for half-duplex operation at 4800 bps on the switched network.

Newer versions of the 208A are offered by AT&T as the 2048A and 2048C models, which are also designed for four-wire leased line operation. The 2048C has a start-up time less than one half of the 2048A, which makes it more suitable for operations on multidrop lines.

Both Bell 208 type modems and CCITT V.27 modems pack data three bits at a time, encoding them for transmission as one of eight phase angles. Unfortunately, since each type of modem uses different phase angles to represent a tribit value, they cannot talk to each other. Table 3.10 lists the V.27 modulation phase shifts with respect to each of the eight possible tribit values. The most common use of 208 and CCITT V.27 modems with personal computers is when the PC is functioning as a remote job-entry computer. Several manufacturers now offer internal and external 208A/B modems, permitting the PC to communicate at 4800 bps over the PSTN or on a leased line.

9600 bps

Three common modems that are representative of devices that operate at 9600 bps are the Bell System 209, the CCITT V.29 and V.32 modems. Modems equivalent to the Bell System 209 and CCITT V.29 devices are designed to operate in a full-duplex, synchronous mode at 9600 bps over

Table 3.10 V.27 Modulation Phase
Shift vs. bit Pattern

Tribit values	Phase change
001	0
000	45
010	90
011	135
111	180
110	225
100	270
101	315

private lines. The Bell System 209A modem operates by employing a quadrature amplitude modulation technique as previously illustrated in Figure 3.19. Included in the Bell System modem is a built-in synchronous multiplexer which will combine up to four data-rate combinations for transmission at 9600 bps. Other vendors market a similar modem without the built-in multiplexer.

With the exception of Bell System 209 type modems, a large majority of 9600 bps devices manufactured throughout the world adhere to the CCITT V.29 standard. The V.29 standard governs data transmission at 9600 bps for full- or half-duplex operation on leased lines, with fallback data rates of 7200 and 8400 bps allowed. At 9600 bps the serial data stream is divided into groups of four consecutive bits. The first bit in the group is used to determine the amplitude to be transmitted while the remaining three bits are encoded as a phase change, with the phase changes identical to those of the V.27 recommendation listed in Table 3.10.

Table 3.11 lists the relative signal element amplitude of V.29 modems, based upon the value of the first bit in the quadbit and the absolute phase which is determined from bits 2–4. Thus, a serial data stream composed of the bits 1100 would have a phase change of 270° and its signal amplitude would be 5.

The resulting signal constellation pattern of V.29 modems is illustrated in Figure 3.28.

Table 3.11 V.29 Signal Amplitude Construction

Absolute phase	1st Bit	Relative signal element amplitude
0,90,180,270	0	3
	1	5
45,135,225,315	0	$\sqrt{2}$
	1	$3\sqrt{2}$

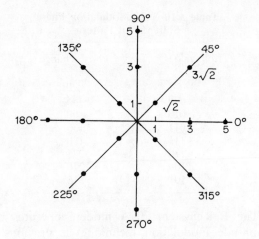

Figure 3.28 V.29 Signal Constellation Pattern

A new CCITT recommendation that warrants attention is the V.32 standard. V.32 is based upon a modified quadrature amplitude modulation technique and is designed to permit full-duplex 9600 bps transmission over the switched telephone network. A V.32 modem establishes two high-speed channels in the opposite direction to one another as illustrated in Figure 3.29. Each of these channels shares approximately the same bandwidth. An echo-canceling technique is employed by V.32 modems which permits transmitted and received signals to occupy the same bandwidth. This is made possible by designing intelligence into the modem's receiver that

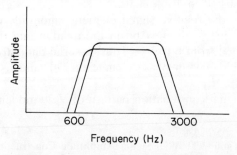

Figure 3.29 V.32 Channel Derivation

A V.32 modem obtains high-speed full-duplex transmission by deriving two channels that share approximately the same bandwidth through the use of an echo-canceling technique.

A summary of the operational characteristics of Bell System and CCITT V series type modems is given in Table 3.12.

permits it to cancel out the effects of its own transmitted signal, enabling the modem to distinguish its sending signal from the signal being received. Unfortunately, echo canceling requires sophisticated circuitry and has resulted in the cost of V.32 modems being approximately twice the cost of V.29 modems that offer the same data rate on leased lines.

A summary of the operational characteristics of Bell System and CCITT V series type modems is given in Table 3.12.

Table 3.12 Modem Operational Characteristics

Modem type	Data rate	Transmission technique	Modulation technique	Transmission mode	Line use
Bell System					
103 A,E	300	asynchronous	FSK	Half, full	Switched
103 F	300	asynchronous	FSK	Half, full	Leased
201 B	2400	synchronous	PSK	Half, full	Leased
201 C	2400	synchronous	PSK	Half, full	Switched
202 C	1200	asynchronous	FSK	Half	Switched
202 S	1200	asynchronous	FSK	Half	Switched
202 D/R	1800	asynchronous	FSK	Half, full	Leased
202 T	1800	asynchronous	FSK	Half, full	Leased
208 A	4800	synchronous	PSK	Half, full	Leased
208 B	4800	synchronous	PSK	Half	Switched
209 A	9600	synchronous	QAM	Full	Leased
212	0–300	asynchronous	FSK	Half, full	Switched
	1200	asynchronous/ synchronous	PSK	Half, full	Switched
CCITT					
V.21	300	asynchronous	FSK	Half, full	Switched
V.22	600	asynchronous	PSK	Half, full	Switched/ leased
	1200	asynchronous/ synchronous	PSK	Half, full	Switched/ leased
V.22 bis	2400	asynchronous	QAM	Half, full	Switched
V.23	600	asynchronous/ synchronous	FSK	Half, full	Switched
	1200	asynchronous/ synchronous	FSK	Half, full	Switched
V.26	2400	synchronous	PSK	Half, full	Leased
	1200	synchronous	PSK	Half	Switched
V.26 bis	2400	synchronous	PSK	Half	Switched
V.26 ter	2400	synchronous	PSK	Half, full	Switched
V.27	4800	synchronous	PSK		
V.29	9600	synchronous	QAM	Half, full	Leased
V.32	9600	synchronous	QAM	Half, full	Switched

Non-standard modems

Due to the requirement of PC users for faster transmission throughput to support file transfer and interactive full-screen display operations, several vendors have designed proprietary operating modems to achieve data rates that would have been beyond the realm of belief several years ago. Some of these modems incorporate data compression and decompression algorithms, permitting data to be compressed prior to transmission and then expanded back into its original form at the modem at the opposite end of the communications path.

Since compression decreases the amount of data requiring transmission the modem can accept a higher data rate input than it is capable of transmitting. Thus, a V.29 operating modem incorporating data compression that has a 2 to 1 compression ratio is theoretically capable of transmitting data at 19 200 bps, even though the modem operates at 9600 bps. Since the compression efficiency depends upon the susceptibility of the data to the compression algorithms built into the modem, in actuality the modem operates at a variable data rate. When no compression is possible, the modem operates at 9600 bps, while the actual throughput of the device increases as the data input into the modem becomes more susceptible to compression.

A second type of non-standard modem reached the marketplace in 1986. More formally known as packetized ensemble protocol modem, this modem incorporates a revolutionary advance in technology due to the incorporation of a high-speed microprocessor and approximately 70 000 lines of instructions built into read only memory (ROM) chips on the modem board.

To better understand the operation of a packetized ensemble protocol modem, let us review the operation of a conventional modem, using the Bell System 212 device for illustrative purposes.

When a Bell 212A modem modulates data, two carrier signals are varied to impress information onto the line. One carrier signal operates at a frequency of 1200 Hz, while the second carrier frequency operates at 2400 Hz, resulting in two paths which enables full-duplex transmission to occur on a two-wire circuit. This is illustrated in Figure 3.30. Thus, at any instant in time data can flow on only two frequencies.

Under the packetized ensemble protocol, the originating modem simultaneously transmits 512 tones onto the line. The receiving modem evaluates the tones and the effect of noise on the entire voice bandwidth, reporting back to the originating device the frequencies that are unusable. The originating modem then selects a transmission format most suitable to the useful tones, employing 2-bit, 4-bit or 6-bit quadrature amplitude modulation (QAM) and packetizes the data prior to its transmission. Figure 3.31 illustrates the carrier utilization of a packetized ensemble modem.

As an example of the efficiency of this type of modem, let us assume that 400 tones are available for a 6-bit QAM scheme. This would result in

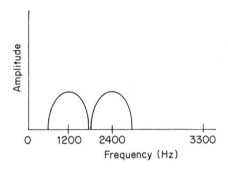

Figure 3.30 Bell 212A Modem Carrier Signals

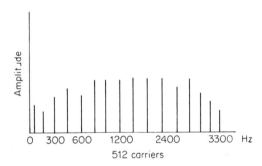

Figure 3.31 Packetized Ensemble Modem

a packet size of 400 × 6 or 2400 bits. If each of the 400 tones is varied four times per second, a data rate of approximately 10 000 bps is obtained. It should be noted that the modem automatically generates a 16-bit cyclic redundancy check (CRC) for error detection, which is added to each transmitted packet. At the receiving modem, a similar CRC check is performed. If the transmitted and locally generated CRC characters do not match, the receiving modem will then request the transmitting modem to retransmit the packet, resulting in error correction by retransmission.

Some of the key advantages of a packetized ensemble protocol modem are its ability to automatically adjust to usable frequencies which greatly increases the use of the line bandwidth and its ability to lower its fallback rate in small increments. The latter is illustrated in Figure 3.32, which shows how this type of modem loses the ability to transmit on one or a few tones as the noise level on a circuit increases, resulting in a slight decrease in the data rate of the modem. In comparison, a conventional modem, such as a 9600 bps device, is designed to fall back to a predefined fraction of its main data rate, typically 7200 or 4800 bps.

To appreciate the advantages of using high-speed modems, let us examine the transmission of a 250-word document, 20 such documents and the

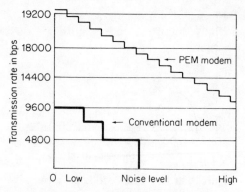

Figure 3.32 Transmission Rate versus Noise
Level

contents of a 360K byte diskette at different data rates. A comparison of
the utilization of 300, 1200, 2400, 4800 and 10 000 bps modems is presented
in Table 3.13. As indicated, a 10 000 bps modem can substantially reduce
the transmission time required to send long files between personal computers
or a personal computer and a mainframe computer. In fact, the retail price
of approximately $1250 for a packetized ensemble modem can be recovered
in less than 1 year through a reduction in communications charges. This will
occur if a personal computer user has a requirement to transmit via a long-
distance telephone call the contents of a diskette just once a week to another
computer.

The original packetized ensemble modem was designed by Telebit
Corporation and is marketed as the Trailblazer. Digital Communications
Associates (DCA) markets two similar modems under license, using the
trademark Fastlink. DCA markets a modem card for insertion into the
system unit of an IBM PC or compatible personal computer and a stand-
alone unit that can be attached to any computer with a standard RS-232
communications port.

In addition to being compatible with other packetized ensemble protocol
modems, these devices are compatible with V.22 bis, V.22, 212A and 103
type modems. This compatibility permits the personal computer user to use
the device for high-speed file-transfer operations when connected to another

Table 3.13 Comparing Throughput Efficiencies

Item to transmit	Transmission rate (bps)				
	300	1200	2400	4800	10 000
1 page 250 words (s)	40	10	5	2.5	1.2
20 pages (s)	800	200	100	50	24
360K diskette (min)	163.84	40.96	20.48	10.24	4.92

packetized ensemble protocol modem as well as to access information utilities, other personal computers and mainframes that are connected to industry standard modems.

Asymmetrical modems

Borrowing an old modem design concept, several vendors have introduced asymmetrical modems for use by personal computers. These modems, in essence, contain two channels which in the early days of modem development were known as the primary and secondary channel.

Originally, modems with a secondary channel were used for remote batch transmissions, where the primary high-speed channel was used to transmit data to a mainframe computer while a lower-speed secondary channel was used by the mainframe to acknowledge each transmitted block. Since the acknowledgements were much shorter than the transmitted data blocks, it was possible to obtain efficient full-duplex transmission even though the secondary channel might have one-tenth of the bandwidth of the primary channel.

In the late 1980s, several modem vendors realized that while high-speed transmission might be required to refresh a PC's screen when the personal computer was connected to a mainframe or for a file transfer, transmission in the opposite direction is typically limited by the user's typing speed or the shortness of acknowledgements in comparison to data blocks of information. Realizing this, modem vendors developed a new category of devices which use wide and narrow channels to transmit in two directions simultaneously, as illustrated in Figure 3.33. The wide-bandwidth channel permits a data rate of 9600 bps while the narrow-bandwidth channel is used to support a data rate of 300 bps. Where these asymmetrical modems differ

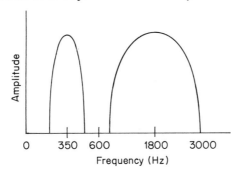

Figure 3.33 Asymmetrical Modem Channel
Assignment

An asymmetrical modem encodes data onto two carrier
signals. High-speed data is encoded onto an 1800 Hz
carrier while low-speed data is encoded onto a 350 Hz
carrier.

from older modems with secondary channels is in the incorporation of logic to monitor the output of attached devices and to then reverse the channels, permitting an attached personal computer to access the higher speed (wider bandwidth) channel when necessary. Although no standards existed for asymmetrical modems when this book was written, several manufacturers were attempting to formulate the use of common frequency assignments for channels. Since a 9600 bps asymmetrical modem has a retail price approximately one-half of a V.32 modem, it appears that consumer use of this type of modem may result in the development of standards.

Modem handshaking

Modem handshaking is the exchange of control signals necessary to establish a connection between two data sets. These signals are required to set up and terminate calls, and the type of signaling used is predetermined according to one of three major standards, such as the Electronic Industry Association (EIA) RS-232-C or RS-449 standard, or the CCITT V.24 recommendation. RS-232-C and CCITT V.24 standards are practically identical and are used by over 98 percent of all modems currently manufactured. To better understand modem handshaking, let us examine the control signals used by 103 type modems. The handshaking signals of 103 type modems and their functions are listed in Table 3.14, while the handshaking sequence is illustrated in Figure 3.34.

The handshaking routine commences when an operator at a PC or terminal at one location dials the telephone number of the remote device. At the remote site, a ring indicator (RI) signal at the answering modem is set and passed to the device that answers the call. For simplicity of illustration, we will assume that the PC user called a mainframe computer. The computer then sends a data terminal ready (DTR) signal to its modem, which then transmits a tone signal to the modem connected to the PC. Upon hearing this tone, the PC operator presses the data pushbutton on the modem, if it

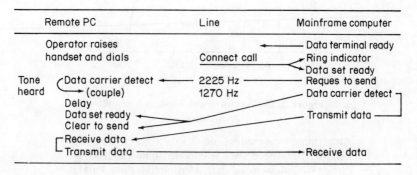

Figure 3.34 Handshake Sequence

Table 3.14 Modem Handshaking Signals and their Functions

Control signal	Function
Transmit data	Serial data sent from device to modem
Receive data	Serial data received by device
Request to send	Set by device when user program wishes to transmit
Clear to send	Set by modem when transmission may commence
Data set ready	Set by modem when it is powered on and ready to transfer data; set in response to data terminal ready
Carrier detect	Set by modem when signal present
Data terminal ready	Set by device to enable modem to answer an incoming call on a switched line; reset by adapter diconnect call
Ring indicator	Set by modem when telephone rings

is so equipped for manual operation. Upon depression of the data button for manually operated modems, the originating modem sends a data set ready (DSR) signal to the terminal, and the answering modem sends the same signal to the computer. At this point in time both modems are placed in the data mode of operation. With automatic operating modems, this handshaking procedure occurs automatically and transparently to the PC operator.

The mainframe computer normally transmits a request for identification to the PC attempting to access the computer as a remote terminal. To do this the mainframe computer sets request to send (RTS) which informs the PC's modem that it wishes to transmit data. The PC's modem will respond with the clear-to-send (CTS) signal and will transmit a carrier signal. The mainframe computer's modem detects the clear-to-send and carrier-on signals and begins its data transmission to the PC. When the mainframe computer completes its transmission it drops the RTS, and the PC's modem then terminates its carrier signal. Depending upon the type of circuit on which transmission occurs, some of these signals may not be required. For example, on a switched two-wire telephone line, the RTS signal determines whether a PC is to send or receive data, whereas on a leased four-wire circuit RTS can be permanently raised. For further information the reader should refer to specific vendor literature or appropriate technical reference publications.

Self-testing features

Many low-speed and most high-speed modems have a series of pushbutton test switches which may be used for local and remote testing of the data set and line facilities.

In the local or analog test mode, the transmitter output of the modem is connected to the receiver input, disconnecting the customer interface from the modem. A built-in word generator is used to produce a stream of bits which are checked for accuracy by a word comparator circuit, and errors are displayed on an error lamp as they occur. The local test is illustrated in Figure 3.35.

To check the data sets at both ends as well as the transmission medium, a digital loop-back self-test may be employed. To conduct this test, personnel may be required to be located at each data set to push the appropriate test buttons, although a number of vendors have introduced modems that can be automatically placed into the test mode at the distant end when the central site modem is switched into an appropriate test mode of operation. In the digital loop-back test, the modem at the distant end has its receiver connected to its transmitter, as shown in Figure 3.36. At the other end, the local modem transmits a test bit stream from its word generator, and this bit stream is looped back from the distant end to the receiver of the central site modem where it is checked by the comparator circuitry. Again, an error lamp indicates abnormal results and indicates that either the modems or the line may be at fault.

The analog loop-back self-test should normally be used to verify the internal operation of the modem, while the digital loop-back test will check both modems and the transmission medium.

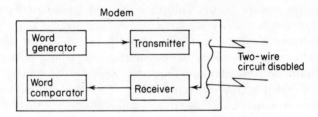

Figure 3.35 Local (Analog) Testing

In local testing the transmitter is connected to the receiver, and the bit stream produced by the word generator is checked by the word comparator.

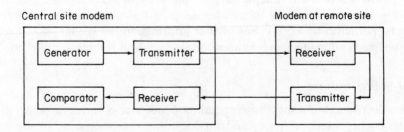

Figure 3.36 Digital Loop-back Self-test

In the digital loop-back test both the modems and the transmission facility are tested.

3.4. INTELLIGENT MODEMS

Due to the popularity of the Hayes Microcomputer Products series of Smartmodems™, the command sets of those modems are the key to what the terms 'intelligent modems' and 'Hayes compatibility' mean. Since just about all modern personal computer communications software programs are written to operate with the Hayes command set, the degree of Hayes compatibility that a non-Hayes modem supports affects the communications software that can be used with that modem. In some cases, non-Hayes modems work as well or even better than a Hayes modem if the software supports the non-Hayes features of that device. In other cases, the omission of one or more Hayes Smartmodem features may require the personal computer user to reconfigure his or her communications software to work with a non-Hayes modem, usually resulting in the loss of a degree of functionality.

The Hayes command set actually consists of a basic set of commands and command extensions. The basic commands, such as placing the modem off hook, dialing a number, and performing similar operations, are common to all Hayes modems. The command extensions, such as placing a modem into a specific operating speed, are applicable only to modems built to transmit and receive data at that speed.

The commands in the Hayes command set are initiated by transmitting an attention code to the modem, followed by the appropriate command or set of commands one desires the modem to implement. The attention code is the character sequence AT, which must be specified as all uppercase or all lowercase letters. The requirement to prefix all command lines with the code AT has resulted in many modern manufacturers denoting their modems as Hayes AT compatible.

The command buffer in a Hayes Smartmodem holds 40 characters, permitting a sequence of commands to be transmitted to the modem on one command line. This 40-character limit does not include the attention code, nor does it include spaces included in a command line to make the line more readable. Table 3.15 lists the major commands included in the basic Hayes Command Set. Other modems, such as DCA's Fastlink employ a command set that can be considered to be a superset of the Hayes command set. While communications software that uses the Hayes command set will operate with this modem, such software cannot utilize the full potential of the modem. This is because the Hayes command set in 1988 only supported a data rate selection up to 9600 bps while the Fastlink modem could be set to a data rate of 19 200 bps by proprietary software commands.

The basic format required to transmit commands to a Hayes compatible intelligent modem is shown below.

AT Command[Parameter(s)]Command[Parameter(s)]. . .Return

Table 3.15 Hayes Command Set

Command	Major commands Description
A	Answer call
A/	Repeat last command
C	Turn modem's carrier on or off
D	Dial a telephone number
E	Enable or inhibit echo of characters to the screen
F	Switch between half- and full-duplex modem operation
H	Hang up telephone (on hook) or pick up telephone (off hook)
I	Request identification code or request check sum
M	Turn speaker off or on
O	Place modem on-line
P	Pulse dial
Q	Request modem to send or inhibit sending of result code
R	Change modem mode to 'originate-only'
S	Set modem register values
T	Touch-tone dial
V	Send result codes as digits or words
X	Use basic or extended result code set
Z	Reset the modem

Each command line includes the prefix AT, followed by the appropriate command and the command's parameters. The command parameters are usually the digits 0 or 1, which serve to define a specific command state. As an example, H0 is the command that tells the modem to hang up or disconnect a call, while H1 is the command that results in the modem going off hook, which is the term used to define the action that occurs when the telephone handset is lifted. Since many commands do not have parameters, those terms are enclosed in brackets to illustrate that they are optional. A number of commands can be included in one command line as long as the number of characters does not exceed 40, which is the size of the modem's command buffer. Finally, each command line must be terminated by a carriage return character.

To illustrate the utilization of the Hayes command set let us assume we desire to automatically dial New York City information. First, we must tell the modem to go off hook, which has an effect similar to manually picking up the telephone handset. Then we must tell the modem the type of telephone system we are using, pulse or touch-tone, and the telephone number to dial. Thus, if we have a terminal or personal computer connected to a Hayes compatible modem, we would send the following commands to the modem:

AT H1

AT DT1,212-555-1212

In the first command, the 1 parameter used with the H command places the modem off hook. In the second command, DT tells the modem to dial (D) a telephone number using touch-tone (T) dialing. The digit 1 was included in the telephone number since it was assumed we have to dial long distance, while the comma between the long-distance access number (1) and the area code (212) causes the modem to pause for two seconds prior to dialing the area code. This two-second pause is usually of sufficient duration to permit the long-distance dial tone to be received prior to dialing the area code number.

Since a Smartmodem automatically goes off hook when dialing a number, the first command line is not actually required and is normally used for receiving calls. In the second command line, the type of dialing does not have to be specified if a previous call was made, since the modem will then use the last type specified. Although users with only pulse dialing availability must specify P in the dialing command when using a Hayes Smartmodem, several vendors now offer modems that can automatically determine the type of dialing facility the modem is connected to and then use the appropriate dialing method without requiring the user to specify the type of dialing. For other non-Hayes modems, when the method of dialing is unspecified, such modems will automatically attempt to perform a touch-tone dial and, if unsuccessful, then redial using pulse dialing.

To obtain an appreciation of the versatility of operations that the Hayes command set provides, assume two personal computer users are communicating with one another. If the users wish to switch from modem to voice operations without hanging up and redialing, one user would send a message via the communications program he or she is using to the other user indicating that voice communication is desired. Then, both uses would lift their telephone handsets and type '+++ (Return) ATH (Return)' to switch from on-line operations to command mode (hang up). This will cause the modems to hang up, turning off the modem carrier signals and permitting the users to converse.

Result codes

The response of the Smartmodem to commands is known as result codes. The Q command with a parameter of 1 is used to enable result codes to be sent from the modem in response to the execution of command lines while a parameter of 0 inhibits the modem from responding to the execution of each command line.

If the result codes are enabled, the V command can be used to determine the format of the result codes. When the V command is used with a parameter of 0, the result codes will be transmitted as digits, while the use of a parameter of 1 will cause the modem to transmit the result codes as words. Table 3.16 lists the Basic Results Codes set of the Hayes Smartmodem 1200. As an example of the use of these result codes, let us assume the following commands were sent to the modem:

138

AT Q0

AT V1

The first command, AT Q0, causes the modem to respond to commands by transmitting result codes after each command line is executed. The second command, AT V1, causes the modem to transmit each result code as a word code. Returning to Table 3.16, this causes the modem to generate the word code 'CONNECT' when a carrier signal is detected. If the command AT V0 were sent to the modem, a result code of 1 would be transmitted by the modem, since the 0 parameter would cause the modem to transmit result codes as digits.

By combining an examination of the result codes issued by a Smartmodem with the generation of appropriate commands, software can be developed to perform such operations as redialing a previously dialed telephone number to resume transmission in the event of a communications session being interrupted, and automatically answering incoming calls when a ring signal is detected.

Table 3.16 Smartmodem 1200 Basic Result Codes Code Set

Digit word	Word code	Meaning
0	OK	Command line executed without errors
1	CONNECT	Carrier detected
2	RING	Ring signal detected
3	NO CARRIER	Carrier signal lost or never heard
4	ERROR	Error detected in the command line

Modem registers

A third key to the degree of compatibility between non-Hayes and Hayes Smartmodems is the number, use and programmability of registers contained in the modem. Hayes Smartmodems contain a series of programmable registers that govern the function of the modem and the operation of some of the commands in the modem's command set. Table 3.17 lists the functions of the first 12 registers built into the Hayes Smartmodem 1200, to include the default value of each register and the range of settings permitted. These registers are known as S registers, since they are set with the S command in the Hayes command set. In addition, the current value of each register can be read under program control, permitting software developers to market communications programs that permit the user to easily modify the default values of the modem's S registers.

To understand the utility of the ability to read and reset the values of the modem's S registers, consider the time period a Samrtmodem waits for a

Table 3.17 S Register Control Parameters

Register	Function	Default Value	Range
S0	Ring to answer on		0..255
S1	Counts number of rings	0	0..255
S2	Escape code character	ASCII 43	ASCII0..127
S3	Carriage return character	ASCII 13	ASCII0..127
S4	Line feed character	ASCII 10	ASCII0..127
S5	Backspace character	ASCII 8	ASCII0..127
S6	Dial tone wait time (seconds)	2	2..255
S7	Carrier wait time (seconds)	30	1..255
S8	Pause time caused by comma (seconds)	2	0..255
S9	Carrier detect response time (1/10 second)	6	1..255
S10	Time delay between loss of carrier and hang up (1/10 second)	7	1..255
S11	Touch-tone duration and spacing time (milliseconds)	70	50..255

dial tone prior to going off hook and dialing a telephone number. Since the dial tone wait time is controlled by the S6 register, a program offering the user the ability to change this wait time might first read and display the setting of this register during the program's initialization. The reading of the S6 register would be accomplished by the program sending the following command to the modem:

AT S6?

The modem's response to this command would be a value between 2 and 255, indicating the time period in seconds that the modem will wait for a dial tone. Assuming the user desires to change the waiting period, the communications program would then transmit the following command to the modem, where *n* would be a value between 2 and 255.

AT S6 = *n*

Compatibility

For a non-Hayes modem to be fully compatible to a Hayes modem, command-set compatibility, result codes compatability and modem register compatability is required. Of the three, the modem register compatability is usually the least important and many users may prefer to consider only command set and response codes compatibility when acquiring intelligent modems.

The rationale for omitting register compatibility from consideration is the fact that many non-Hayes modem vendors manufacture compatible modems using the default values of the Hayes Smartmodem registers. This enables those manufacturers to avoid building the S registers into their modems, reducing the size, complexity and many times also reducing the price of their modem. Thus, if the default values of the S registers are sufficient for the user and the modem under consideration is both command set and result code compatible the issue of register compatibility can normally be eliminated as an acquisition factor to consider.

Benefits of utilization

With appropriate software, intelligent modems can be employed in a variety of ways which may provide the user with the potential to reduce the cost of communications as well as to increase the efficiency of the user's data-processing operations. To obtain an understanding of the benefits that may be derived from the use of intelligent modems, let us assume that our organization has a number of sales offices geographically dispersed throughout many states. Let us further assume that each sales office uses a personal computer to process orders, which are then mailed to company headquarters for fulfillment.

Due to postal delivery time or other factors, the delay between receiving an order at a sales office and its transmittal to company headquarters may be unacceptable. Since the order-processing delay is making some customers unhappy, while other customers citing faster competitor delivery time have been canceling or reducing their orders, management is looking for a way to expedite orders at a minimum cost to the organization.

Although a person in each sales office might be delighted to call a computer system at corporate headquarters at the end of each day and use a mainframe program to enter orders, this activity would operate at the speed of the person entering the data, communications costs would be high since the session would occur during the day, and last minute orders might not get processed until the next day unless the person performing the data entry activity agreed to stay late. Since each sales office is assumed to have a personal computer, another method we may wish to consider is the utilization of personal computers to expedite the transmittal of orders between the sales offices and the company headquarters.

Since the personal computer in each sales office is already used to process orders and prepare a report that is mailed to headquarters, one only has to arrange for the transmission of the order file each day, since the program that produces the report would only have to be sent to company headquarters once, unless the program was revised at a later date. Then, after a personal computer at company headquarters receives the order file, it would use that file as input to its copy of the order-processing program, permitting the report to be produced at company headquarters.

Due to the desire to automate the ordering process at a minimal cost, it might be advisable to perform communications after 11 p.m. when rates for the use of the switched telephone network are at their lowest. Since it would defeat the purpose of communications economy to have an operator at each sales office late in the evening, a communications program that provides unattended operation capability would most likely be obtained. This type of communications program would require the use of an intelligent modem at the company headquarters location as well as at each sales office location. Then, the communications software program operating on a personal computer at company headquarters could be programmed through the use of macro commands or menu settings to automatically dial each sales office computer at a predefined time after 11 p.m., request the transmission of the order file and then disconnect after that file had been received. The communications program would then dial the next sales office, repeating the file transfer procedure. At each sales office, a similar unattended communications program would be operating in the personal computer at that office. Upon receiving a call, the intelligent modem connected to the personal computer would inform the computer that a call had been received and the program would then answer the call, receive the request to transfer the order file, transmit that file to the distant computer and then hang up the telephone. To prevent anyone from dialing each sales office, most unattended communications programs permit password access to be implemented, enabling the user to assign appropriate passwords to the call program that will enable access to the files on the called personal computer.

3.5 MODEM SELECTION

A large number of parameters may be considered by some PC users in the modem-selection process, while other users, due to their application requirement, may be content to examine only a limited number of parameters. Table 3.18 lists the major modem-selection parameters one should consider as well as some of the more popular choices available for selection for many parameter categories.

Alternate voice/data capability is normally accomplished by a switch on the modem. If one wishes to use one's PC to dial friends and switch between voice and data this feature should be considered.

Automatic modem features run the gamut from automatic dialing and answering of calls to line sound monitoring and redialing of the last number dialed. Normally, the command set used to implement the features is more important than any one feature offered by a specific modem vendor. This results from the fact that most asynchronous communications programs are written to operate with the Hayes command set and if one' automatic modem features do not correspond to this command set one's software choices may be limited.

Table 3.18 Modem-selection Parameters

Alternate voice/data switch
Automatic features – autodial, autoanswer, redial
Asynchronous character bit length
Bundled with software
Compatibility – modulation and command set
Configuration – stand-alone or card
Data rate – 300, 1200, 2400
Data format – asynchronous, synchronous
Half-/full-duplex on two-wire lines
Interface to the telephone network
Originate/answer mode
Power source
Security feature – dialback/password
Self-testing features and indicators
Stored log-on/telephone numbers
Telephone dialing method – pulse or rotary

The asynchronous character bit length actually refers to the number of data bits and stop bits an asynchronous modem supports. Typically, most modems support 7 or 8 data bits and 1 or 2 stop bits.

Concerning software bundling, many modem vendors package an asynchronous communications program with their hardware. Although such packages offer a convenient and usually more economical method to obtain hardware and software, as all modems are not equal neither are all communications programs. Thus, one should carefully check the features of the communications software program if its acquisition is of major importance to the modem purchaser.

With respect to compatibility, one should consider both modulation compatibility and command-set compatibility. The former governs the types of other vendor modems your modem can communicate with while the latter governs the software programs that can be used to implement the intelligent features of the modem if it is so equipped.

As previously discussed in this chapter, one can obtain an external or stand-alone modem or a modem built onto a card that must be inserted into an expansion plot in the PC's system unit. There are many advantages to internal modems, to include eliminating the cable requirement between the PC and modem as well as resulting in less desk space being required. Since 2400 bps modems consume much more power than 300 or 1200 bps modems, users with a PC should examine the power consumption of other devices installed in their PC. This is because a PC has a 65 watt power supply while the PC XT has a 135 watt power supply and the PC AT has a 192 watt power supply.

Although a 2400 bps modem can transmit and receive information twice as fast as a 1200 bps modem, a higher data rate may not always be best. Since no one can type at the rate of 300 characters per second, it makes little sense to access an information utility at 2400 bps for interactive query–response applications if the utility charges more per connect hour at the higher data rate. On the opposite side of the spectrum, if one expects to transmit and receive a large volume of data, higher-speed modems, such as those operating at 2400 bps, may be more appropriate for one's situation. In such cases, the savings from reduced transmission durations may exceed the cost of the higher-speed modem after only several months of usage.

If one's PC is to communicate synchronously or bisynchronously, one must obtain a synchronous modem. Although most PCs presently communicate asynchronously, synchronous transmission normally permits a higher level of data transfer to occur. Some modems, such as the Bell System 212A and compatible devices, can operate either asynchronously or synchronously based upon the setting of a switch in the modem. Due to advances in technology, by the end of the decade one might expect 9600 bps modem cards to cost no more than 300 bps modem cards cost today.

Most modems currently marketed can be interfaced to the telephone network via a modular plug which is inserted in a wall-mounted jack. The most popular jacks used are RJ11, RJ12 and RJ13. Normally if you are making a single line connection, your cable from the modem will be inserted into an RJ11 wall jack. For a multiline installation, the cable is usually connected to an RJ12 or RJ13 telephone jack. The information pages in the front of your local telephone book usually contain a detailed explanation of the type of telephone jack required and the requirements for notifying the telephone company of the installation of the modem to the telephone line.

If one expects to originate and answer calls an originate/answer mode modem is an absolute requirement. Otherwise, the frequency assignments between your modem and the distant device will be incompatible since the distant modem would most likely be an originate-mode modem which, as previously explained in this chapter, cannot communicate with another originate-mode modem.

Although most external modems obtain power from a transformer with a wall plug that directly plugs into a standard a.c. outlet, several manufacturers currently offer a series of modems that obtain power from their connection to the telephone line. While this feature may not appear to be significant, it can alleviate the necessity of long extension cords when one wishes to connect one's modem to a telephone jack that is remotely located from a conventional power outlet. For modem boards, power is obtained from the system unit of the PC they are installed in. Since a 1200 bps modem usually requires four times the power of a 300 bps modem, readers are cautioned to check the power requirements of all components in a fully populated PC as the sum of the power of all components in operation can conceivably exceed the maximum output of the PC's 65 watt power supply.

Due to the mass media exposure of various 'hackers' and the popularity of the movie *War Games* several vendors have marketed security modems.

These modems usually incorporate such features as dialback to the transmission originator to verify the location of the call origination party or incorporate a password-checking mechanism. While such modems are normally sold for use at a mainframe computer center, they can also be considered for use with a PC that operates as a corporate bulletin board or with a multi-user PC system that permits dial-in access. By using this type of modem, the PC user can reduce the probability of unauthorized access into his or her PC.

Although self-testing features are usually associated with expensive high-speed modems, many manufacturers of low-speed modems have incorporated this feature into their products. By pressing a button, issuing a command or toggling a switch, one can place the modem into its self-test mode. If the modem performs a local test, a word generator in the modem transmits a predefined message to the transmitter, which is then strapped to the receiver, bypassing the telephone line, hence the term local test. The receiver demodulates the data, which is then sent to a word comparator in the modem which checks the message content against the content it expects to receive. If the transmitted messages matches the expected message, a green light is normally displayed to indicate that the modem has passed its self-test. If the message demodulated by the receiver does not match the value in the word comparator, a red light is usually displayed, indicating that the modem failed its self-test and that it requires service. Other modems have diagnostic features built into the modem which permit the device to be tested via the telephone from a remote diagnostic center, permitting the vendor or a company's technical control center to remotely check the operational status of one's modem.

Most modems contain a series of light-emitting diode indicators on the front panel of the device that display the status of the modem's operation. Typical indicators include a power indicator which is illuminated when power to the modem is on, a terminal-ready indicator which is illuminated when the attached PC or terminal is ready to send or receive data, a transmit data indicator that illuminates when data is sent from the attached device to the modem, a receive data indicator that illuminates when data is received from a distant computer or terminal, and a carrier detect signal that illuminates when a carrier signal is received from a distant modem. Other indicators on some modems include an off-hook indicator that illuminates when the modem is using the telephone line and a high-speed indicator on dual speed modems that illuminates whenever the modem is operating at its high speed. Table 3.19 lists the most common modem indicator symbols, their meaning and the resulting status of the modem when the indicator is illuminated on the front panel of the modem.

While most modems obtain the telephone number to be dialed from a dialing directory in a software program, several modems are marketed with the capability to store both telephone numbers and log-on sequences required to access mainframe computers. These modems usually contain a limited

Table 3.19 Common Modem Indicator Symbols

Symbol	Meaning	Status
HS	High speed	ON when the modem is communicating with another modem at 2400 baud
AA	Auto answer/answer	ON when the modem is in auto answer mode and when on-line in answer mode
CD	Carrier detect	ON when the modem receives a carrier signal from a remote modem. Indicates that data transmission is possible
OH	Off hook	ON when the modem takes control of the phone line to establish a data link
RD	Receive data	Flashes when a data bit is received by the modem from the phone line, or when the modem is sending result codes to the terminal device
SD	Send data	Flashes when a data bit is sent by the terminal device to the modem
TR	Terminal ready	ON when the modem receives a Data Terminal Ready signal
MR	Modem ready/power	ON when the modem is powered on
AL	Analog loopback	ON when the modem is in analog loopback self-test mode

amount of complementary metal oxide semiconductor (CMOS) storage whose low power requirements are satisfied by a small battery in the modem.

Although a large part of the United States has touch-tone dialing, many areas can only accept rotary or pulse dialing. Normally a modem that provides auto-select touch tone or pulse dialing is preferable, since it provides the PC user with the ability to access long-distance discount telephone services such as MCI or Sprint, whose access requires touch-tone dialing. Even if you do not use a long-distance service requiring touch-tone dialing and are presently located in an area serviced by pulse dialing, the auto-select feature will provide you with the capability to take advantage of the quicker dialing capability of touch-tone if it should be offered in your area without having to replace your modem.

With modem technology one of the most rapidly evolving fields, the reader is cautioned that the parameters presented in Table 3.18 should be used as a guide and not as an all-inclusive list of parameters to consider in selecting the most appropriate modem to satisfy one's requirements.

CHAPTER FOUR

Communications Software

In this chapter, we will first review the major communications software features that should be considered in selecting an appropriate program to satisfy one's telecommunications requirements. Then, using the discussion of these parameters as a foundation of communications software knowledge, we will examine several commercial general-purpose communications programs as well as the rationale and utilization of programs that provide the user with specific terminal emulation capability. Concluding this chapter will be a discussion of micro-to-mainframe software and the key features included in many of these program packages.

4.1 SOFTWARE FEATURES

The effect of members of the IBM PC series on users requiring desktop computation is probably as pronounced as that of the telephone and duplicating machine on all business users. Today it is difficult to find a business, educational institution, or government agency that does not have a large and growing base of personal computers.

The variety of uses to which personal computers can be put is limited only by the user's imagination and by the machine's physical constraints. While word processing and electronic spreadsheet programs are by far the most common applications, no less important is the machine's ability to communicate information. In fact, the range of personal computer applications that depend on data communications is to pervasive that in a few short years it will be hard to imagine any PC without the ability to communicate.

One of the main problems facing IBM PC users is the selection of appropriate communications software. Today, literally hundreds of such programs are marketed, ranging in scope from simple line-by-line TTY emulators to programs that mimic specific types of terminals. They may also include such features as file transfer, unattended operation, and automatic sign-on and sign-off procedures for accessing bulletin boards and mainframes.

Different programs offer a variety of features that the user may wish to consider. Table 4.1 lists forty-five of the most common features of communications programs in alphabetical order. This table can serve as a checklist in comparing specific programs. Alternatively, users with the opportunity to test or analyze programs prior to purchase may wish to rate the capability of each package according to those features deemed important.

Many of these features are interrelated in function. Some programs may not treat them separately but may incorporate them into another utility. Thus, the specifications and operational characteristics of each program should be investigated thoroughly.

Hardware utilization

The first set of features to be considered includes those that the user might first encounter when examining communications programs. An initial question is, or should be, 'Which programs will work on the hardware available?' Memory, the number and type of disk drives and storage media, and the presence of a hard disk will affect how a communications program can be utilized.

Drive Use and Requirements

With different hardware configurations, personal computer disk storage capability can significantly vary. For example, the IBM PC can range in storage from a machine containing one single-sided drive capable of storing 160K bytes to a configuration with two dual-sided drives, each disk storing up to 380K bytes. Based on these storage-capacity differences, both the medium that the communications program is distributed on and the number and type of disk drives it requires for operation should be checked for compatibility with the user's hardware.

Memory Requirements

Most communications programs have memory requirements ranging from 64K to 192K bytes. However, integrated programs that include communications may need as much as 384K to 640K bytes of memory. Although most IBM PCs, for example, are now shipped with at least 256K bytes installed, older PCs had as little as 16K bytes. Thus, users may have to expand their microcomputers' memory prior to using certain programs.

Modem Compatibility

Communications programs may support a specific type of intelligent modem, several such modems, or both intelligent and nonintelligent devices. Compatibility with an existing modem can be ensured by checking the command set supported by the communications program. In some cases the communications program will list a few specific modems supported. The

Table 4.1 Common Features of Communication Programs

| | Utilization Performance | | | | | | |
Feature	Hardware	Software	Operational	Dialing	Transmission	Efficiency	Flexibility	Security
Automatic operations supported				•				
Buffer control								
Character-transfer support								
Clock display								
Communications port selection			•			•		
Control-character transfer							•	
Copy protection								•
Data compression								
Dialing directory				•				
Dialing from the keyboard				•	•			
Dialing method (tone/pulse)				•	•			
Disk-directory access								
Display-width selection								
Documentation						•	•	
Drive use and requirements								
Editing capability			•					
Encryption capability			•					
Error detection and correction						•	•	
Exit to OS command level								•
File closing						•	•	•

File-transfer capability
File-viewing capability
Foreground/background operations
Journalization
Line-feed control
Lowercase/uppercase conversion
Memory requirements
Mid-session prompts/help capability
Mode selection (menu/command)
Modem compatibility
OS command use
OS version requirements
Pacing capability
Preconfigured dialing directory
Printer control
Programmable-key capability
Programmable macros
Protocol setting
Screen-dump capability
Selectable data rate
Stripping/converting characters
Switchable printer ports
Terminal emulation
Transmission mode
Unattended operation capability

command set of the user's modem should be checked against those supported by the program.

Printer Control

The ability to turn a printer on and off is supplied by most communications programs. Since an attached letter-quality printer operates at a slower rate than a dot-matrix printer, such a device would probably not be able to keep pace with a long response or a long file transmitted by the distant machine. To overcome this limitation, some programs use a segment of memory as a printer spooler, enabling the simultaneous printing and down-line loading of data when the printer cannot keep up.

If the communications program does not have this capability, an alternative is to transfer a file and then list its contents. Without a printer spooler, the user can only print and receive data simultaneously when the speed of the printer exceeds the data-transfer rate of the communications line. Otherwise, the receive buffer in the communications program will probably overflow, resulting in the loss of data. Data-flow overrun may even cause a program to terminate the session.

When a simultaneous-print option is activated, some communications programs strip control characters prior to sending data to the printer, while others send all data, including control characters, to the printer. Certain control characters adversely affect the printer. Transmitted form-feeds waste paper, while XOff characters disconnect any printer designed to respond to flow control. Suspending the printer may cause the microcomputer keyboard to lock and not respond to any keystrokes until the printer is manually revived.

Software utilization

Clearly, the proper hardware is required to run a communications program on an IBM PC. Just as important is the program's compatibility with the machine's software environment, in particular its operating system (OS).

OS Version Requirements

Many communications programs written in BASIC or another higher-level language operate under most, if not all, versions of an IBM PC's OS. By and large, though, assembly-language programs are not OS independent, since they may use certain function calls that are available only at or above a particular OS revision level. Thus, for example, one program may require an IBM PC with a disk operating system (DOS) of version 2.X or above, while another program operates with DOS 1.X or higher.

OS Command Use

Many packages let the user execute operating-system commands through the communications program. Programs that have this feature allow users to delete and rename files, display disk directories, format a disk, or perform other operations without first leaving the communications program. This feature can be especially advantageous under certain situations, such as transferring a file onto the PC when there is insufficient room for the file on the disk. Unfortunately, this usually occurs when the only storage medium available is a newly purchased box of blank, unformatted disks. With the ability to use operating-system commands, files can be deleted from a storage disk or a new disk formatted without leaving the communications program.

Operational considerations

One communications program category of features frequently overlooked is the interaction of the program with the user. Many program features have a pronounced effect upon the efficient operation of the program by the user. In addition, a communications package must also be compatible with the user's level of expertise and need for convenience, clarity, and ease of use.

Mode Selection (Menu/Command)

For the first-time user, a menu-driven communications program makes the various options easier to understand and to use. However, users may reach a level of expertise where it is simpler to type commands than to go through a series of menus to accomplish a given task. At the opposite end of the spectrum are command-driven programs. These programs may be more difficult to master but, once learned, more efficient than their menu-driven counterparts.

To strike a balance through the advantages and disadvantages associated with menu- and command-driven software, some programs let the user select the mode of operation. For example, the user might switch from menu-driven to command-driven mode after obtaining a degree of familiarity with the program.

Mid-Session Prompts/Help Capability

Some communications programs employ extensive prompt messages that make it difficult for the user to set an option incorrectly. Others provide limited prompting but may compensate for this lack with extensive help or assistance displays that appear in response to a predefined key sequence.

Figure 4.1 illustrates the PC-Talk III command summary that is displayed in the upper right portion of the screen when the Home key is pressed on

PrtSc	= print screen contents
PrtSc	= contin. printout (or PgUp)
Alt-R	= Receive a file (or PgDn)
Alt-T	= Transmit a file (or PgUp)
transmit:	pacing '=p' binary '=b'
tran/recv:	XMODEM '=x'
Alt-V	= View file Alt-Y = delete
Alt-D	= Dialing directory
Alt-Q	= redial last number
Alt-K	= set/clear Func keys (Alt-J)
Alt-	= set/clear temp Alt keys
Alt-E	= Echo toggle Alt-M = Message
Alt-S	= Screendump Alt-C = Clearsc
Alt-P	= communications Parameters
Alt-F	= set program deFaults
Alt-L	= change Logged drive
Alt-W	= set margin Width alarm
Alt-Z	= elapsed time/current call
Alt-X	= eXit to DOS
Ctrl-End	= send sustained Break signal

Figure 4.1 PC–TALK III Command Summary

the keyboard. Since this program is command-driven, it is quite easy to forget many of the commands that are not used frequently. This help screen, while limited to a display of the available commands, may be sufficient for many users.

Documentation

It is difficult to make full use of a sophisticated communications program without good documentation that indicates explicitly how each feature works. In addition, a good index is imperative, since thumbing through a manual wastes both time and communications dollars when the user is connected to a remote service.

Clock Display

Like a fancy box of chocolates, interactive communications can easily become addictive. Calling long distance or using a value-added carrier that charges a fee based on the duration of the connection can quickly escalate communication costs. Search charges from information utilities or data-retrieval services may exceed $100 per connect-hour. Therefore, a mechanism to display the duration of a call can serve as a reminder that it may be time to terminate the session.

Many communications programs display the duration of a session. Some programs automatically display the elapsed time while others display the time only when the user enters a predefined command or control code.

Although this feature may be deemed frivolous by anyone with a wrist watch, once used, it can become like that indispensable box of chocolates.

Dialing

Once a software program has been found compatible with your requirements, it will almost certainly be used to set up a call over a switched public telephone network. Initiating a call involves dialing, which may be from a preconfigured or a user-developed dialing directory. Dialing has a number of aspects which are discussed in the following paragraphs.

Automatic Operations Supported

A communications program may support a wide variety of automatic features. These can be as simple as control of an attached modem, or as sophisticated as automatic sign-on to an information utility or time-sharing environment on a corporate mainframe. Such sign-on tools are actually programmable macros, and will be considered under a separate category. However, control of an attached modem lets a program automatically dial, answer calls, redial numbers that are busy, and hang up the telephone when the session is over or when a call in progress ends due to loss of carrier.

Even with a nonintelligent modem, the user should try to obtain a communications package that supports both manual and automatic operations, since the hardware can then be upgraded without a change of software. Of course, the command set that the software supports should be examined to insure that it will operate with the user's new, intelligent modem.

Due to the popularity of the Hayes Smartmodem, most vendors marketing intelligent modems have designed their products to be compatible with the Hayes command set. However, some programs support other command sets. Table 4.2 lists nine representative 1.2-kbps modems from six vendors. In some instances, the modems are not compatible with the Hayes command set. Other modems are either directly compatible or are built to recognize dual command sets. In addition, other modems, such as the Hayes 2.4-kbps unit and the DCA Fastlink have command sets that are supersets of the Hayes 1.2 kbps device. Thus, programs written to work with the lower-speed modem will operate with the higher-speed device, but they may not take full advantage of specific features of those modems.

Dialing Method (Tone/Pulse)

Most intelligent modems work with both touch-tone and pulse telephone-dialing methods. Therefore, to make the most of an intelligent modem, the communication program may translate the dialing method requested into an

154

Table 4.2 Representative Modem Command Sets Supported

Vendor/Modem	Command set supported
AT&T Information Systems	
Model 4000	AT&T
Dataphone II 2212C	AT&T
Case Rixon	
Executive	Case Rixon, Hayes
Cermetek Microelectronics	
Info-Mate 1200-TPC	Hayes
General DaatComm Industries, Inc.	
212/ED	GDC, Hayes
Acculine 1200	Hayes
Microcom, Inc.	
SX1200	Microcom
ERA 2/1200	Hayes
Universal Data Systems	
FasTalk 1200	Hayes

appropriate modem command. Without this capability, it may be necessary to adjust a modem setting in order to change the dialing method.

Dialing Directory

Programs can incorporate dialing directories ranging in scope from a simple listing of telephone numbers to a set of sophisticated entries, in which each entry includes the number to be dialed, a text description of the destination, and parameter settings. Figure 4.2 lists a partially completed dialing-directory screen from the PC-Talk III communications program. Up to four screens of 15 entries each, or a total of 60 dialing entries, can be maintained on a file created and accessed by the program.

Initially, the directory is empty. Default communications parameters are 300 bps, even parity, seven data bits, and one stop bit, since this is the most common setting for accessing mainframes and information utilities. As users add entries to the dialing directory, they can easily change the default parameters as well as the four rightmost columns, which affect the echoing of transmitted characters to the screen, letting a remote personal computer user know the status of file transfers (messaging), replacing of received characters (stripping), and how frequently new lines of data are sent (pacing). Once the parameters are set, selecting a particular entry tells the program to dial the number and to use the entry's parameters.

Some programs permit only ten entires, or even fewer. This number may be sufficient for many users. However, if requirements grow, the only way to add a new entry is to remove an existing one. Thus, the prospective

```
===Dailing directory 1===        Modem dialing command = ATDP
Long distance service +* =

                                  _*=
Name                Phone *      Comm Param   Echo  Mesg  Strip  Pace
1-FEINET            971-1001     300-E-7-1     N     N     N      N
2-FEINET *2         527-1800     300-E-7-1     N     N     N      N
3-UVA *1            924-0280     300-E-7-1     N     N     N      N
4-UVA *2            924-7401     300-E-7-1     N     N     N      N
5-MACON                 2053     1200-E-7-1    Y     N     1      N
6-----------------  - --- --- ----  300-E-7-1  N     N     N      N
7-----------------  : --- --- ----  300-E-7-1  N     N     N      N
8-----------------  - --- --- ----  300-E-7-1  N     N     N      N
9-----------------  - --- --- ----  300-E-7-1  N     N     N      N
10----------------  - --- --- ----  300-E-7-1  N     N     N      N
11----------------  - --- --- ----  300-E-7-1  N     N     N      N
12----------------  - :-- --- ----  300-E-7-1  N     N     N      N
13----------------  - --- --- ----  300-E-7-1  N     N     N      N
14----------------  - --- --- ----  300-E-7-1  N     N     N      N
15----------------  - --- --- ----  300-E-7-1  N     N     N      N

Dial Entry *:       | or ...  Enter:  R to revise or add to directory
                                      M for manual dialing
                                      F/B to page through directory
                                      X to exit to terminal
                    | For long distance service, precede entry * with +/-
```

Figure 4.2 PC–TALK III Dialing Directory

purchaser should consider the number of entries as well as how flexibly new ones can be added.

Dialing from the Keyboard

Since all dialing directories are finite in size, the ability to enter a telephone number from the keyboard can save the user a considerable amount of effort. If the communications program permits dialing only through a directory entry and the directory is full, it may be necessary to remove an entry in order to dial.

Preconfigured Dialing Directory

Some communications programs contain a dialing directory whose parameters are preconfigured for major information utility services, such as CompuServe, Dow Jones, and The Source, among others. Normally, preconfigured dialing directories do not contain telephone numbers for the entries, since the program's purchaser could be located anywhere in the United States or abroad and any number included would probably not reflect the most economical telephone number to use.

The preconfiguration of transmission parameters may eliminate many minutes or hours of future effort; however, a word of caution is in order.

At least one vendor lists 800-numbers in the dialing directory along with the parameter settings required to access several information utilities. Unfortunately, these 'toll-free' numbers are not free, since the information utilities add a surcharge to the user's connect time when access is via an 800-number. It is usually much less expensive to go through a value-added carrier that might just be a local call away.

Transmission

Another category of features includes those directly involved in the transmission, reception, and flow of data across a telecommunications link. These features are examined in the following paragraphs.

Transmission Mode

Since various mainframes operate in either half- or full-duplex, a communications program should permit users to switch between these two transmission modes. Depending on the settings of the PC and the destination machine, either zero, one, or two characters may be displayed for each character typed on the keyboard.

If the PC is in a half-duplex transmission mode, each time a key is pressed the character is echoed to the display as well as transmitted. If the remote computer is also operating half-duplex, the character is not echoed back and a single character is displayed for each one transmitted. If, however, the remote machine is in full-duplex, the character will be echoed back to the PC and two characters will be displayed for each one sent. The obvious solution is to change the PC to full-duplex to match the remote device.

With the PC in full-duplex and its remote partner in half-duplex, no character will be displayed when a key is pressed. This is because the PC transmits but does not echo the character to the screen while the remote unit receives the character and also does not echo it. Again, the solution is to change the transmission mode of the PC.

Terminal Emulation

Most of the original communications programs first written for use with personal computers transmitted and received data on a line-by-line basis. These programs did not take advantage of the screen-display capability of the personal computer and simply emulated Teletype-style transmission.

More sophisticated terminal emulation can cause problems for the personal computer user. For instance, a terminal from Digital Equipment Corporation (DEC) might not work with an IBM mainframe in full-screen mode, because it does not recognize many of the control codes used by the mainframe for cursor positioning, character attributes, and similar screen-control functions. To enable a personal computer to operate as a specific type of terminal, it became necessary to develop emulation software to convert these control codes into equivalents that the microcomputer recognizes. Similarly, the codes used to represent functions on the personal computer had to be converted into their mainframe equivalents. Thus, users wishing to use a PC for local processing and to act as a specific type of terminal must look for a package with the appropriate emulation capability.

Character Transfer Support

IBM PC applications involving communications ordinarily transmit data in seven-bit ASCII. However, memory-image files can be transferred only in an 8-bit representation. Also, the IBM PC and its compatibles use an extended ASCII character set, with 8-bit characters used to obtain ASCII characters from 128 to 255. In many cases, programs written in Basic use these extended-ASCII characters, which would preclude program transfers between personal computers if the communications program did not support 8-bit ASCII transmission. Thus, the communications programs should support 8-bit data transfer if the user wants to send binary data or programs that use extended ASCII characters.

Another area where character transfer is important involves using a mainframe as an intermediate-storage device for personal-computer-to-personal-computer transmission. Figure 4.3 illustrates how an existing corporate network could be employed to support such communications, eliminating most direct data transfers between personal computers.

If the mainframe supports only conventional 7-bit ASCII, the communications program must be able to break each 8-bit byte to be sent to the mainframe into two 7-bit ASCII characters (actually two 4-bit nibbles,

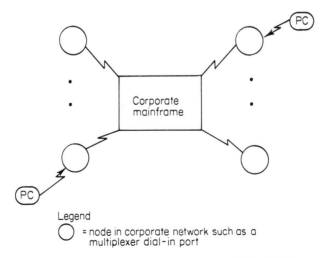

Figure 4.3 Using the Corporate Network for PC-to-PC Transmission

padded with zeros in the last three positions). It must also be able to reconstruct data retrieved from the mainframe. Needless to say, both personal computer programs need this feature.

File Transfer Capability

If the user has to transmit or receive binary files, the program must be able to transfer non-ASCII data. The same goes for transmitting tokenized Basic programs, in which certain key combinations are used by IBM to represent Basic keywords. Tokenizing cuts down on storage requirements but uses 8-bit ASCII, so the communications program must have an 8-bit capability.

This should not be confused with the ability of some programs to transfer 8-bit ASCII data. These programs work only some of the time because an 8-bit binary string being transmitted may accidentally have the same bit composition as an end-of-file mark, which could abnormally end the file transfer.

Stripping/Converting Characters

Some characters transmitted from a mainframe or information utility can interfere with the intended operation of a personal computer. Others can be a display nuisance. For example, an ASCII 127 character is sometimes used for timing delay. In such cases, the mainframe sends a variable number of these characters between lines, thinking that an attached electromechanical printer needs time to return its print-head to the home position. If the communications program does not automatically strip this character, it will appear on the IBM PC screen similar in size to a hotel from a Monopoly game. Not only does this clutter the display, but it also shifts each line a number of positions to the right. Since there are occasions where the user may wish to retain pad characters, some programs have an option for specifying which characters, if any, should be stripped from the incoming communications buffer.

Another character transmission area that can result in personal computer trouble is when a mainframe or information utility transmits an ASCII 126 character (control-z on an IBM PC) to mark the end of a response to a PC request. If received data were being logged to disk, the operating system might interpret the ASCII 126 as an end-of-file mark, which would cause any information in the file following this character to be inaccessible. The rest of the file would have been logged to disk, but the disk operating system would see an end-of-file mark. The only way to retrieve such a file would be with a special utility program.

To alleviate such misinterpretations, the communications program should contain a character-conversion feature. All ASCII 126 characters would be converted to ASCII 32 (space) characters. Similarly, a character-conversion feature could change XOFFS to spaces, which could keep the printer running.

Buffer Control

Communications programs use a buffer, which is a portion of random-access memory, for temporary storage when transmitting and receiving data. As the buffer fills, a flow-control procedure incorporated into most programs prevents the buffer from overflowing and thus keeps received data from being lost. The common method of implementing flow control is for the program to transmit an XOFF character when its receive buffer is between one-half and two-thirds full. If the transmitting device recognizes the XOFF, it will temporarily stop transmitting, so that the communications program can process the data in its receive buffer. Then, after the buffer is emptied or reduced to a predefined value, the program transmits an XON character to tell the distant device that it may resume transmission.

Since some mainframes implement flow control with characters different from XON and XOFF, users who anticipate accessing a variety of mainframes may wish to consider a program that lets them select flow-control characters via a parameter table., Without such a feature, sending an XOFF will not halt the mainframe. Under certain situations, such as when receiving data and printing it concurrently, the buffer on the PC can overflow, resulting in data loss.

Pacing Capability

Pacing control, intended to keep buffers from overflowing, can involve one of three methods. The host can slow down the transmission of files to a remote personal computer by pausing for a set amount of time between each transmitted line. Certain mainframes do not permit a connected device to send a line of data until the device receives a prompt from the host (typically an asterisk or question mark). Therefore, some communications programs may wait for the receipt of the prompt before they transmit the next line. A third pacing mechanism is known as character-receipt delay. Here, the user specifies how many characters must be received from the mainframe before the program may transmit new line of data.

Of the three pacing methods, transmission upon prompt-character receipt is the most efficient, as it lets the user specify the exact character string that must be received from the mainframe before the program sends the next line of data. With time pacing, the user must specify an interval (in seconds or fractions of a second) as the worst-case time that it will take the mainframe to process each line of data.

A mainframe's response time is a function of its current load and of the activity to be performed. Therefore, pausing for a set interval between lines can result in bloated connect time and transmission charges, since this method does not take advantage of the fact that some lines of data can be processed more quickly than others. Since impulse noise can destroy characters, specifying a number of characters that must be received from the mainframe before the microcomputer continues may cause an infinite wait. To avoid this situation, some communications programs that use this method permit manual user intervention or automatic transmission of the next line after a predefined time delay.

Performance efficiency

Of penultimate concern to most users is how a program functions once a connection to the target computer has been made and the program is mediating a session. One general set of requirements involves the software's efficiency. This element can show up in anything from compression, which hastens the transfer of files and reduces waiting time, to disk directory access, which can improve the user's productivity.

Selectable Data Rate

For remote communications, most programs let the user select a variety of data-transfer rates from 110 to 9600 bps. This range is normally sufficient for many users. However, the introduction of some modems that can operate at data rates up to 19.2 kbps means that programs limited to 9.6 kbps may not operate with such modems or fail to use the modem at its highest data-transfer capability.

In other instances, the user might cable a personal computer directly to a mainframe's communications channel and transfer data up to 19.2 kbps. Similarly, this speed may not be achievable unless the communications program can support it. Thus, the maximum data rate supported by the program should be checked for both local connections and remote connections if the personal computer is to be directly cabled to a mainframe.

This form of connection means that the personal computer must communicate with remote devices through a second asynchronous adapter. If the communications program does not support multiple adapters or if there is only one adapter in the microcomputer, a fallback switch may be installed as illustrated in Figure 4.4. By means of the fallback switch, either a directly connected mainframe or a modem for remote communications may be accessed through a single adapter.

Data Compression

Several communications programs incorporate data-compression techniques. These range from simple blank suppression to sophisticated encoding schemes that reduce the actual quantity of data transferred up to 50 percent or more. For lengthy file-transfer operations, a data-compression feature can significantly reduce transmission time and thus communications cost. Obviously, the computer at the other end of the data link must have the

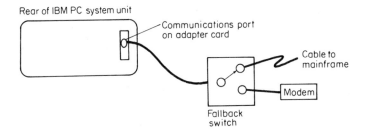

Figure 4.4 Using a Fallback Switch

Through the use of a fallback switch, one communications adapter can share two communications paths; however, only one path can be accessed at a time.

same communications program, since compression techniques are not standardized and are normally proprietary to each software vendor.

Although data compression can be useful, it must be disabled in order to access a computer that does not have a similar program. Otherwise, data transferred in a compressed mode would not be in recognizable to the other device. Thus, the program must allow the user to turn off compression.

To transfer large files with a communications program that lacks data compression, the user can take advantage of stand-alone utility programs offered on the market that compress and decompress files. Compressed files could be transmitted and then decompressed with another copy of the utility program.

Error Detection and Correction

For file-transfer operations, the probability of an error occurring increases with the length of the file. The communications program should be able to detect the occurrence of an error, as well as to automatically correct the error without intervention. Typically, the program first detects that an error has occurred within a data block and then asks the other device to retransmit that block.

A wide variety of methods is used to detect and correct transmission errors. A simple checksum can be formed by adding up the ASCII values of the characters in a block and dividing this sum by a fixed number. More sophisticated algorithms use polynomial checking.

One of the more popular error detection and correction methods is incorporated into the XMODEM protocol created by Ward Christensen. In this protocol's error-handling technique, data is grouped into 128-byte blocks. A checksum for each block is formed by adding the ASCII values of all 128 characters and dividing the sum by 255. Then the quotient is discarded and the remainder is appended to the block as the checksum.

At the receiving device, a similar operation is performed on the received data. If the locally computed checksum matches the transmitted checksum, the data is considered to have been received correctly. If not, the receiver will ask the transmitting device to retransmit the block.

Although the above method of error detection and correction is extensively implemented by most noncommercial bulletin boards and in many commercial software programs, it does have several deficiencies. For one thing, it is a stop-and-wait protocol, where block number $N+1$ cannot be transmitted until block number N is acknowledged. Also, after nine negative acknowledgements are received, the communications session will terminate and file transfer must restart from the beginning. Another limitation is the probability of receiving an undetected error, which is higher with the error-detection method used by the XMODEM protocol than with a cyclic redundancy-checking algorithm.

One or more of these limitations can be avoided by carefully selecting a communications program. The program should accommodate full-duplex transmission, permitting a number of unacknowledged blocks to remain outstanding, and should implement a more sophisticated error-detection and -correction scheme. Among these protocols are Blast (blocked asynchronous transmission) from Communications Research Group, Microcom Networking Protocol (MNP) from Microcom Inc., and X.PC from Tymnet. Obviously, the destination computer must support the same protocol.

Foreground/Background Operations

Similarly to what is made possible by printer buffers, a few communications programs permit users to perform file-transfer operations while doing other work. This feature frees the microcomputer for other operations during lengthy file transfers and normally increases productivity. Other programs include the capability print information to include screen images and files at the same time the user performs other operations.

Programmable Key Capability

Some communications programs have a rigidly structured macro language. Others let the user assign a string of information for transmission to what is known as a programmable key. In this way, the user may define values associated with certain command-key combinations as well as the function keys on IBM PCs and compatible computers. Pressing these keys during a session will cause the associated string to be transmitted. Both the number of keys that can be programmed and the length of the string that can be assigned to each key should be examined since they vary considerable between programs.

Programmable Macros

A macro is a command that can be stored and executed with a single keystroke. With these programmable macros, the user can store passwords and other log-on sequences and execute them with a single keystroke. This lets the user avoid the repetitive process of typing commands each time a mainframe computer or information utility is to be accessed. Since the number of macros varies between communications programs this is another feature that should be investigated prior to selecting a communications program.

Control Character Transfer

The most common way to tell mainframes to terminate a previously initiated operation is to send a break signal. This signal should not be confused with, for example, the Ctrl+Break (control and break) key combination on the IBM PC keyboard, which terminates the current operation and returns the user to command mode. Instead of transmitting a character, the break signal causes a stream of binary zeros to occur on a line for approximately one-tenth of a second, which tells the mainframe to stop what it is doing and return to its operating system command level.

Normally, the personal computer's communications program will issue a break signal in response to a predefined character sequence being typed on the keyboard. Since the break signal is indispensable for host operations, micro-to-mainframers should learn how to tell the communications package to send one. Unfortunately, not all mainframes recognize a break signal, in which case an ability to transmit control characters from the keyboard becomes important. As as example, some mainframes rcognize a control-C (ASCII 3) as a signal to terminate the current operation. Communications software that does not allow the transmission of control characters may force the user to resort to the inelegant solution of pulling the plug and then reconnecting to the mainframe.

Disk Directory Access

For file-transfer operations, an ability to check the contents of a floppy or hard disk without exiting to the operating system can be a valuable tool. Some communications programs not only let the user specify the disk drive and display files on the default drive (that is, the drive that the operating system will go to on a command that lacks a drive identifier) but also display the amount of storage available on the drive. This feature can be quite handy for down-line loading a file, since it indicates whether or not there is sufficient room to store the file.

For example, the communications program might indicate 10 240 available bytes of storage on the data disk, while the remote machine indicates that the file to be transferred contains 12 288 bytes. The disk obviously has insufficient storage. The user may then install a new disk, or perform an operating system command to delete an existing file, making room for the new one. (The ability to exit to the operating system command level will be examined as a flexibility issue.)

Editing Capability

The ability to edit documents from within a communications program varies widely. Some packages provide only a backspace key. Others let the user perform full text editing of messages and files. To do this, the communications program stores data in an edit buffer and then transfers the edited data to a disk or to the communications port. Without this capability, users must store data on disk, leave the communications program, and then initiate a word processor or text editor to perform the desired editing.

Screen-Dump Capability

Members of the IBM PC family have a built-in command to send a dump of the screen image to an attached printer. Several communications programs have taken this feature one step further, permitting screen images to be stored to disk. Some will also time- and date-stamp each screen image as they are appended to a predefined file. If the program offers a 'view' option, the user can then look at selected screen images saved to disk during a prior communications session. Without this option, a user might have to end communications and run a word processor or text editor to view previously saved screen dumps.

File Closing

Only a few programs close all open files to ensure that data is not lost if the transmission line drops during a file-transfer session. Some programs are quite sophisticated, not only closing and saving whatever information was received during a partial file transfer but also allowing the user to resume file transfer at the point where the disconnection occurred. This permits data to be appended to a file or to the portion of a file already received.

Unattended Operation Capability

Some communications programs, such as electronic bulletin-board programs, permit remote users to access and use all or a portion of the personal computer's hardware and software. This feature can be useful for unattended file transfers and electronic mail centralization. It does, however, require the habit of checking the mailbox on a periodic basis.

Performance flexibility

From within a communications session or normal command mode, a number of features can make a program more flexible. Users with non-standard screens will appreciate the ability to select display, while such features as editing capability benefit all users.

Protocol Setting

This can mean as little as setting such parameters as the number of data bits, the type of parity, and the number of stop bits transmitted with each character or as much as specifying the type of error detection and correction to be used for transferring files. The more sophisticated programs let the user transfer data files with no error checking, with the XMODEM protocol, or with a vendor-proprietary cyclic redundancy check. Programs offering a menu of schemes permit a wider scope of potential communications, since there is no universally standardized error-detection and -correction mechanism used with PC operations.

Communications Port Selection

Expansion slots for adapter cards can support several asynchronous communications ports. Although most users have only a single modem, a serial printer could be run through the second communications port. Thus, being able to select which port is transmitting data provides some users with additional flexibility and may eliminate a time-consuming recabling process, if, for example, the printer is on port 1 with the modem on port 2, but the program inflexibly assumes that the modem will always be on port 1, the user must change cables.

Switchable Printer Ports

For users with both a letter-quality and a dot-matrix printer attached to their microcomputers, the ability to switch printer ports through the communications program can be a convenient feature. Users might select the letter-quality device to print electronic messages from the home office that are to be reproduced for distribution to other employees. The dot-matrix printer could rapidly list data that does not require high-quality printing. If this feature is not supported, a fallback switch between one printer port and the two printers could be installed as previously illustrated in Figure 4.4. Then the user could switch manually between printers.

Display-Width Selection

When a television is used as an IBM PC display easily readable 80-column text cannot be displayed. In this case, the communications program should be able to operate in either 40- or 80- column display mode. Similarly, if the program emulates a 132-column display terminal and the hardware includes a special graphics-display board, the program can make full use of the hardware. Some programs emulate 'wide display' terminals by means of a horizontal scrolling mechanism. The program should be compatible with any specialized hardware used to display the full wide-display terminal screen.

Journalization

The journalization feature lets the user record communications sessions. Some programs can log all transactions to a disk file or printer, while other programs let the user journalize selectively (everything transmitted, everything received, or both).

For users of the IBM PC and compatible computers operating under DOS release 2.0 or later versions, a journalization feature is built into the operating system. Users can send a journal to the printer through DOS by pressing the Ctrl+PrtSc (control and print-screen) keys simultaneously.

File-Viewing Capability

This feature permits the user to view files generated by a screen-to-disk dump. It may also permit the display of both text and tokenized Basic files. If a Basic file in tokenized form is listed on the screen, it will appear unintelligible. Communications packages with a file-viewing capability interpret the Basic program without requiring that the user exit and create an ASCII version of the file. The reasons for listing such a file while in a communications program are twofold. First, the user may wish to preview a program as it is down-line loaded from a mainframe or utility. Secondly, and perhaps more importantly, the user may want to up-line load a certain program but has to scan a few files first to make sure the right one is sent.

Exit to OS Command Level

Just about every communications program provides a simple mechanism to exit the program and re-enter the personal computer's operating system. If this feature is not offered, the operating system must be reinitialized and the program terminated each time another program is invoked, which may be awkward and inconvenient.

Lowercase/Uppercase Conversion

Some mainframe computers support only uppercase letters. To be able to communicate with such machines, a program must peform a lowercase-to-uppercase conversion prior to transmitting data. If the program does not include this feature, an alternative is to use the 'Caps Lock' key to ensure that conversational-mode communications are in uppercase.

Line-Feed Control

This option lets the user adjust the program's actions based upon the presence or absence of line feeds after carriage returns. If neither the communications program nor the computer at the other end of the data link adds line feeds after each transmitted line during file transfer, the data received will be treated as one long, continuous line. Thus, it would not be listable or usable. In conversational mode, each line received overprints the previous line displayed on screen, which makes it difficult to conduct a dialogue with another device. If the communications program adds a line feed to each received line and the remote device adds one to each transmitted line, transferred data files and data received in conversational mode will appear double spaced. A communications program may include the option to enable or inhibit line feeds after carriage returns.

Security performance

Safeguarding user data is a familiar concern, but few users realize that the copy protection they can find so irritating is merely a security precaution taken by software vendors.

Encryption Capability

A few communications programs incorporate a security-mode data-transfer feature. Typically, this feature uses modulo-2 addition, adding together the binary value of the data to be transferred and a binary key that the program generates in a byte-by-byte fashion. At the other end of the data link, modulo-2 subtraction is used to reproduce the original text. Figure 4.5 illustrates modulo-2 addition and subtraction which forms the basis for the encryption of data.

Since this form of encryption obviously requires the same program at both ends of the data link, an alternative method is a stand-alone file-encryption program. With this method, data can be encoded prior to its transmission, independently of the communications program. However, the program must support 8-bit data transfers, since most file-encryption programs result in the conversion of 7-bit ASCII into a binary file. As long as the recipient has as similar file-encryption program and knows the key used to encode the data, the original text can be reconstructed.

```
Original character – A              01000001
Key                                 00001011
Modulo-2 addition                   ----------

  Transmitted data – F              01001010

Received data                       01001010
Modulo-2 subtraction of key         00001011
                                    ----------

Reconstructed data                  01000001
```

Figure 4.5 Encryption is Based upon Modulo-2 Mathematics

When encryption is in effect a key is added to each byte prior to its transmission. The receiver's program subtracts the key to restore the data to its original value.

Copy Protection

To ensure that users obey their licence agreement, several communications software vendors have implemented a variety of copy protection schemes. Some suppliers let the user transfer the program to a hard disk, but protect their program by requiring that the original disk be inserted in a disk drive before the hard-disk copy is run. The program then checks periodically to make sure the 'master' disk (the one purchased by the user) is in the drive. Under such a scheme, the user can perform file transfers from disks with a configuration consisting of one disk drive and one hard disk. However, it is necessary to first transfer all down-line loaded files to the hard disk and then, after leaving the communications session, copy the files from the hard disk to one or more floppy disks.

Another approach to copy protection is to imbed a certain code, normally the serial number of the program, into the software. When one personal computer communicates with another using the same program, a check is initiated. If the two codes match, communications between the two computers is inhibited. Since this protection scheme permits the user to make an unlimited number of copies of the program as well as to transfer it to a hard disk and operate it without a master disk, it may be preferred to other schemes that limit operational flexibility.

4.2 COMMUNICATIONS PROGRAM EXAMINATION

In Section 4.1, approximately 50 features common to communications software written for operation on personal computers were examined. Using the information as a base, this section will focus its attention upon the utilization of four popular communications programs, relating the features presented in the referenced section to the operational capabilities, constraints and limitations of these programs.

The programs examined in this section were selected based upon the distinct market each program appears to be developed to satisfy. One program is basically a teletype emulator that is distinguished by its simplicity of operation. A second program was selected due to its enhanced file-transfer ability and the large number of versions of the program that operate on a variety of microcomputers, minicomputers and mainframe computer systems. The third program provides the user with a rich environment of configurable communications parameters as well as the capability to convert their personal computer into a variety of specific types of terminals due to the comprehensive emulation capability of that program. The last program examined in this seciton contains a comprehensive script programming language which enables users to easily automate just about all communications functions.

It should be noted that the three programs reviewed in this section were selected for illustrative purposes only and should not be construed as a positive or negative endorsement of any particular vendor product. In addition, readers are cautioned that it is the policy of many vendors to update their programs on a periodic basis and a feature currently missing or lacking in capability on the version of software examined by the author may be added or revised in a later release.

PFS: Access

This communications program marketed by Software Publishing Company was designed for the person that desires the ability to access information utilities and mainframe computers for interactive communications on a line-by-line (TTY emulation) basis. Basically, the term TTY references any type of terminal device that sends and receives data asynchronously on a line-by-line basis, uses the 7-level ASCII character code and incorporates an RS-232-C interface. In comparison to terminal devices that operate on a full-screen oriented basis, the TTY is considered to be a dumb device. This is due to the characteristics of the device precluding, as an example, the display of numerous fields on a terminal display screen, permitting a terminal operator to rapidly tab between different fields and enter or modify data accordingly.

The PFS: Access diskette contains a SETUP program that permits the user to modify the program to work with different equipment, such as a serial printer or a fixed disk. By entering the command SETUP, the user can configure the program to support a specific type of printer as well as to indicate to the program the adapter address of the connection to the printer. Although this may appear trivial, it allows users with a letter quality printer connected to LPT1 and a dot matrix printer connected to LPT2, as an example, to direct printing to the faster dot-matrix printer without requiring the user to recable their printers. Printers supported by PFS: Access include the IBM Color and Graphics printers, C.Itoh, Epson, Epson with Graftrax Plus, IDS, NEC, and Okidata models. Other options on the SETUP menu permit the user to turn color on or off, install PFS: Access onto a fixed disk, and exit to the operating system. Since the program is copy protected, users are limited to five attempts to install a copy of the program on their fixed disk. A separate program called BACKUP on the distribution diskette permits the user to make one backup of the program.

The Main Menu

The program is initiated by entering the command ACCESS at the DOS command level, resulting in the display of its main menu which is illustrated in Figure 4.6.

```
          1. CompuServe          6. Other Service
          2. Dow Jones           7. Other Service
          3. EasyLink            8. Other Service
          4. MCI Mail            9. Choose Modem
          5. THE SOURCE          E. Exit

                       Selection:

          Copyright 1984 Software Publishing Corporation
  F1-Help                                            F10-Continue
```

Figure 4.6 PFS: Access Main Menu

The first time the main menu is displayed the user should select option 9 to initialize the program for the type of modem they will be using. In addition to selecting the appropriate modem, the user can also indicate, to the program, the communications port connected to the modem and whether their telephone supports rotary or touch tone dialing. Figure 4.7 illustrates the Choose-modem menu displayed as a result of entering 9 from the PFS: Access main menu. In this example a Hayes Smartmodem 300 was selected and the program was informed that the modem was connected to the first communications port (COM1:) and that a touch-tone dialing service was available for use.

Once the modem parameters are entered the program will redisplay the main menu, enabling the user to select a service to dial.

As indicated in Figure 4.6, PFS: Access is preconfigured for the communications parameters of five information utilities and electronic mail vendors. If one of the prelisted services is selected, all the user is required to enter is a telephone number to access the service.

```
┌─────────────────────────────────────────────────────────────────┐
│    1. Bitzcomp PC:IntelliModem        8. Transcend PC ModemCard   │
│    2. Hayes Smartmodem 300            9. Transcend PC ModemCard 1200│
│    3. Hayes Smartmodem 1200/1200B    10. US Robotics Password     │
│    4. IBM PCjr built-in              11. Ven-Tel PC Modem Plus    │
│    5. Novation 103 Smart-Cat         12. Ven-Tel PC Modem Plus 1200│
│    6. Novation 103/212 Smart-Cat     13. Acoustic                │
│    7. POPCOM Model X100              14. Others                   │
│  Selection: 2                                                     │
│  Modem connects to COM1: or COM2: COM1:                          │
│  Rotary or Touch Tone (R/T): T                                   │
│  F1-Help       ESC-Main Menu      F10-Continue                  │
└─────────────────────────────────────────────────────────────────┘
```

Figure 4.7 Choose-modem Menu

Service Information

Suppose that a user decides to add a new service to the main menu. By selecting option 6 from that menu, a blank service information menu is displayed. The user can then enter the service name, the telephone number to be dialed, whether or not an automatic sign-on should be created and the appropriate communications settings required to access the service.

Figure 4.8 illustrates the completion of the service information menu by the user to access CompuServe's Infoplex message-switching system. Since the telephone used by the author was connected to a switchboard where an '8' must be dialed to access long distance, the telephone number was prefixed by that digit. In addition, since it can require up to two seconds to gain access to the long-distance network, the digit 8 was followed by two commas, where a comma imbedded in a telephone number causes the program to issue a command to the modem to delay approximately one second prior to dialing the next number.

Automatic Sign-On

One of the more interesting features of PFS: Access is the program's capability to generate an automatic sign-on if the user enters a Y in response

```
┌─────────────────────────────────────────────────────────────────┐
│                         Service Information                       │
│                                                                   │
│          Service name: Infoplex                                  │
│          Telephone number: 8,,404,237 3003                       │
│          Create automatic sign-on (Y/N): N                       │
│                                                                   │
│                         Communications Settings                   │
│                                                                   │
│          Modem speed: 300                                         │
│          Data bits (7 or 8): 7                                   │
│          Stop bits (1 or 2): 1                                   │
│          Parity (none, odd, even, mark, space): EVEN             │
│          Half or full duplex (H/F): F                            │
│                                                                   │
│          F1-Help      Esc-Main menu      F10-Continue            │
└─────────────────────────────────────────────────────────────────┘
```

Figure 4.8 Service Information Menu

to the 'create automatic sign-on' option on the service information menu. When this option is requested the program automatically builds a file during the sign-on process consisting of the user's service prompts and responses until the user presses a function key to terminate the activity once the sign-on process is completed. Thereafter, the user can simply select the service from the main menu and the program will automatically dial and initiate the appropriate sign-on procedure.

Program Limitations

Although the procedure for generating an automatic sign-on is the easiest of many communications programs available on the market it can be best appreciated when compared to the complex macro coding required by some programs; unfortunately only one automatic sign-on can be created for each of the eight service options on the ACCESS Main Menu. In fact, one of the program's major limitations may be its inability to store more than eight service menus and their associated telephone numbers and communications parameters.

Although the user can substitute the communications information associated with a new service for previously entered or preconfigured information, only a maximum of eight entries are permitted at one time. While this should be sufficient for most home users and many businesses, users with a requirement to communicate with more than eight remote locations may prefer a program with a more extensive dialing directory.

Another limitation is the failure of the program to recognize the loss of carrier signal. When this situation occurs the keyboard becomes locked and after a few moments of puzzlement a glance at the attached modem will result in a recognition of the problem. Service can be restored by first pressing the F3 (disconnect) key, which causes the main menu to be redisplayed, and then selecting the previously used service to re-establish communications. If the user has an internal modem or an external device that does not indicate the presence or absence of carrier, puzzlement concerning what happened when the carrier is dropped may extend beyond a few minutes. PFS: Access, another 'user-friendly' program, would be greatly improved if it could detect the loss of carrier and display an appropriate message on the screen.

Another interesting feature of PFS: Access is its ability to save between 15 and 50 or more screens of information with the number of screens saved depending upon the service accessed. This information is saved in memory and the user can employ the Home, PgUp, PgDn, End, or arrow keys to scan previously saved information. In addition, users can also save information to disk as well as transmit previously created files; however, the absence of an error-detection and -correction mechanism in the version of the program used by the author made error-free file transfers a risky proposition, especially when the quality of the telephone circuit is dubious.

A new release of this program corrects this deficiency by incorporating the popular XMODEM protocol for file-transfer operations.

For persons that desire a measure of privacy in their communications the program includes an ecryption feature that limits the legibility of a transmitted document to the sender and receiver knowing the correct privacy code.

PFS: Access is limited to basic teletype terminal emulation. It lacks many of the more sophisticated features contained in other communications programs. The package lacks, as has been noted, an extended dialing directory. It will not strip characters, such as pad characters, or convert a code in one word-processing format to its equivalent in another. Unattended operations, such as auto-answer or timed call origination, are not supported, nor is pacing (pausing between characters so that the computer can keep up). However, for users who can live happily without such features, this simple and relatively easy-to-use program may suffice.

Blast

BLAST, an acronym for Blocked Asynchronous Transmission, is a powerful communications program marketed by the Communications Research Group of Baton Rouge, Louisiana. The key features that separate this communications program from the majority of personal computer communications programs currently marketed are its efficiency in conducting file-transfer operations and the numerous versions of the program that operate on a wide variety of personal computers, minicomputers, and mainframe computer systems.

Most communications programs, such as those employing the XMODEM protocol, implement error correction by using a stop-and-wait data-transfer technique. Under this technique the receiving station must send back an affirmative acknowledgement (ACK) prior to the transmitting device being able to transmit the next data block. Regardless of the data transmission rate, this technique causes a considerable amount of idle periods to occur on the line. In addition, under certain conditions which include the occurrence of an abnormal amount of line noise, a file-transfer operation terminates and most communications programs require the operator to reinitiate the entire file transmission sequence, even if 99 per cent of the file has been successfully transmitted prior to the communications session abnormally terminating.

To alleviate the previously discussed problems, BLAST employs a proprietary protocol which resembles the operation of modern synchronous data link control protocols. BLAST, as its name implies, blocks asynchronous data into data blocks for transmission similar to the method used by XMODEM and other protocols. Where BLAST varies from XMODEM and other protocols is in its ability to perform simultaneous transmission and reception of data, permit data blocks to be acknowledged out of sequence, and in its error-recovery procedures.

174

Data blocks transmitted by BLAST are continuously interleaved with cyclic redundancy checking (CRC) characters and acknowledgement (ACK) characters as illustrated in Figure 4.9. Since these blocks slide past one another in two directions at the same time, the term 'sliding window' transmission is normally associated with this technique. This permits, for example, the receiver to acknowledge a data block while the transmitting device continues to transmit data. By eliminating the stop-and-wait feature associated with most other asynchronous personal computer communications programs, BLAST can increase the throughput of file-transfer operations by 50 percent or more in comparison to programs employing a stop-and-wait error-detection and -correction method.

Another key feature of BLAST is its ability to have up to 16 blocks of data outstanding and not acknowledged. This permits up to 16 000 characters to be transmitted before an ACK or NAK must be received and again serves to increase the program's throughput.

Concerning error recovery, BLAST provides the user with the ability to resume transmission at the point where it was interrupted. This can be a valuable feature when one has transmitted a large portion of a lengthy file and a sudden line hit or other transmission impairment breaks the transmission session. Without this capability, one would have to restart the file-transfer process from the beginning.

Not only Microcomputers

The organization of BLAST is such that it conforms to four of the seven layers in the International Standards Organization (ISO) Open Systems Interconnection (OSI) model. These are the application, presentation, session, and transport layers. The application module in the program provides the command interface between the user and the program while the presentation module provides the interface between the program and the operating system it operates under. The later module translates the disk

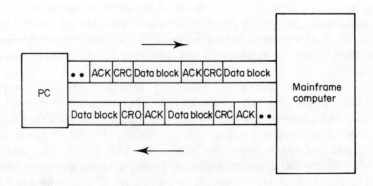

Figure 4.9 BLAST Employs a 'Sliding Window' Protocol

and data formats between the operating system and the actual transmission, which provides the mechanism for any system executing BLAST to perform file-transfer operations with another system operating the program. The other two layers of the program perform communications maintenance functions. Housekeeping for the application in progress counting the number of blocks sent, making sure that not more than 16 are out at once, computing and displaying the percentage of the file that has been sent, is handled by the session module. The transport module takes care of the data transfer and the sequencing of the blocks.

Due to its architecture, BLAST provides file-transfer capability for over 85 computers and 20 operating systems. In addition to operating on the IBM PC series and compatible personal computers, versions of BLAST are available for use under Apple DOS 3.3, CP/M and CP/M-86, DEC RSTS and RSX, IBM MVS and VM/CMS and AT&T and Berkley UNIX operating systems, among others. The range of personal computer, microcomputer, and mainframe computer systems that BLAST operates upon reads like a *Who's Who?* listing of the computer industry, making it difficult to find a system not supported.

For error-free PC-to-mainframe communications, a device known as a BLAST box is required to be connected to mainframe computers when personal computers use versions of BLAST preceding version 7.4. The BLAST box is a protocol converter which converts the 8-bit full-duplex BLAST protocol received from a personal computer into a 7-bit half-duplex format which is supported by most mainframe computer front-end communications processors.

Versions 7.4 and above support Release B of the BLAST protocol in addition to the original BLAST protocol, permitting error-free communications with IBM mainframes, Wang VS systems and Hewlett-Packard computers without requiring the use of the BLAST box. Here, each mainframe is assumed to have BLAST host computer software installed, which, in conjunction with personal computers operating BLAST versions 7.4 and above eliminate the need for a BLAST box. This host software executes as a foreground application program, enabling remote users to invoke the program from a time-sharing operation (TSO) session. Once the host software is invoked, file transfers to and from the remote user occur using the BLAST file transfer protocol.

Operation

BLAST is a menu-driven program that is distributed on diskette. Although MS/DOS BLAST REV 7 was used in preparing this section experience with the use of the earlier REV 6 of the program provided a first-hand illustration of the evolution of a communications software program. While the file-transfer efficiency of both versions of the program remains the same, and far more efficient than most if not all other programs, significant differences in the operation and utilization of both the program and the user's manual were noted. Not only is REV 7 easier to use due to its improved menu structure, but the manual that comes with the program has evolved from a publication which lacked clarity to a very respectable user's manual that incorporates one of the best sections covering communications concepts encountered in technical literature.

One example of the problems with REV 6 documentation concerned the modem switch settings. To use the program with a Hayes Smartmodem 1200, switches 1 and 6 must be positioned up, a fact originally buried deep within section six of the documentation. Since the factory settings of switch 6 is down, upon selecting the dial phone number option in the program the user received the message '#### YOU MUST HANG UP PRESENT CALL BEFORE DIALING OR ANSWERING ####.' Unfortunately, selecting the 'HANG UP PHONE' option in the program had no effect on this switch setting and the user who did not examine and reset his or her modern configuration switches to the appropriate positions was probably in for a frustrating experience. In REV 7 this vital information is moved forward to the 'Getting Started' section of the user manual, where it logically belongs. Although most of the changes between revisions were a marked improvement, unfortunately the method of copy protection was not. Under REV 6 copy protection was based upon the serial number of the program, that is, no file transfer between two computers operating BLAST would occur if during the file-transfer initialization process both serial numbers matched. This permitted the program to be easily transferred to a fixed disk an unlimited number of times. Under REV 7 the copy-protection scheme was changed and a program called 'HDCOPY' on the distribution diskette will only copy the software onto a fixed disk for a specified number of installations.

Program Execution

Executing the program can be as simple as entering the command BLAST, or users can enter a command line consisting of the command followed by one or more optional parameters to configure the program to their specific requirements to include their hardware environment. Some of the optional parameters that can be included in the command line enable input to be read by the program from a file in place of the keyboard, permit all activity to be logged to a specific output file, denote the desired communications port to be used by the program, instruct the program to use an existing configuration file containing communications parameters and other settings, and enable printing to be logged to a port other than LPT1.

Permitting command input to be read from a file allows BLAST to operate unattended, providing users with the capability to take advantage of off-hour data transfer when rates are normally lower. Included in the program is a sophisticated set of batch-control commands that enables the user to essentially program BLAST to perform such functions as dial a number at a specified time, repeat dialing until the value of a counter is reached if the dialing failed, transfer one or more files and disconnect after the file transfer is completed.

Main Menu

Execution of the program results in the display of the BLAST main menu which is illustrated in Figure 4.10. This menu is one of five basic menus in the program that permits the user to request program functions and respond to prompt messages generated by the program.

The selection of T, E, C or L options in the main menu results in the display of additional menus that have options relative to the major function of the menu. Selecting the T option from the main menu turns the user's computer into a dumb terminal capable of transmitting and receiving data on a line-by-line basis to include the transfer of files. The resulting terminal/modem menu also permits the user to set options that govern such modem control functions as the dialing of a number, answering an incoming call, and the hanging-up of a current connection.

The E option in the main menu results in the program entering the 'error-free' mode in which file transfers are conducted using the proprietary BLAST full-duplex, sliding-window protocol. This option can only be used with another computer operating a version of BLAST. Selecting the L option in the main menu results in the display of a local functions menu. This menu permits the user to request a variety of file-reference operations to include the listing of file names and the display of files on the screen as well as the erasing and renaming of files.

When the program is initially used, option C should be selected first from the main menu. This option allows the user to customize one or more

```
                              MAIN MENU

        T-terminal/modem functions C-change configuration      Q-quit program
        E-error-free  mode            L-local functions

                          Enter desired option:

                  -------------------- LOCAL DISPLAY AREA --------------------



        ---------------------------------------------------------------------------

                              BLAST REV 7 . 2 . 1
                          Blocked ASynchronous Transmission
                        (c) 1984 Communications Research Group, Inc.
                              Serial No. 0208700158
```

Figure 4.10 Blast Main Menu

configuration parameters to meet the user's requirements with respect to the communications and terminal specifications.

As the result of selecting option C from the BLAST main menu, the program's configuration management menu will be displayed. This menu is illustrated in Figure 4.11.

Configuration Management

Although many of the parameters listed in the configuration management menu are self-explanatory, several are not and warrant specific attention due to the flexibility they afford users of the program.

The configuration management menu shows the default settings of this menu when the program is initialized. Listed directly under the menu heading are six options that govern the 24 parameters in the menu. The user can change parameters by entering a C, load a previously saved configuration file (option L), save a newly created or modified configuration file (option W) or change the receive and/or transmit translation tables (options R and T). The last two options permit the user to specify character stripping or conversion by displaying a translation table that users can modify to satisfy their requirements. Thus, users accessing some mainframes might change ASCII 127 to ASCII 32 to convert a pad character, displayed on the screen of some computers as a Monopoly house, to a space character.

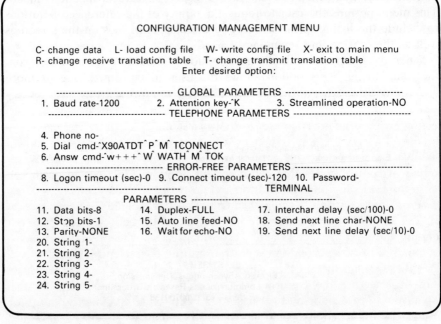

Figure 4.11 Configuration Management Menu

Under the global parameters section of the configuration management menu the attention key setting of ^K (Control + K key pressed at the same time) denotes the default key combination to be pressed to interrupt current program processing and return the user to a menu level. This key can be redefined to suit the user's preference. Once users become familiar with the overall operation of the program they can set the streamlined operation option to YES, resulting in the program skipping certain intermediate menus when entering the terminal and file-transfer modes of operation.

The dial command under option 5 in the telephone parameters list enables the user to define the connection string that is generated when the 'dial a phone number' option is selected from the program's terminal/modem menu. The default value sets the timeout to 90 seconds (^90), uses the Hayes command to tone dial (ATDT), has the desired telephone number substituted for the ^P entry, issues a return (^M) and traps the CONNECT message returned by the Hayes modem.

The answer command defines the connection control string transmitted to answer an incoming call. The disconnect command defines the control string issued by the program when the 'hang up current call' option is selected from the program's terminal/modem menu. The control strings are preconfigured for a Hayes or Hayes-compatible modem and must be changed by the user to operate with another type of modem.

The error-free parameters are used to specify various program options that are applicable to file-transfer operations using the program's proprietary protocol. The log-on timeout parameter enables the user to specify the time interval in seconds for which the program will try to establish handshaking with a remote system prior to declaring a long-on timeout. A default value of zero causes the program to continuously attempt to log-on to the remote system.

Once handshaking is completed the 'connect timeout' option specifies the time interval for which BLAST will wait for a response from the remote system prior to timing out. The 'password' option in the error-free parameter section enables the program user to specify a string that is used as a password to control access to their system by a remote user in the error-free mode. Finally, five user-definable strings in the configuration data enable the setting of control codes that cause certain program functions to occur, or cause the user's log-on identification and password to access remote systems to be preset to a string. Examples of control codes include ^E, which causes BLAST to wait for a transmitted character to be echoed back prior to sending the next character, and ^Dxx which causes the program to delay xx hundredths of a second between transmitting characters. Unfortunately, once these strings are set they can be used from the terminal/modem menu only by selecting the 'send string' option from that menu. Ideally the expansion of preconfigured strings to govern both communications and printer-control functions would increase the capability of the program since it would, for example, permit the user to put the printer into a compressed-print mode. Another enhancement would be the ability to associate printer control of the strings to the function keys or another easily remembered key sequence.

File-transfer Operations

If BLAST was a United States Marshall instead of a communications program it would probably be known as the fastest gun in the country. Although numerous variables to include the workload on a remote system and the quality of a dial-up circuit affect the overall throughput of a file-transfer operation, several tests conducted by the author verified laboratory and government agency reports concerning the transmission efficiency of the program. Transmitting a specially created file three times under BLAST showed the program to be 32–57 percent quicker than four other programs used by the author. The difference would have been greater but for monetary constraints that precluded calling an associate in Europe to observe the difference in effect of satellite delay between BLAST and other programs that are ill-suited for such operations.

To use the BLAST error-free mode requires one to first access the program's terminal modern menu from the main menu by selecting option T. The result of this selection is illustrated in Figure 4.12. Assuming the user has either previously loaded a configuration file or modified the parameters of the configuration management menu to meet their requirements, selecting option D from the terminal/modem menu causes the program to dial the predefined number. Once a connection to another system running BLAST is obtained the user can press the attention key to return to the main menu and select the E option to enter the error-free file-transfer mode of operation.

After selecting option E in the main menu the program displays a menu of options relating to the program's error-free mode. The resulting menu displayed is illustrated in Figure 4.13.

```
-------------------------- TERMINAL/MODEM MENU --------------------------
A- answer   H- hang up        C- turn capture ON   B- send break   X-  exit
D- dial     1-5-send string 1–5   U- upload text file   L- local functions

Enter desired option (or ⟨return⟩ only to become terminal):
```

Figure 4.12 Terminal/Modem Menu

```
OPTIONS FOR ERROR-FREE MODE

I-   interactive local command input              S-  slave mode
F-   read local commands from a command file      X-  exit to main menu

                    Enter desired option: i
```

Figure 4.13 Options for Error-free Mode

Normally the user originating the call with only one file to transfer will enter I when the menu in Figure 4.13 is displayed. Regardless of the selection (except option X), BLAST attempts to synchronize itself with the remote system. In this synchronization process each BLAST-operated system transmits a lower case p with even parity at one-second intervals. The program then clears the previously displayed menu and displays the message 'Waiting for log-on with remote system . . .'. Once log-on is successful the program displays a message to that effect and displays an error-free communication menu, which is partially illustrated in Figure 4.14 Options in this menu permits the user to transmit and receive binary and text files as well as send messages between systems and send file management commands to the remote system (option R). As the file transfer is conducted BLAST provides the user with a display of the line quality in terms of 'good block' throughput as well as the percentage of the file transfer that is completed and the number of blocks remaining to be transferred.

```
              ERROR-FREE COMMUNICATIONS MENU

  S-  send file    ST- send text file   M-  send message     R-  remote functions
  G-  get file     GT- get text file    L-  local functions  C-  continue display
                                                             X-  exit to main menu

                          Enter desired option: S
```

Figure 4.14 Error-free Communications Menu

BLAST-II

During 1987, a Beta test copy of Communications Research Group's latest version of BLAST – to be marketed as BLAST-II – was examined. This program should be commercially available by the time you read this book.

The major change between BLAST-II and previous versions of this program is the incorporation of a 'Lotus' type command interface. In BLAST-II, commands can be selected from menus by moving the highlight bar over the command and pressing the return key or by simply typing the first letter of the command. Since this method of command selection was pioneered by Lotus Development Corporation in their very popular 1-2-3 spreadsheet, most users will immediately feel very comfortable using BLAST-II.

A total of five BLAST menus are included in the BLAST-II System. Figure 4.15 illustrates the top portion of the offline menu. Each menu screen is divided into five parts, with the top line displaying current information to include the menu name, current directory and mode. Line 2 displays the options for selection which, as indicated in Figure 4.15, include select, new, modify, write, remove, local, and online. The third part of the screen, line 3, displays a description of each option as the user moves the highlight bar from one option to another. The fourth part of the screen is known as the

```
BLAST        Offline                        C:\BLAST              MENU
Select   New   Modify   Write   Remove   Local   Online
... select a system setup from the directory
                                                    F1-help = ESC-exit =

    ==== Setup Directory ================================================
    demoline ....CRG BLAST demonstration line ...........  ..............................

    default ...............................................................  ...........................................
```

Figure 4.15 BLAST–II Offline Menu

scroll area, which displays all activity in the terminal mode. Finally, the fifth screen part is the bottom status line which displays a variety of information to include the current system date, elapsed time in a session, system time and the high status of data carrier, CTS, XOFF, the Insert and Num Lock keys.

Through the use of the 'select' option, the user can load a previously created Setup file. The 'new' option enables the user to create a Setup file while 'modify', 'write' and 'remove' perform the indicated function with respect to previously created and saved Setup files. Here, the Setup file defines all the parameters that are required for the user to talk to another computer.

Figure 4.16 shows the display of the demonstration Setup file included with BLAST-II. Although many of the entries in Figure 4.16 are self-explanatory, there are certain entries which warrant a description.

By entering a Userid and Password, BLAST-II will automatically log-on to another system once the connect option in the Online menu is selected. This is easily accomplished with the 'Lotus' interface by selecting 'online' to obtain the online menu and then selecting the 'connect' option in that menu.

The data rates supported by BLAST-II include 300, 600, 1200, 2400, 4800, 9600, 19 200 and 38 400 bps. The protocol entry permits either BLAST or the XMODEM checksum protocol to be selected for error-free file-transfer operations.

BLAST-II supports VT52, VT100 and Data General D200 terminal emulation as well as TTY line-by-line communications. The 'auto LF in' and 'auto LF out' options permit line-feed characters to be appended to incoming or outgoing data. Since some mainframe computers echo characters while other computers transmit a prompt character in response to each line in a file uploaded to the mainframe, the 'wait for echo' and 'prompt char' options can be used to control the appropriate response for the system one will establish communications with. Two other options – 'char delay' and 'line delay' – can also be used to control the uploading of data. Here, 'char delay' defines the time between characters being transmitted while 'line

```
BLAST    Offline    demoline        C:\BLAST            MENU
Select  New  Modify  Write  Remove  Local  Online
... system setup ready, switch to the ONLINE menu
============================================================ F1-hel = ESC-exit =

  ╔═══════════════════════════════════════════════════════════════════════╗
  ║ Setup for : demoline                                                    ║
  ║                                                                         ║
  ║      Description: CRG BLAST demonstration line                          ║
  ║     Phone Number:                               Emulation: VT100        ║
  ║      System Type: demo                      Attention Key: ^K           ║
  ║ Originate/Answer: ORIGINATE                   Full Screen: NO           ║
  ║           Userid:                              Local Echo: NO           ║
  ║         Password:                               AutoLF In: NO           ║
  ║        Comm Port: COM1:                        AutoLF Out: NO           ║
  ║       Modem Type: HAYES                      Wait for Echo: NO          ║
  ║        Baud Rate: 1200                        Prompt Char: NONE         ║
  ║           Parity: NONE                         Char Delay: 0            ║
  ║         Protocol: BLAST                        Line Delay: 0            ║
  ║    Logon Timeout: 480                     XON/XOFF Pacing: YES          ║
  ║  Connect Timeout: 480                      DTR/CTS Pacing: NO           ║
  ║  Transfer Passwd:                          7 Bit Channel: YES           ║
  ║      Script File:                           Packing Size: 84           ║
  ║         Log File: blastlog                                             ║
  ║   Translate File:                                                       ║
  ║    Keyboard File:                                                       ║
  ╚═══════════════════════════════════════════════════════════════════════╝

01/25/87 |  CTS |        |  00:00:25 |        | 11:45 am

BLAST    Online                demoline        C:\BLAST            MENU
Connect  Terminal  CaPture  Upload  Filetransfer  Script  Local  Disconnect
... become a terminal to the remote system
============================================================ F1-help = ESC-exit :
```

Figure 4.16 Demonstration Setup File

delay' defines the time between transmitted lines. These options are normally set for mainframe computers incapable of flow control.

Other interesting and valuable options are Log and Script files. The Log file enables a record of the communications session to be recorded to the filename entered for this option. Similarly, the inclusion of a Script file name results in the execution of macro commands included in the file when BLAST is initiated. Although the BLAST-II script language is similar to BASIC, unfortunately, Communications Research Group defined the language commands differently from BASIC commands that perform similar functions, forcing users to remember, as an example, that PUT instead of PRINT displays data on the display while ASK instead of INPUT prompts the user with a string and places the response into a variable. In spite of this, the script language is both powerful and easy to master as indicated by a portion of a Script file displayed in Figure 4.17, with comments defining each macro command included in the file through the use of the pound sign (#) prefix.

```
SET @PHONENO="8,555-1212"      # Sets number to dail
SET @ BAUDRATE="2400"          # Sets data rate
WAIT UNTIL 21:00               # Dial when rates cheaper
START                          # label
CONNECT                        # become a terminal to remote system
  IF OK GOTO FILE              # Connection established
  LET @X=X+1                   # increment count
  IF@X=3 GOTO START            # try again
CURSOR 10,10                   # Position cursor
PUT"3 Attempts failed"         # Display message
DISCONNECT                     # hang up modem
FILE                           # beginning of file transfer
```

Figure 4.17 Script File Example

Both menu commands and language commands can be included in Script files to control the program. In Figure 4.17, CONNECT and DISCONNECT are examples of two BLAST-II menu commands, while the remaining macros are a few of the language commands included in the program. To understand the use of commands in Script files, we will examine the BLAST online menu which is illustrated in Figure 4.18.

As indicated in line 2 of Figure 4.18, the online menu provides the reader with 8 options for selection. By selecting CONNECT, BLAST-II will automatically dial and log-on to a remote system using the system and modem type defined in the Setup file. The TERMINAL option makes BLAST act as an interactive terminal to the remote system while the CAPTURE option results in the capture of all incoming text to a file. UPLOAD is used to transfer a text file to a remote system without using an error-checking procedure, while the FILE TRANSFER option transfers a file to the remote system using BLAST's error-checking protocol.

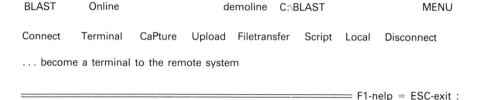

Figure 4.18 BLAST II Online Menu

The LOCAL option results in the display of a LOCAL menu, which enables the user to perform a variety of file operations on his or her system to include listing directory entries, renaming files, typing files and printing files. Similar operations can be performed on a remote system through the use of the remote menu, which is accessible if the FILETRANSFER option in the online menu is selected.

The SCRIPT option enables a previously programmed macro file to be executed while the DISCONNECT option results in a log-off of the remote system and the hanging-up of one's modem.

With the ability to transfer data at rates up to 38.4 kbps and the support of most intelligent modems to include Digital Communications Associates Fastlink, the ease of use of BLAST-II will probably make this communications software program very popular.

Terminal emulation concepts

Prior to discussing the third communications program, an explanation of terminal emulation may be beneficial for those readers not familiar with this subject area.

A large variety of communications software programs are marketed for use with personal computers. These programs range in functionality from basic teletype (TTY) emulation programs that transmit and receive information on a line-by-line basis to more sophisticated programs that enable the personal computer to appear to the mainframe computer as a specific type of terminal. Programs in the latter category are required if one wishes to access mainframe applications that were written to work with a particular type of terminal and display information on a full-screen basis. In addition, an appropriate terminal emulator enables terminal display attributes, such as inverse video, blinking, underlining, and so on to be generated on the personal computer's display. In such cases, the communications program must convert the personal computer's character set to the character set of the terminal emulated and vice versa, to include a conversion of terminal display-control character sequences as well as printer-control character sequences.

One of the most popular terminals whose attributes are emulated in software is the Digital Equipment Corporation VT 100. The VT 100 is an asynchronous, 7-bit ASCII character code RS-232-C terminal. Unlike a TTY, the VT 100 has a degree of intelligence which provides it with the ability to support full-screen operations. The VT 100 works with all DEC mainframes and minicomputers and replaced an older terminal known as the VT 52. The large number of software packages providing VT 100 emulation capability is a tribute to the popularity of the terminal which works with the large base of DEC VAX computer systems. In fact, because of the popularity of this terminal, its system of cursor addressing has been recognized by the American National Standards Institute (ANSI) as standard 3.64. Thus, an ANSI 3.64 terminal, in effect, is a DEC VT 100 look alike. An enhanced version of the VT 100, called the VT 220, was recently introduced by DEC and can be expected to result in the development of VT 220 emulators by many communications software vendors.

Keyboard and Command Code Differences

Although the keyboard of a personal computer is very similar to most asynchronous terminal keyboards, there are usually a few important differences between the keyboard of the terminal being emulated and the personal computer's keyboard. When no direct one-to-one mapping is possible, most communication programs require a two- or three-key sequence to be entered on the personal computer to obtain the desired emulated key.

Table 4.3 shows a portion of the command codes recognized by a few popular asynchronous ASCII coded terminals. Note that an application program developed on a mainframe to use the functions of any one of the three terminals listed in Table 4.3 cannot be used with another terminal shown in that table. The incompatibility between the command codes recognized by a personal computer and the command codes recognized by such terminals normally precludes using a personal computer for anything other than line-by-line transmission, known as TTY, or teletype terminal emulation. To enable a personal computer to emulate one or more specific terminals, the communications software program must convert the ASCII control codes that perform screen functions into the equivalent codes of the terminal being emulated. Similarly, the command codes generated by the mainframe computer that believes it is communicating with a specific type of terminal must be converted into the command codes recognized by the personal computer. Thus, a personal computer communications software program that emulates a Hazeltine Executive 80 terminal, for example, transmits the characters ESC, FF to the host computer when the cursor up key on the personal computer keyboard is pressed, while a program that emulates a Televideo 950 terminal transmits the VT character, and so on.

Table 4.3 Terminal Command Code Differences

| Function | Terminal | | |
	Hazeltine Executive 80	IBM 3101/20	Televideo 950
Cursor up	ESC,FF	ESC,A	VT
Cursor down	ESC,VT	ESC,B	LF
Cursor right	DLE	ESC,C	FF
Cursor left	BS	ESC,D	BS
Cursor home	ESC,DC2	ESC,H	RS
Erase screen	ESC,FS	ESC,L	ESC,*
Erase to end of line	ESC,SI	ESC,I	ESC,T
Erase to end of page	ESC,CAN	ESC,J	ESC,Y

Similarly, upon receipt of the character representing the cursor up function, a communications emulation program operating on an IBM PC, for example, translates it into the RS character (ASCII 30), which is the function code for cursor up on the PC.

Emulation Categories

Since every asynchronous communications software program written for use with a personal computer enables this device to operate as a teletype by transmitting and receiving data on a line-by-line basis, all such programs can be classified as terminal emulators. Once teletype terminal emulation is eliminated from consideration, asynchronous emulation programs can be classified into three general categories – specific terminal emulation, multiple terminal emulation, and user-definable terminal emulation programs. It should be noted that while some programs fall into only one category, the scope of other programs permits them to fall into two or three of the preceding categories.

Examples of specific terminal emulation programs include the SmarTerm 100, SmarTerm 125, SmarTerm 240 and SmarTerm 400 programs from Persoft Inc. SmarTerm 100 permits an IBM PC to function as a Digital Equipment Corporation VT 100 series terminal, such as the VT100, VT101, VT102, or VT52. This program implements most of the features of VT100 terminals on an IBM PC to include character attributes, line and character insertion and deletion and full local printer support. All VT100 keys are mapped to PC keyboard keys, permitting a PC operator to use popular DEC full-screen editors. In addition, SmarTerm 100 permits both ASCII and binary programs or data files to be transferred to and from the host computer. Although SmarTerm 100 supports two 132-column video boards available for use in the PC, on systems without direct 132-column display capability the program uses horizontal scrolling of the conventional 80-

column display to permit users to view any portion of the internally maintained 132-column display area.

Persoft's SmarTerm 125 expands Digital Equipment Corporation VT100 terminal emulation to the VT125, adding graphics functions support of DEC's Remote Graphics Instruction Set (ReGIS). Subject to some hardware limitations, SmarTerm 125 emulates all functions of the VT125 ReGis language on an IBM PC to include position, curve, vector, text, downloadable character sets, shading, multiple writing planes, and custom writing patterns as well as DEC macrograph facilities. Due to the graphics emulation cability of SmarTerm 125, PC users can use a variety of popular mainframe graphic products to include SAS/GRAPH and DEC graph.

Persoft's SmarTerm 240 emulates DEC VT 100 and VT 220 text display terminals as well as Tektronix 4010/4014 and DEC VT 640 graphic display terminals. The software includes an extensive on-line help facility and supports binary data transfer via the XMODEM and KERMIT protocols as well as including a proprietary binary transfer protocol.

Another product in the PERSOFT SmarTerm series that warrants attention is SmarTerm 400. This program allows an IBM PC to function as a Data General Corporation D100, D200, or D400 terminal as well as to enable ASCII or binary program and data file transfer between an IBM PC and a host computer system that believes it is communicating with a Data General terminal. Like other members of the SmarTerm series, SmarTerm 400 implements virtually all features of the previously listed Data General terminals on the PC. In addition to the PERSOFT series of specific terminal emulators, many communications programs usually incorporate a VT100 emulation capability into their program or offer this popular emulator as an option.

Multiple product user-defined terminal emulation

One of the most comprehensive multiple product terminal emulation programs was developed by Softronics. Known as Softerm PC, this program supports basic TTY terminal emulation, as well as including exact emulations of 24 popular terminals and providing all keyboard and display functions, together with the support of both conversational and block mode data transfer. A list of the specific terminals emulated by Softerm PC are listed in Table 4.4. In addition to the specific terminals listed in Table 4.4, Softerm PC includes a general-purpose, user-defined terminal emulator which enables the user to specify the parameters required for the emulation of a terminal's attributes not specifically included with the program.

The program's user-defined terminal emulation capability provides TTY standard carriage return, line feed, and backspace processing while permitting user definitions for most of the common terminal functions. Functions that are user definable with Softerm PC are listed in Table 4.5.

Table 4.4 Softerm PC Terminal Emulators

TTY Compatible	Hewlett Packard 2622A
ADDS Regent 20	Honeywell VIP 7205
ADDS Regent 25	Honeywell VIP 7801
ADDS Regent 40	Honeywell VIP 7803
ADDS Regent 60	IBM 3101 Model 10
ADDS Viewpoint	IBM 3101 Model 20
Data General D200	Lear Siegler ADM-3A
Datapoint 3601	Lear Siegler ADM-5
DEC VT52	Televideo 910
DEC VT102	Televideo 925
Hazeltine 1400/1410	Televideo 950
Hazeltine 1500	User Defined
Hazeltine 1520	

Table 4.5 Softerm User-definable Terminal Functions

Answerback		
Home cursor		
clear screen		
Erase to end-of-line		
Erase to end-of-screen		
Insert line		
Delete line		
Printer	On	Off
Inverse video	On	Off
Low intensity	On	Off
Underline	On	Off
Blink	On	Off
Cursor up		
Cursor down		
Cursor right		
Cursor left		

Program Features

Besides providing a comprehensive set of terminal emulation modules, Softerm is a program rich in communications features. The program provides one of the most explicit methods of defining the user's hardware environment encountered in any program. In addition, the program contains many features that other programs lack. Examples of a few of these features include the ability of the user to set the cursor definition and foreground and background colors to be displayed, to log screen images to disk, and a comprehensive printer control definition capability to include defining the page length and width as well as the folding or truncation of long lines and other printer information.

The cursor definition feature permits the user to have the screen cursor displayed as an underline, partial block, half block, or full block. If a color monitor is used, one can select from a set of eight colors the specific foreground and background colors to be displayed. Between the cursor and color definitions one can explicitly configure their display to meet their personal visual preferences.

Another valuable feature included in Softerm is a FORTRAN 77 source program that can be used to obtain micro-to-mainframe protocol compatibility. When transferred to a user's mainframe computer, this program enables the mainframe to obtain transmission compatibility with the Softerm protocol known as Softrans. Softrans incorporates as CRC-16 polynomial algorithm for error-free block transfer of data as well as a data-compression algorithm to enhance line efficiency. In addition to the Softrans protocol, users of Softerm can also specify the use of an XMODEM protocol contained in the program for file-transfer operations. Since Softerm's user manual exceeds 350 well-documented pages, the major problem faced by many users of this program will probably involve becoming familiar with the wealth of features included in the program and their utilization.

Operation

The program's 'communications agent' is loaded the first time Softerm is executed as well as upon user command thereafter. Illustrated in Figure 4.19, this program module automatically tests the PC's system configuration for the presence of standard communications and printer ports COM1–COM4 and LPTI–LPT3, setting default values for all ports encountered. As illustrated in Figure 4.19, the IBM PC used to operate the program contained two communications (COM) ports and two printer (LPT) ports. If the default settings of the communications agent do not accurately reflect the user's attachment of devices, one can easily toggle the field values to select the most appropriate entry from a series of predefined program entries. This is accomplished by using the Tab key to position an inverse video field over the appropriate display choice one wishes to change. Then, one can use either the space bar or the cursor-positioning keys to toggle through the available choices, pressing the Enter key to inform the program to accept the entry displayed.

Since no device was connected to the COM2 and LPT2 ports, nothing was selected for these field values. Similarly, since a Hayes Smartmodem was to be used with a tone dialing line, these field entries were selected as indicated in Figure 4.19.

Softerm version 1.01.04 used by the author supported 18 modems, permitting the user to simply press the space bar or cursor key once the inverse video field was positioned under dialer type to select the appropriate modem.

```
  SOFTERM PC                                    Version 1.01.04

┌─────────────── Communications Agent System Definition ──────────────┐

  Port         I/O  Address  Connected To  Using     Dialer Type      Dial Mode

  COM1         $03F8         Computer      Modem    Manual
  COM2         $02F8         Printer
  COM3         $0000
  COM4         $0000

  LPT1         $03BC         Printer
  LPT2         $0278         Printer
  LPT3         $0000

┌──────────────────────────── Directory Paths ───────────────────────┐

  System Files:       C: \SOFTERM
  Temp Files:         A:
  All Other Files:    C: \SOFTERM
```

Figure 4.19 Initial Communications Agent Display

As illustrated in Figure 4.19, another capability obtained from the utilization of the communications agent is the ability of the user to specify three categories of directory paths. The directory paths for the system files and the "All Other Files" category are initially set to the current directory; however, they can be easily changed to reflect the user's operational requirements. Similarly, the Temp files directory path has a default value to the diskette (drive A) and can also be changed.

```
  SOFTERM PC                                    Version 1.01.04

┌─────────────── Communications Agent System Definition ──────────────┐

  Port         I/O  Address  Connected To  Using     Dialer Type      Dial Mode

  COM1         $03F8         Computer      Modem    Hayes            Tone
  COM2         $02F8         Nothing                Smartmodem
  COM3         $0000
  COM4         $0000

  LPT1         $03BC         Printer
  LPT2         $0278         Nothing
  LPT3         $0000

┌──────────────────────────── Directory Paths ───────────────────────┐

  System Files:       C: \SOFTERM
  Temp Files:         C: \SOFTERM
  All Other Files:    C: \SOFTERM
```

Figure 4.20 Modified Communications Agent

From the directory paths information contained in Figures 4.19 and 4.20 the reader will note that the Softerm program was placed on a fixed disk (drive designator C:) under a directory labeled Softerm.

Although the contents of the Softerm distribution diskettes can be transferred to a fixed disk an unlimited number of times, to operate the program requires the user to place the original system diskette into the PC's A drive since the program implements copy protection in this manner.

Once the appropriate information is defined to the communications agent the user must press the Alt + Enter keys for the program to accept the current screen format. For persons used to simply pressing the Enter key to conclude an operation, the program's reliance on numerous Alt + other key combinations may require a period of adjustment to these key sequences. Fortunately, simply remembering the Alt + ? combination displays an appropriate help screen matching the user's point of progress in the program, which is usually sufficient to permit one to rapidly move through the program.

System Definition

After the communications agent system definition is completed a default port definitions screen will be displayed. This screen consists of a column of fields that correspond to the options available for each port defined to the communications agent as illustrated in Figure 4.21. Since the options for some ports are not applicable to other ports, a significant number of blank entries appear in the table. As an example of this, consider COM1

```
 SOFTERM PC                                    Version 1.01.04

 ┌───────────────────── Default Port Definitions ─────────────────────┐

 Port                          COM1        LPT1

 Bits/Character                8
 Parity                        None
 Stop Bits                     1
 Speed                         1200
 RCV Pacing                    Xon/Xoff
 XMIT Pacing                   None
 Fill Character
 Fills After CR
 Fills After LF
 Fills After FF
 LF After CR                               Yes
 Page Length                               66
 Page Skip                                 6
 Hardware FF                               Yes
 PageWidth                                 80
 Fold Long Lines                           Yes
 Graphic Char Set                          No
```

Figure 4.21 Default Port Definition Menu

which is an IBM PC serial communications port for which only six options are applicable.

Like all definition menus in the program, the user can easily change a port definition by moving an inverse video bar over the item to be changed and simply pressing the space bar or cursor key until the desired parameter from a list of parameters available for that option is displayed.

The bits/character option toggles between a value of 7 and 8, while the choices available for parity are none, odd, even, mark, and space. The stop bit field toggles between 1 and 2, while the serial port option speed can be set to a value from 50 to 9600 bits per second.

The 'RVC pacing' option defines the type of pacing control the program will use when receiving data and this option is obviously only applicable to a COM port connected to a computer. This option can be toggled between XON/XOFF, DTR, and none, with a DTR selection allowing the data terminal ready signal to be used for pacing control. For data transmissions the XMIT pacing option indicates whether or not the diagram should respond to a pacing signal when transmitting data.

When a printer is attached to a COM port the FILL CHARACTER option permits the user to have the program generate a pad character or a user-specified character to provide pacing control for nonintelligent printers that do not respond to XON/XOFF. In addition, the user can specify the number of characters (fill after CR) to be transmitted to the printer after a carriage return, after a line feed (fill after LF), or after a form feed (fill after FF) is transmitted as well as whether or not the program should automatically generate a line feed (LF after CR) after each carriage return in the data being transmitted.

While the preceding options are more comprehensive than encountered in most communications programs, Softerm also includes six additional printer port options to enable the user to configure hard copy output in almost every way one can imagine. These options permit the user to specify the length in lines (page length) of forms used in their printer, the number of lines to be skipped over (page skip) when printing a page, and whether or not the printer has the capability to form feed (hardware FF) when sent an ASCII form-feed character. The 'page width' option defines the number of columns available on the printer while the 'fold long lines' option indicates whether print lines exceeding the number of printer columns are to be folded or truncated. The last printer port option, 'graphic char set', permits the user to indicate whether or not the printer has the capability to print graphic characters. If not, the program will automatically translate such characters into spaces for all printing operations.

Video and Printer Definition

The third and final screen in the communications agent permits the user to define video and printer definitions, the latter function being not only extremely useful upon occasion, but probably a unique attribute of Softerm that should be incorporated into all programs that the user may wish to use with a printer.

Figure 4.22 illustrates the video and printer definitions menu. The 'printer macro strings' permits users to predefine up to ten command strings that can be used to initialize one's printer to a desired printing format. Thereafter, whenever a Softerm print function or utility requests a printer command string, the user can simply press a function key to initiate one of the predefined character sequences. Thus, pressing function keys could be used to place one's printer in an emphasized print mode, compressed print mode, and so on.

After the Communications Agent system definition is completed the Softerm Setup Options screen is displayed as illustrated in Figure 4.23. From this menu users can select a specific terminal emulation activity (load emulation), change communications parameters (terminal options), and

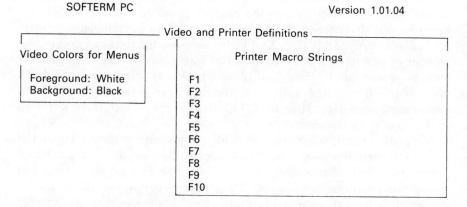

Figure 4.22 Softerm Printer and Definition Menu

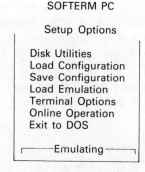

Figure 4.23 Softerm Setup Options Menu

perform other basic functions to include going on-line or exiting the program to DOS.

When the 'load emulation' option is selected, initially the selection 'TTY compatible' will be displayed under 'emulating' on the screen illustrated in Figure 4.23. By using the space bar or cursor-positioning keys, one can toggle through the 24 emulations available for selection in this program.

Once the appropriate emulator is selected one can then utilize the emulator with the previously configured communications, display, and printer parameters initialized by using the communications agent or one can select the terminal options menu to change one or more parameters. Different configurations can be saved to disk using the 'save configuration' option and recalled by using the 'load configuration' option.

The 'disk utilities' option illustrated in Figure 4.24 permits the user to display the current directory as well as to rename and delete files and set a default path through a hierarchical file structure without having to exit the program.

Once the 'on-line operation' option is selected from the Softerm menu, the only deficiency in this otherwise extremely powerful program became noticeable. When this option is selected, the screen clears and the cursor is positioned at column 1, row 1, with no notification of what the user is to do next.

Only from trial and error or reading the manual (which is not simple when faced with over 350 pages of reading material) does one determine that one should press the Alt + 2 keys followed by the F2 key to obtain a pop-up display of the program's dial utilities menu. As illustrated in Figure 4.25, selecting this option permits the user to generate and retrieve dialing directory information as well as to print one's directory, terminate a call (hang up), or dial the number associated with a name in the directory which Softerm calls the 'phone book.'

Although initially this procedure may be frustrating to a novice, after a short period of time working with the program one will appreciate the

```
Configuration Name:
Current  Path:        C:\SOFTERM
          SOFTERM PC

   Disk Utilities

   Display Directory
   Rename File
   Delete File
   Set Default Path

   Alt-Esc Cancels
```

Figure 4.24 Disk Utilities

SOFTERM PC

Dial Utilities Options

Add Phone Book Entry
List Phone Book
Print Phone Book
Dial Number
Hangup

Alt Esc Cancels

Figure 4.25 Dial Utilities Menu

capabilities of the dial utilities. Users can build a virtually unlimited dialing directory since additions to the phone book are logged to disk file named Softerm.Fon. Once entered, selecting the dial number option permits the user to simply enter the name of the desired entry to be dialed and the program automatically searches the phone book and retrieves and displays the telephone number and communications parameters of the matching name previously entered into the phone book. Next, the user can change any entry or, if satisfactory, have the number dialed by pressing Alt + Enter keys.

RELAY Gold 2.0

Although this communications program is similar in ease of use to PFS:Access, its wealth of sophisticated features sets it apart from all but a handful of programs. Its key features include an editor with English-like commands that could justify the purchase of the program by itself, a script language that is probably more comprehensive than that available in any communications program, and numerous areas of capability that make this program a pleasure to use. Examples of the latter include a 'learn' mode of operation which enables a user to generate a script file automatically as he or she signs onto a time-sharing computer or information utility and a 'hot' key, which enables users to toggle back and forth between RELAY Gold and DOS.

Due to the comprehensive nature of the RELAY Gold script language, our discussion of this program will focus upon its use.

Figure 4.26 illustrates the RELAY Gold main menu. By pressing the F3 key, the user causes a 'Directory of computers' to be displayed. This directory consists of preconfigured parameters and protocols that can be selected or changed by simply moving the cursor to the appropriate entry and modifying the data or pressing the F1 key to have the program call the selected computer. Figure 4.27 illustrates a portion of the RELAY Gold Directory of Computers. If a telephone number is entered for the entry line where the cursor is located, upon pressing the F1 key the program will

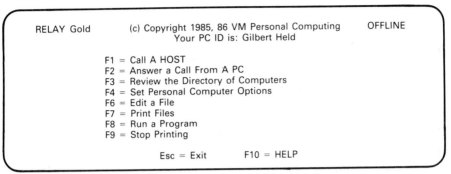

Figure 4.26 RELAY Gold Main Menu

automatically dial that number and use the parameters assigned to the selected computer entry. Otherwise, a screen prompting the user to enter the desired telephone number will be displayed.

From an examination of the 'Type' and 'Notes and Comments' columns in Figure 4.27, the reader will note another sophisticated feature of RELAY Gold – its capability to work with a 3278 emulation board as well as emulate different types of conventional asynchronous terminals. In addition to this, RELAY Gold is one of a handful of communications programs that can provide the user with 3270 terminal emulation capability without requiring the use of special hardware. This capability is obtained by the use of another VM personal computing software product on the mainframe, which in conjunction with RELAY Gold on a PC results in protocol conversion through software.

```
                        Directory of Computers

   Name          Telephone Number  Speed   Type    Notes and Comments

   3278                            NONE   COAX   MODEL: 3278 emulation board
   A HOST                         1200   TTY    MODEL: Full duplex host
   A PC                           1200   RELAY  MODEL: A PC Using RELAY
   COMPSERV                       1200   TTY    MODEL: CompuServe
   DIALCOM                        1200   TTY    MODEL: ITT Dialcom
   DOWJONES                       1200   TTY    MODEL: Dow Jones News
   EASYLINK                       1200   TTY    MODEL: EasyLink
   FIDO                           1200   TTY    MODEL: FIDO bulletin board
   IBM7171                        1200   VT100  MODEL: IBM 7171 as a VT100
   MODEM   MODEM                  1200   TTY    Type directly to your MODEM

       Use PgDn and PgUp to scroll the Directory. Press ENTER when finished.
   F 1 = Call Name at Cursor          F 2 = Answer Name at Cursor
   F3 = Add a New Name in Directory   F4 = Review Connect Options
        By Copying Entry at Cursor         for Name at Cursor

                    Esc = Quit      F10 = HELP
```

Figure 4.27 Directory of Computers

```
Review Connect Options for Computer Named: TYMNET

COMn Port Number?    1 (1,2)              Logon Script Filename?        GILTEST
File Protocol?       R (R,S,N,K,X,C)      Function Key Filename?
Parity Code?         I (I,N,E,O,M,S,7,8)  Translation Filename?
Local Echo?          N (Y,N)             Full or Half Duplex?          F (F,H)
Auto Linefeed?       N (Y,N,X)           Flow Control (XON/XOFF)?      Y (Y, N, R, X)
Stop Bits?           1 (1,2)              Turnaround Character?         11 (00-FF)
Answerback Char?     00 (00-FF)          Script Control Char?          00 (00-FF)
Send LF with CR?     N (Y,N)             Show Control Characters?      N (Y, N)
                                         Delay After Each Line?        0 (0-99)

                     Esc = Quit          F10 = HELP
```

Figure 4.28 Connection Options for TYMNET Computer Directory Entry

The RELAY Gold program comes preconfigured to support a variety of terminal emulations.

Once the Directory of Computers is displayed, the user can check or modify the communications parameters assigned to that option by pressing the F4 key. Figure 4.28 illustrates the screen display for the TYMNET entry in RELAY Gold's Directory of Computers. The log-on script filename called GILTEST contains a file of commands which will enable the user to automatically log-on to TYMNET and access the CompuServe electronic mail system through the Tymnet packet network.

Script Language

RELAY Gold's script language can be used to create programs to automatically log-on to a system, perform unattended operations at predefined times and, if the user wishes, to build a bulletin board due to the comprehensive scope of the language. The script language consists of three basic elements – variables, functions and commands. All script language variables start with an ampersand (&) and can be classified as system, local user and global user. System variables such as &DATE and &TIME are predefined by RELAY Gold. Since one script can call another, local user variables are for use in the current script while Global user variables have values which are common to all scripts.

The other two elements in the script language are functions and commands. Like variables, functions start with an ampersand. Thus, &FSIZE (fileid) would return the number of characters in a disk file named by the parameter fileid. Commands are words followed by operands, such as SET MSPEED 2400 which sets the modem's speed to 2400 bps, SEND C"CPS" which transmits the string CPS followed by a carriage return, and SMSG"XYZ" which displays the message XYZ on line 25 of the PC's display.

To obtain an appreciation of the versatility of the RELAY Gold script language, consider the actions that occur when one wishes to access the CompuServe InfoPlex electronic mail service through the Tymnet packet network. As illustrated in Figure 4.29, upon accessing the Tymnet node what appears to be a line of jibberish is received at the user's PC. In reality, the Tymnet node transmits the message 'please type your terminal identifier' at a 300 bps data rate. If the user's modem operates at a higher data rate as is the case in this example, the initial line of transmission is garbled, since it takes a short period of time for the modems at the Tymnet end of the data link to adjust to the modem speed of the person accessing the network. Next, the user types his or her terminal identifier, which for a PC is the letter A, either uppercase or lowercase. This identifier is not echoed back by Tymnet and as a result does not appear in Figure 4.29.

After the user enters his or her terminal identifier, Tymnet displays the node and port number at which the user gained access to the packet network. In this example, the user accessed Tymnet on port 6 of node 5660. Next, Tymnet asks the user to log-in, which in effect is a prompt message for the user to enter the destination to which he or she wishes Tymnet to route the user. Here, the user entered the characters CPS to inform Tymnet that a route to the CompuServe computer is requested. After Tymnet performs the routing to CompuServe, the CompuServe computer displays a welcome message, followed by requests for the user to enter his or her UserID, password, address and code.

The preceding log-on sequence to Tymnet, routing to CompuServe, and log-on to the CompuServe InfoPlex electronic mail service can be easily automated. Figure 4.30 illustrates the creation of the RELAY Gold script file GILTEST.SCR which accomplishes the activity previously described. As illustrated, the file was created in the RELAY Gold editor.

```
x | x | ˙|xxx< ˙xx˙x
–5600--006–
please log in: CPS

host: WELCOME TO COMPUSERVE 3373

User ID: 48102, 7776
Password:
Address ? HELD
Code ?
InfoPlex 1E(311) -- Ready at 08:15 EST 30-Jan-87 on T10QFM

Type/HELP for help on InfoPlex commands

   0 Messages pending
```

Figure 4.29 Accessing CompuServe's InfoPlex Electronic Mail Service Through Tymnet

```
Editing C:GILTEST. SCR in path \RELAY                                    19 Lines

===>
* * * TOP OF FILE * * *
ON TIMEOUT GOTO -EXIT              ;* if wait exceeded exit
WAIT 60 UNTIL "xxx"                ;* get initial msg
SEND N"a"                          ;* identify terminal type
WAIT 60 UNTIL "please"             ;* receive please log on msg
SEND 60 UNTIL "ID:"               ;* where we want to go
SENDC"48102,7776"                  ;* user ID request
WAIT 60 UNTIL "Password:"          ;* send our ID
SEND C"#####"                      ;* receive request for password
WAIT 60 UNTIL "Address ?"          ;* send password
SEND C"HELD"                       ;* receive address request
WAIT 60 UNTIL "Code ?"             ;* send address
SEND C"#######"                    ;* receive code request
STOP                               ;* send it
-EXIT                              ;* thats all folks
SMSG "Tymnet not responding – try
later"

* * * END OF FILE * * *
```

Figure 4.30 Creating a Script File

The semicolon asterisk (;*) sequences denote the beginning of comments and are ignored by the RELAY Gold script language processor. The ON TIMEOUT GOTO-EXIT command will result in a branch to the label -EXIT whenever any following WAIT commands in the script file time out. To understand how the WAIT command operates, consider the second line in the script file GILTEST.SCR illustrated in Figure 4.30 – WAIT 60 UNTIL "XXX". This command causes the IBM PC to wait up to 60 seconds to receive the string "XXX". If the string is received within that time period, the next line in the file is executed, otherwise the program branches to the label -EXIT due to the ON TIMEOUT statement at the beginning of the file.

Two types of SEND commands were used in the example contained in Figure 4.30. The SEND N"string" command causes the string contained in quotes to be transmitted without a carriage return while a SEND statement with the character C preceding a quoted string adds a carriage return to the end of a string. As indicated in Figure 4.30, a sequence of 'trapping' portions of expected transmissions from the system to be accessed followed by transmitting the appropriate requested information enables a user to easily automate his or her log-on procedure.

Although complex branching, looping and variable operations were omitted from the example, the reader should note that complex communications procedures and operations can also be easily automated with RELAY Gold. Thus, readers requiring the use of a powerful and versatile script language should consider this program.

Fitting the requirement

Each of the four communications programs examined in this chapter can be used to satisfy a distinct set of end-user communications requirements.

If one wishes to be on-line in a minimum amount of time and is not concerned with specifically tailoring the program to the hardware environment PFS: Access is one of many similar programs that can satisfy this type of requirement. Most users require less than one hour to become conversant with the program and a minimal background in communications terminology should be more than sufficient for persons to use this program effectively.

For fast and efficient file-transfer operations BLAST is probably the premier communications program. In addition, due to the comprehensive series of microcomputers, minicomputers and mainframes for which versions of the program are available, this program is the solution to the incompatibility problems faced by many large businesses operating a diverse mixture of computer systems.

While Smarterm is a power-packed communications software program with a comprehensive set of terminal emulators, its many options and the degree of personal computer and communications terminology usage make it a difficult program to master. Although the author thoroughly enjoyed using its many features, persons with minimal communications requirements are best advised to look elsewhere for a teletype terminal emulator. If the user wants a program beyond teletype emulation, desires to configure the hardware environment and wishes the flexibility of many terminal emulation capabilities in one program then this program deserves consideration.

For the communications user who wishes to automate log-on, file transfer and other features, RELAY Gold offers perhaps the most comprehensive script language of all programs. In addition, its numerous features to include the script 'Learn' mode and a hot key make this program a must for persons desiring to automate repetitive operations.

4.4 MICRO-TO-MAINFRAME SOFTWARE

Although the title of this section can refer to a variety of communications products, micro-to-mainframe software is usually more sophisticated than the communications programs previously examined in this chapter. Normally, micro-to-mainframe software implies the use of a communications program on a PC which operates in conjunction with one or more software programs operating on the mainframe. Table 4.4 lists four of the key micro-to-mainframe functions included with many software packages fitting into this category.

In comparison to simple file transfer which is transparent to data content, micro-to-mainframe software includes the capability to both transfer and reformat data. As an example of this capability, consider a general ledger program and its data files residing on a mainframe computer. Although the

Table 4.6 Micro-to-mainframe Software Functions

File transfer and format convrsion
Virtual disk storage
Task customization and automation
Multilevel security

general ledger data files could be downloaded into a PC with conventional communications, such files would probably be incompatible with spreadsheets and database programs that operate on an IBM PC. When using a micro-to-mainframe software package, the PC user obtains the capability to transfer data from spreadsheet and database files on the PC to the mainframe, in a file format that the general ledger program can accept. Similarly, general ledger files downloaded to the PC will be translated in a spreadsheet or database file format based upon parameters supplied by the PC user to the program operating on the PC.

Virtual disk storage capability on the mainframe enables the PC user to allocate mainframe storage in increments, ranging from 16K or 32K bytes to megabytes. Once a virtual disk is established, the software package enables the PC to treat each disk as an individual disk drive. Access to information stored on the mainframe is then accomplished via one or more virtual disks using standard PC DOS commands. Depending upon the vendor marketing the software package, the virtual disk interface on the mainframe will be interfaced to a particular vendor's mainframe database program, such as IDS, IMS or another program. Another advantage accruing from the use of virtual disks is the ability it affords different types of personal computers to share files without worrying about disk interfaces. Thus, different types of PCs, such as an Apple Macintosh and an IBM PC could access the same virtual disk to retrieve common information or transfer information between the two personal computers.

Some micro-to-mainframe packages enable users to customize and automate tasks, permitting file transfer, data extraction, data reformatting and other tasks to be automated. Some software packages use a series of menus to create 'task lists,' while other packages enable the PC user to express the desired tasks in the form of a series of macro commands. Where these programs differ from the script languages previously discussed in this chapter is in their ability to work in conjuncton with software on a mainframe.

In comparison to most communications software programs which either have an encryption option or lack other security features, micro-to-mainframe packages normally incorporate a variety of security-related functions. These functions can include password-controlled access to virtual disks as well as to files, records and fields within a file.

CHAPTER FIVE

Packet Networks and Information Utilities

Until the early 1970s, access to mainframe computer systems was accomplished either through entry into a particular organization's data communications network or through the use of the public switched telephone network. Since then, a third method of accessing mainframe computers has rapidly gained the acceptance of both the business and home computer user requiring access to a variety of computer facilities of independent organizations located at geographically dispersed locations. This method of communications is known as packet switching. For many persons requiring access to information utilities, a packet network can be viewed as a transmission expressway, providing a fast, reliable and inexpensive method of communications to numerous locations throughout the United States and abroad.

In this chapter, we will first focus our attention upon packet switching technology and the utilization of such networks to access information utilities. Then, we will examine the use of several information utilities and the services and facilities they offer users.

5.1 PACKET NETWORKS

The first packet-switching network was developed by the Advanced Research Projects Agency (ARPA) of the US Department of Defense. The initial goal of this network was to permit a wide variety of computer resources located throughout the United States to be simultaneously accessed via a common network by research personnel. To permit simultaneous access to computer facilities in an efficient manner required the development of a new type of data communications network, employing a technique known as packet switching.

Packet switching

Packet switching is a technique where data is broken into shorter sections known as packets. Each packet is forwarded over the network's communications facilities whenever it is ready to be transmitted, independent of the remaining data. This technique then permits many devices to share a common communications facility by time as illustrated in Figure 5.1. The simplified packet network illustrated in Figure 5.1 shows two packet network nodal points, with three mainframe computer systems connected to the two nodes.

The packet network node is normally a minicomputer-based computer system which forms and routes packets to other destinations on the network. If access to a node is from a non-packet forming device, such as an asynchronous terminal or personal computer, the node breaks the transmission into segments called packets. During the packet-assembly process, address and control information is appended to the data in the packet as illustrated in Figure 5.2. Similarly, when packetized data is received at its final destination, the header information is stripped from the packet prior to the node transmitting the data to the device connected to that node. This process is known as disassembly, with the term PAD normally associated with a device that performs packet assembly and disassembly operations

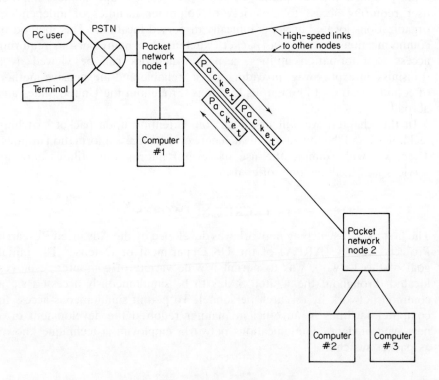

Figure 5.1 Simplified Packet Network

In a packet network, minicomputers at each node assemble data into packets for transmission over the network's facilities.

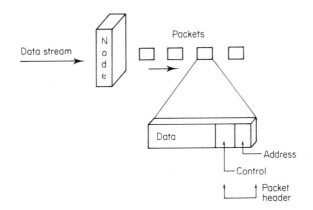

Figure 5.2 Packet Assembly

During the packet assembly process, non-packetized data
is packetized, with address and control information
appended to each packet.

and which is used to enable devices incapable of forming packets to
communicate with packet networks.

X.25

The CCITT X.25 recommendation forms the basis for the flow of data
within and to and from public packet data networks. The first draft of the
X.25 recommendation was published in 1976, with major changes to the
standard occurring in 1980 and 1984. Formally titled 'Interface Between
Data Terminal Equipment (DTE) and Data Circuit Terminating Equipment
(DCE) for Terminals Operating in the Packet Mode on Public Data
Network', the latest version of the X.25 recommendation provides a precise
set of procedures for communications between DTE and DCE in a packet
environment. Here, the DCE is a network node processor, normally a
minicomputer operating specialized software. The DTE is a programmable
device located at an end-user facility, such as a front-end processor,
intelligent terminal or mainframe computer which supports the X.25 protocol.

Since no dumb terminals and until recently very few personal computers
supported the X.25 protocol, such terminal devices cannot communicate
directly to a network node. This is because dumb terminals and most PCs
communicate as 'character' mode devices, whereas network node processors
and mainframe computers operating X.25 software communicate as 'packet'
mode devices. Thus, dumb terminals and most PCs must communicate with
a special network DTE known as a PAD, which converts the data stream
of the terminal or personal computer into the X.25 protocol. The PAD can
be located at the packet network node or at the end-user's facility.

To standardize the conversion of asynchronous to X.25 data flow, three
CCITT recommendations were developed – X.3, X.28 and X.29. The X.3

recommendation defines such parameters as data rate, the escape character and the flow-control technique, enabling the PAD to operate with a specific type of terminal, personal computer or mainframe computer. By the appropriate setting of these parameters, the PAD is able to correctly interpret the data stream received from the device communicating with it. Similarly, the device communicating with the PAD is able to understand the PAD when these parameters are set correctly.

The X.3 Packet Assembly/Disassembly (PAD) parameters which are used to control start–stop terminals within an X.25 network are listed in Table 5.1.

Each of the PAD parameters has two or more possible values. Ten of the more commonly altered parameters and their possible values are dealt with in the following paragraphs.

2:n Echo

This parameter controls the echoing of characters on the user's screen as well as their forwarding to the remote DTE. Possible values are:

0   no echo
1   echo

Table 5.1 X.3 Parameters

X.3 parameter number	X.3 meaning
1	PAD recall
2	Echo
3	Selection of data forwarding signal
4	Selection of idle timer delay
5	Ancillary device control
6	Control of PAD service signals
7	Procedure on receipt of break signal
8	Discard output
9	Padding after carriage return
10	Line folding
11	Binary speed
12	Flow control of the terminal pad
13	Line feed insertion after carriage return
14	Padding after line feed
15	Editing
16	Character delete
17	Line delete
18	Line display
19	Editing PAD service signals
20	Echo mask
21	Parity treatment
22	Page wait

3:n Selection of data forwarding signal

This parameter defines a set of characters that act as data forwarding signals when they are entered by the user. Coding of this parameter can be a single function or the sum of any combination of the functions listed below. As an example, a 126 code represents the functions 2–64, which results in any character to include control characters being forwarded. Possible values of parameter 3 are:

0   no data forwarding character
1   alphanumeric characters
2   character CR
4   characters ESC, BEL, ENQ, ACK
8   characters DEL, CAN, DC2
16   characters ETX, EOT
32   characters HT, LF, VT, FF
64   all other characters: $X'OO'$ to $X'IF'$

4:n Selection of Idle Timer Delay

This parameter is used to specify the value of an idle timer used for data forwarding. Possible values of this parameter include:

0   no data forwarding on time-out
1   units of 1/20 second, maximum 255

7:n Procedure on Receipt of Break Signal

This parameter specifies the operation to be performed upon entry of a break character. Possible values of this parameter include:

0   nothing
1   send an interrupt
2   reset
4   send an indication of break PAD
8   escape from data transfer state
16   discard output

Similar to parameter 3, parameter 7 can be coded as a single function or as the sum of a combination of functions.

12:n Flow Control of the Terminal PAD

This parameter permits flow control of received data using X-ON and X-OFF characters. Possible values are:

0   no flow control
1   flow control

13:n Line Feed Insertion After Carriage Return

This parameter instructs the PAD to insert a line feed (LF) into the data stream following each carriage return (CR). Possible values are:

    0 No LF insertion

    1 Insert an LF after each CR in the received data stream

    2 Insert an LF after each CR in the transmitted data stream

    4 Insert an LF after each CR in the echo to the screen

The coding of this parameter can be as a single function or a combination of functions by summing the values of the desired options.

15:n Editing

This parameter permits the user to edit data locally or at the host. If local editing is enabled, the user can correct any data buffered locally, otherwise it must flow to the host for later correction. Possible values of this parameter include:

    0   no editing in the data transfer state

    1   editing in the data transfer state

16:n Character Delete

This parameter permits the user to specify which character in the ASCII (International Alphabet Number 5) character set will be used to indicate that the previously typed character should be deleted from the buffer. Possible values for this parameter include:

    0   no character delete

  1–127   character delete character

17:n Line Delete

This character is used to enable the user to specify which character in the character set denotes the previously entered line should be deleted. Possible values are:

    0 no line delete

  1–127 line delete character

18:n Line Display

This parameter enables the user to define the character which will cause a previously typed line to be redisplayed. Possible values are:

    0 no line display

  1–127 line display character

20:n Echo Mask

This parameter is applicable only when parameter 2 is set to 1. When this occurs, parameter 20 permits the user to specify which characters will be echoed. Possible values include:

   0   no echo mask (all characters echoed)
   1   no echo of character CR
   2   no echo of character LF
   4   no echo of characters VT, HT, FF
   8   no echo of characters BEL, BS
   16   no echo of characters ESC, ENQ
   32   no echo of characters ACK, NAK, STX, SOH, EOT, ETB and ETX
   64   no echo of characters defined by parameters 16, 17 and 18
   128   no echo of all other characters in columns 0 and 1 of International Alphabet Number 5 and the character DEL

The X.28 recommendation defines the commands and procedures for establishing (call request) and disconnecting calls (call clear). The X.29 recommendation defines the procedures for the exchange of PAD control information and how user data is transferred between a packet mode DTE and a PAD or between two PADs.

In essence, PADs are concentration devices which have the capability to multiplex between 2 and 64 or more character-mode devices onto an X.25 data link. Some PADs simply convert an asynchronous character stream into a synchronous X.25 data format while other PADs are designed to provide 2780, 3780 and 3270 protocol conversion to X.25.

In actuality, when we refer to packet-switching standards we normally refer to the X.25 recommendation and related packet network standards. These related standards include the previously discussed X.3, X.28 and X.29 recommendations as well as the X.75 and X.121 recommendations.

X.75 describes the procedures for the interconnection of packet-switched networks. X.121 is the international numbering plan for public data networks. Together, these standards permit the user of one packet network, as an example, to access a computer connected to a different packet network.

X.25 Layers

The X.25 recommendation defines three functional layers which correspond to layers 1–3 of the ISO Reference Model described in Chapter 1.

The X.25 physical layer (level 1) is defined by the CCITT X.21 recommendation. Unlike RS-232-C or the V.24 interface that uses control signals on pin connectors, the X.21 interface employs the transmission of coded character strings across as 15-pin connector to define standard interface functions. Due to the limited availability of communications equipment with an X.21 interface, the CCITT approved an interim interface, X.21 bis. X.21 bis is functionally equivalent to the RS-232-C and V.24 interfaces in which a separate function is assigned to each pin in the 25-pin connector.

The X.25 link layer (level 2) is responsible for the transmission of packets of data between the user (DTE) and the node (DCE) without error. A data link control procedure very similar to HDLC is used, which adds control fields to the data packet as illustrated in Figure 5.3. As discussed in Chapter 1, the flag fields serve as the beginning and ending frame delimiters, while a 16-bit frame check sequence field provides the error-detection capability for the frame. The link layer is responsible for subdividing the user's data into packets which normally contain 128 characters. Some X.25 networks use 32, 256, 512 or 1024 character packets, with the packet size transparent to the user. When two packet networks are interconnected, X.75 defines the procedures for the orderly exchange of data between dissimilar sized packets.

The third X.25 layer is known as the packet layer. Level 3 defines the procedures for establishing and clearing calls and the exchange of packets between a DTE and DCE. Level 3 software prefixes the required packet control information to the user's data, after which it initiates level 2 software to create the X.25 frame. Included in the packet control information field are three subfields, known as octets since they consist of 8 bits. The first octet defines the logical channel group while the second octet defines the logical channel number used. Together, these two octets provide the routeing information which directs the packet to flow over a defined logical channel. The third octet, packet type identifier, defines the type and resulting function of the packet. Examples of packet types include call request, DCE clear, DTE clear, DCE RR (receiver ready) and DTE RR.

Methods of connection

One can connect a terminal, personal computer or a company's mainframe computer to a packet network in several ways. Figure 5.4 illustrates a few

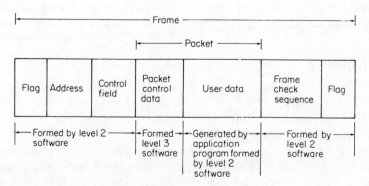

Figure 5.3 The X.25 Frame

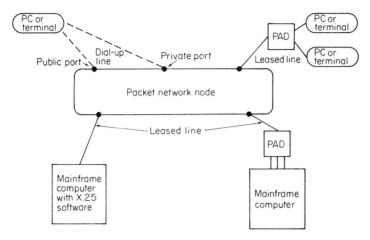

Figure 5.4 Packet Network Interface

Individual or grouped terminals and PCs can be connected to a packet network via the switched telephone network or by using leased lines. In comparison, mainframe computers are always connected to a packet network by a leased line.

of the more common methods employed to interface a packet network. Note that a public port is a published telephone number that is available for all users to dial. In actuality, each node has a group of telephone numbers connected to a telephone rotary which causes an incoming call to be switched to the next available number if the dialed number is busy. To insure one never encounters a busy signal, many packet networks have private ports which are telephone numbers reserved for the exclusive use of a particular customer.

In an office environment where many terminals and PCs may require the use of a packet network, a PAD could be installed at one's facility. The PAD would directly assemble and disassemble packets at one's location and communicate with the packet network node via a leased line obtained from the telephone company.

Two basic methods can be used by independent businesses as well as information utilities to connect their mainframe computers to a packet network. If an organization's mainframe computer has X.25 software that performs packet assembly and disassembly of data, they can connect their mainframe via a leased line directly to a packet network node. This is illustrated in the lower left portion of Figure 5.4. If such software does not operate on their mainframe, they can install a PAD at their location to perform the packet assembly and disassembly function as illustrated in the lower right part of Figure 5.4.

A packet-switched network consists of a large number of microcomputer-based nodes interconnected to one another via high-speed data links. These data links resemble a mesh topology and are used by the minicomputers at the nodes to dynamically route packets of user data to their final destination. If traffic becomes too heavy on one link or a link failure occurs, the network control center in the packet network will sense such conditions and automatically inform the computer-based nodes in the network to perform alternative routeing of data. Since hundreds or thousands of users can be simultaneously connected to the nodes of a packet network in larger cities, the utilization of the lines connecting most nodes in the packet network is high. In turn, this high utilization permits the cost per individual users of a packet network to result in an economical means of performing communications.

Utilization costs

As an example of the cost element associated with packet networks, we will first examine the cost of using the public switched telephone network. Here the cost of a long-distance call varies based upon the time the call was initiated, its duration, the distance between the called and calling parties and whether or not operator intervention was required. During business hours, a coast-to-coast call might cost 50¢ per minute while a call after 11 p.m. might be reduced to 30¢ per minute. Translated into an hourly rate, users can expect to pay between $18 and $30 per hour for such calls. In comparison, the cost of using a packet network is independent of the distance of the transmission. The principal cost elements are based upon connect time and the amount of data transmitted, the latter charged on the basis of kilopackets or kilocharacters.

During prime time, which is usually 8 a.m. to 5 p.m., Monday through Friday, the average cost of accessing a mainframe computer via a packet network is approximately $5 per hour. During that hour you might transmit and receive 128 000 characters. If the packet network charges $1 per kilopacket, this adds an additional cost of $1 if data is packetized 128 characters per packet, resulting in a total cost of $6 per connect hour. In actuality, for interactive applications most packets are transmitted only partially filled. Thus, responding to a mainframe prompt by transmitting 'RUN PROGRAM' results in the transmission of a packet consisting of 11 data characters and 117 pad characters which are inserted into the packet to fill it to 128 characters if that packet size is used by the packet network. Due to this a good 'rule of thumb' is to expect one's packet charges to equal 10 percent of one's connect charges. Even so, the cost associated with using a packet network can be significantly less than dialing long distance.

For non-prime time usage of packet networks, most networks have a flat rate per hour, typically ranging from $2 to $4 per connect-hour. This pricing mechanism is designed to encourage the use of such networks by the home computer hobbyist and businesses that can delay transmission until after normal working hours, representing the awareness of the packet networks that a good portion of their facilities is unused after prime time. Although a company using a packet network to access their mainframes would first establish an account with the network, users accessing most information utilities may never see a separate bill for the use of such facilities. This results from the fact that the cost of accessing the information utility via a packet network may be included in their general fee structure while other services may include a separate line item in their monthly bill to cover the cost of using the packet network.

Figure 5.5 illustrates a general comparison between the cost of using the PSTN, WATS, a leased line and a packet network. This comparison is for individually located terminals or personal computers accessing a common mainframe based upon varying levels of communications ranging from 0 to 50 hours of usage per month. It was assumed that a terminal or personal computer accessing a mainframe was located at a distance of 650 miles from the mainframe. Thus, for comparison purposes, the cost of a leased line was assumed to be $800 per month, while the cost of the use of the PSTN was assumed to be $20 per hour. For WATS, a cost of $15 per hour was assumed. In comparison, a packet network cost of $5.50 per hour to include both the correct time and character cost was assumed.

A few words of caution are in order concerning the costs plotted in Figure 5.5. First, although the use of a packet network for an individually located terminal or personal computer appears to be the most economical, Figure 5.5 does not take into consideration the cost of connecting the mainframe computer to the packet network. This cost is based upon the type of facility used to connect the mainframe to the packet network as illustrated in the lower portion of Figure 5.4 as well as the data rate used to connect the

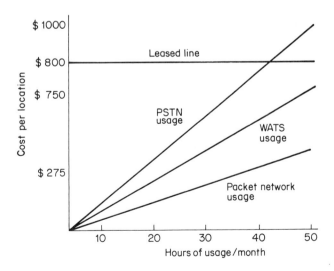

Figure 5.5 Cost Comparison – PSTN, WATS, Leased Line and Packet Network Usage

mainframe computer or PAD to the packet network. This latter cost based upon data rate is due to many packet networks furnishing both a leased line and pair of modems for a set monthly fee to connect the end-user's mainframe computer to the packet network.

Assuming that the cost of a leased line, pair of modems and PAD is $2000 per month, this cost must then be included in any analysis performed to determine the most economical data transportation facility. If there are 10 individual terminal or PC locations, the packet network usage cost illustrated in Figure 5.5 must be adjusted upward by $200 per month. This figure represents the monthly mainframe connection cost ($2000) divided by the number of individual terminal or personal computer locations (10). Thus, if a personal computer or terminal had no usage for the month the cost per location would be $200.

A second consideration in evaluating the economics of using packet networks is the situation where many personal computers or terminals are collocated. Although one could use a PAD to connect to the packet network to reduce one's packet network costs, if there are more than three or four devices collocated and one's individual monthly usage is high, it is usually more economical to install a leased line to the mainframe and a pair of high-speed modems and multiplexers. Figure 5.6 illustrates the use of a pair of eight-channel multiplexers to permit up to eight collocated terminals and personal computers to share access to a mainframe computer.

Since a pair of eight-channel multiplexers can be purchased for approximately $3000 while two high-speed modems (14 400 bps) would cost approximately $6000, a user's one-time cost for the facilities to connect up to eight personal computers and terminals to a distant mainframe would be $9000. Assuming the distance between location 1 and location 2 is 650 miles, the monthly cost of the leased line would be $800.

If each personal computer and terminal averages 50 hours of usage per month, the cost of using a packet network for data transportation is $2750 plus $2000 to connect the mainframe to the packet network, a total cost of

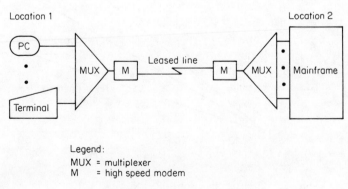

Legend:
MUX = multiplexer
M   = high speed modem

Figure 5.6 Using Multiplexers

$4750 per month. Then, over the course of a year the use of the packet network costs $57 000. In comparison, the networking structure illustrated in Figure 5.6 costs $9600 for the line and $9000 for the equipment, a total first year cost of $18 600. For following years the cost difference would become even more pronounced since the equipment illustrated in Figure 5.6 was assumed to be purchased during the first year.

Although the preceding cost comparisons were generalized, they do illustrate several key concepts concerning the economics associated with the use of packet networks. When only one or a few terminal devices are collocated and there are many such terminals distributed over a wide geographical area, the use of a packet network is normally the most economical data transportation facility. If there are only a few terminal devices and their connect time requirements per month are low, then the PSTN is usually the most economical data transportation facility. If there are many collocated terminals with large connect time requirements, then the installation of a leased line and multiplexers and high-speed modems is normally the most economical method to provide a data transportation facility.

Access

In examining the method employed to access packet network facilities the use of Tymnet, a commercial packet network operated as a subsidiary of McDonnell Douglas, will be used for illustrative purposes. Tymnet was established in the early 1970s and its initial network served 30 cities in the United States. At that time, the company used 2400 bps lines to interconnect locations served in each city and its support of end-users was limited to asynchronous transmission. By the late 1980s, the company's packet network had expanded to over 600 cities in the United States and approximately 50 foreign countries, with 56 kbps or higher-speed lines used to interconnect equipment at each city. In addition to asynchronous support, Tymnet added a variety of synchronous protocol support, to include IBM 2780 and 3780 remote job entry, IBM 3270 interactive bisynchronous and SDLC support as well as other protocols.

One of the major reasons for the growth in the usage of packet networks is the ease by which such networks permit access to computer-based services connected to their facilities. For example, a person who wishes to use the Tymnet packet network would first dial the Tymnet access number nearest to his or her location. This call could be made to one of approximately 600 locations throughout the United States and abroad, which almost assures persons of the ability to access a Tymnet node with a local telephone call.

The telephone call is answered by a minicomputer at the Tymnet node, which places a familiar high-pitched tone known as the carrier signal onto the line. When you have connected to the network, Tymnet displays a request for the user to enter his or her terminal identifier.

The Tymnet terminal identifier is a letter ranging from A to G as well as I and P which is used to enable the packet network to optimize its performance to the user's terminal. In general, the terminal identifier tells the network the code of the terminal, its data rate and the number of pad characters that should be sent from the packet network to the terminal to compensate for the line feed/carriage return delay built into most electromechanical devices. On Tymnet, the identifier A is used to indicate there are no line feed or carriage return delays and is normally entered by users accessing this network with a personal computer or CRT terminal.

If access to Tymnet occurs at a data rate other than 300 bps, the network's 'Please type your terminal identifier' message appears garbled. Once the terminal identifier is entered, Tymnet displays the remote access node number the user is connected to followed by the node's port number. This information is displayed in the form -NNN-PPP-, with NNNN being the node number while PPP is the port number. After these numbers are displayed, Tymnet will display the message 'please log in:'. At this point, the end-user would enter the network address of the facility he or she wishes Tymnet to route them to. Figure 5.7 illustrates the procedure required to access the CompuServe InfoPlex electronic mail system through the Tymnet network. Note that the prompt 'User ID:', 'Password:', 'Address?' and 'Code?' were issued by the CompuServe computer connected to the Tymnet network.

```
ATDT9,746-2739

CONNECT 1200

x⌊  |   x   'x
'  xxx<'xx'xx<'x' < xx@ x<'x'xx@xxxx<˜ x'x<˜ xx<'xxx|xx@xxxx'|xx'xx@xx<'x<Ixx<
 ˜xx@xxxx@xxx<'xxa
-5660-002-
please log in: ccppss

host: WELCOME TO COMPUSERVE 1133

User ID: 40802,7776
Password:
Address ? Held
Code ?
InfoPlex 1E(311) -- Ready at 09:55 EST 20-Jan-87 on T05QCE

Type /HELP for help on InfoPlex commands

  0 Messages pending
/bye

Off at 09:55 EST 20-Jan-87

host: call cleared (c 0,d 0): dte originated
```

Figure 5.7 Access to CompuServe's InfoPlex Electronic Mail System via Tymnet

Once a session is completed and you log-off the CompuServe computer in a normal manner, Tymnet transmits a 'disconnected' message in the form of a call cleared as indicated at the bottom of Figure 5.7. This is a packet-switching message which indicates that the connection previously established between Tymnet and CompuServe has been cleared. Then, you receive the Tymnet message 'please log in' again. At this point, you can enter a new address or hang up your telephone to disconnect from Tymnet.

Since several information utilities to include CompuServe have expanded the scope of their operations to include the establishment of a packet network, it is difficult to make a clear distinction between packet network operators and information utilities. In general, the author tends to view a packet network operator as a company whose primary business is the transportation of data through their network to the computer systems of other organizations. On this basis, Table 5.2 lists the five major packet network operators in the United States. Several of these networks provide true global access, as not only do they have network nodes in many overseas locations but, in addition, have one or more interconnections to foreign packet networks.

Table 5.2 Major Packet Network Operators

ADP Autonet Automatic Data Processing 175 Jackson Plaza Ann Arbor, MI 48106	GTE Telenet 8229 Boone Blvd. Vienna, VA 22180
AT&T Information Systems 1 Speedwell Ave. Morristown, NJ 07960	Tymnet, Inc. 2710 Orchard Parkway San Jose, CA 95134
General Electric Information Services Company 401 North Washington St. Rockville, MD 20850	

Network information

Many packet networks have an information facility that users can access without cost to obtain such information as their dial-up access telephone numbers, international access cost and locations served as well as other relevant information. For Tymnet users, this packet network's Information Directory can be accssed by simply typing INFORMATION after the 'please log in:' message is generated by the network. Figure 5.8 illustrates the nine topics users can select from the Tymnet Information Directory.

From the Information Directory, users can obtain valuable information. As an example, a person traveling to Copenhagen might access the International Access Information portion of the directory and request information about Denmark. Doing so he or she would obtain the point of

1. HELP IN USING THE INFORMATION SERVICE
2. DIAL-UP ACCESS INFORMATION
3. PUBLIC DATA BASE AND TIMESHARING SERVICES AVAILABLE OVER TYMNET
4. INTERNATIONAL ACCESS INFORMATION
5. X.25 PRODUCTS CERTIFIED BY TYMNET
6. COMMUNICATIONS PRODUCTS VERIFIED BY TYMNET
7. HOST TYPES CURRENTLY INTERFACED ON TYMNET
8. TYMNET SALES OFFICE DIRECTORY
9. TYMNET TECHNICAL AND USER DOCUMENTATION
TYPE THE NUMBER OF THE DESIRED MENU ITEM FOLLOWED BY A CARRIAGE
RETURN:

Figure 5.8 Tymnet Information Directory

contact and telephone number of the Danish Post Telegraph & Telephone
(PTT) representative that coordinates packet network facilities as well as a
price list in Danish Kroner of different types of packet network services
available in that country.

Features

Table 5.3 lists nine of the more common features associated with the use
of packet networks. Due to the inclusion of these features or added values,
most packet-switching networks are also known as value-added carriers.

Automatic baud detection is the ability of the network node to sample
the width of the data pulses and adjust its speed to the device requiring
access to the network. Most networks support 0–2400 bps asynchronous dial-
in data transmission.

By the use of a terminal identifier the packet network may perform code
conversion, permitting, as an example, a PC using the ASCII character set
to communicate with a mainframe using the EBCDIC code. Since data is
transferred between network nodes using a sophisticated error-detection
and -correction method, very low error rates occur once data reaches a
packet network node. In addition, the mesh structure of these networks
permits highly reliable service, since nodes are usually interconnected by at
least two paths and packets are automatically routed around any link that

Table 5.3 Packet Network Features

Automatic baud detection
Automatic code detection
Low transmission error rates
Reliable service
Efficient handling of peak traffic loads
Electronic mail facilities
Usage and accounting reports
International access
Protocol conversion

may become inoperative. Similarly, the mesh structure permits packets to be routed over less heavily used circuits, to increase the level of performance on the overall network when traffic on any one link exceeds a certain level.

Usage and accounting reports provided by value-added carriers can include a variety of information which is basically dependent upon the type of features users select during the month. As an example, basic access through a packet network might result in a listing of network nodes accessed, destination node and duration of each network session to include the characters transferred during the session. If users employed other features of the packet network to include sending electronic mail or obtaining international access, the usage and accounting report would identify this. In general, the communications manager of an organization using a packet network to provide access to his or her computational facilities receives this report on a monthly basis. When used correctly, this report can assist the communications manager in assessing whether to upgrade or contract communications facilities as well as to determine if packet network usage costs warrant the consideration of an alternative networking procedure.

Since many packet networks basically cover the entire United States and provide international access from a large number of foreign locations, a logical development was the offering of electronic mail facilities to corporate users. Several packet networks offer electronic mail subsystems that can be accessed for an additional fee. Such systems provide subscribers with an electronic mailbox, which is their address for receiving electronic messages. In addition, many electronic mail systems interface the Telex and TWX networks as well as AT&T Mail, MCI Mail and other mail systems, permitting hard-copy messages to be generated electronically to distant locations where they are then distributed on conventional media. Although electronic mail is a very popular service offering of packet networks, we will defer a detailed examination of this capability until later in this chapter when we cover information utilities. This is due to the higher popularity of electronic mail services provided by vendors that are best categorized as information utilities.

One of the fastest growth areas in the use of value-added carriers involves the protocol conversion features offered by such communications companies. Due to the large base of asynchronous terminals and personal computers, one of the earliest protocol conversion efforts involved the development of software by value-added carriers to enable asynchronous devices to access IBM 3270 mainframe applications. In effect, value-added carriers added protocol conversion software to the minicomputers they installed at a customer's location which previously provided a PAD facility between a user's mainframe computer and the packet network. Typically, this software converted the line-by-line transmission of the terminal or personal computer into a full-screen format to include character attributes and screen-positioning information acceptable to the mainframe, making the mainframe think it was communicating with an IBM 3270 type terminal. When the mainframe

220

transmitted a full screen of information, the protocol conversion software would convert the character attributes and screen positioning information into the appropriate character codes that the terminal or personal computer was built to work with. Due to the large number of different types of personal computers most protocol conversion assumes that the personal computer operates as a DEC VT100 device. This simplifies the protocol conversion software development process since that software only has to translate character attributes and screen positioning information into the appropriate VT100 character codes. Then, any VT100 emulator operating on an IBM PC, Apple Macintosh, DEC Rainbow or other type of personal computer will be able to correctly communicate in full-screen mode of operation with a mainframe that believes it is connected to a 3270 type of display station.

With the market success of asynchronous to 3270 protocol conversion, value-added carriers began to offer users many additional types of conversion software. Figure 5.9 illustrates Tymnet's protocol conversion services that were available or under development in 1987.

The Tymnet 3270 BISYNC and 3270 SNA host computer interfaces permit multidropped 3270 BSC and SDLC terminals to be connected to the user's mainframe via the Tymnet network. Figure 5.10 illustrates how a multidrop line connecting a series of BISYNC or SDLC terminal devices to include IBM PCs with SDLC adapter boards could be connected to a mainframe via Tymnet. One example of the economics associated with this networking strategy would be the situation where an organization has three terminals or personal computers located in three suburbs of Dallas that have to access the corporate mainframe in New York as 3270 devices. By routing the multidrop line from the three Dallas suburbs into a Tymnet node in Dallas, the cost of a leased line from Dallas to New York is eliminated. Although

	Host protocol						
	ASYNC	3270 BISYNC	3270 SNA	X.25	SDLC	2780/ 3780 HASP	2946
ASYNC	A	A	A	A			A
3270 BISYNC	A	A	A	A			
3270 SNA	U	U	A	U			
X.25	A	A	A	A	A		
SDLC				A	A		
2780/3780 HASP	A			A		A	
2946	A			A			A

Terminal protocol

A = Available
U = Under development

Figure 5.9 Tymnet Protocol Conversion Services

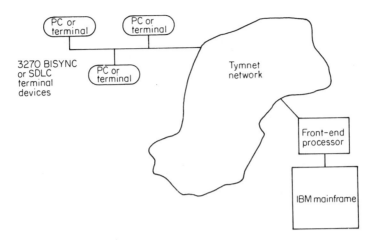

Figure 5.10 Multidrop Network Access Through Tymnet

the user's organization will be billed for the interface at the mainframe and terminal node to support 3270 transmission, this cost may be less than the cost of a leased line between Dallas and New York.

5.2 INFORMATION UTILITIES

In tandem with the growth of packet networks, there has been a corresponding increase in both the number of and scope of coverage of organizations that can be classified as information utilities. Basically, an information utility can be categorized as an organization whose primary business is the selling of access to information; however, many firms in this category have expanded the scope of their operations to include the establishment of their own packet network as well as offering subscribers such features as electronic mail and electronic shopping.

Due to the growth of packet networks, information utilities have been able to rapidly expand their subscriber base. Since telecommunications access to such utilities is very economical via a packet network, students, small businesses and other persons who might normally be excluded from using the facilities of an information utility via long-distance telephone calls have become subscribers. In turn, the rapid increase in the subscriber base and utilization of information utilities has created an increased demand for the utilization of packet networks. Thus, by the mid-1980s, the growth in the utilization of packet networks and information utilities was strongly related to one another.

Utility overview

Table 5.4 lists 11 organizations that can be classified as both information utilities and database vendors. It should be noted that each of these organizations provides services to its subscribers for profit and should not be confused with free bulletin board systems, the latter basically being PC-based systems permitting only one user to access the system at a time. Although a bulletin board system may contain valuable programs and other information that can be retrieved by users accessing such systems, most of the features associated with information utilities to include simultaneous conversation between two or more subscribers, on-line database searches, electronic mail with hard-copy delivery and encyclopedia searches are not available to bulletin board users.

The category of database listed to the right of each vendor in Table 5.4 indicates the major focus of the vendor. In some situations, this could be misleading, as several information utilities provide subscribers with a variety of additional services in addition to database searches, while some vendors limit their services strictly to database retrieval. In addition, information utility/database vendors with the indicator 'numerous databases', in certain situations may be able to provide subscribers with access to one or more databases subscribers might normally associate with a vendor that emphasizes a specific area. As an example, BRS provided subscribers with access to over 50 databases in such areas as business, sciences and medicine, humanities, social science and education.

Table 5.4 Major Information Utilities/Database Vendors

AgriData (Agricultural)
AgriData Resources, Inc.
205 West Highland Ave.
Milwaukee, WI 53203

Auto-Cite (legal)
Bancroft Whitney Publishing Co.
Aqueduct Bldg.
Rochester, NY 14694

BRS (numerous databases)
1200 Route 7
Latham, NY 12110

Chemical Abstracts Service
P.O. Box 3012 (chemistry)
Columbus, OH 43210

CompuServe (numerous databases)
5000 Arlington Centre Blvd.
Columbus, OH 43220

Data Resources, Inc. (economic)
24 Hartwell Ave.
Lexington, MA 02173

Dialog Information Services (numerous databases)
3460 Hillview Ave.
Palo Alto, CA 94304

Disclosure II (corporate financial reports)
Warner Financial Services
605 Third Ave.
New York, NY 10158

Dow Jones News Retrieval Service (financial)
Dow Jones & Co., Inc.
P.O. Box 300
Princeton, NJ 08540

Newsnet, Inc. (on-line publications)
945 Haverford Rd.
Bryn Mawr, PA 19010

The Source (numerous databases)
Source Telecomputing Corp.
1616 Anderson Rd.
McLean, VA 22102

Database inquiry considerations

Ten important factors one may wish to consider prior to subscribing to an information utility to utilize its database search facilities are listed in Table 5.5. Here the access method refers to both the type of terminals and PCs that can access the information utility as well as its interconnection to one or more major packet networks or its own such network. Although the number of on-line databases is important to subscribers, the types of databases access provided and the fees associated with their usage can be equally important. In addition to an initial subscription fee, many vendors have a monthly minimum usage fee that is billed to the subscriber regardless of usage or the fact that they may have taken a month's vacation. Since the connect price per database can vary drastically, one should carefully check the fees associated with the databases one anticipates using prior to subscribing to a particular service. With the cost per connect-hour varying from a minimum of $6 to well over $100 depending upon the database accessed, there can be significant economic differences between using different services. Similarly, the search features offered can have an impact upon the economics associated with the retrieval of data. Some services permit limited Boolean operators that combine keywords, causing the subscriber to perform many searches, while other services permit the use of complex operators which enable the retrieval of the desired information in fewer searches. Finally, some services permit subscribers to order documents while on-line, alleviating extended periods of connect time to print out such documents. To better understand the utilization and features offered by information utilities, we will examine one on-line financially oriented service and the electronic mail facilities of several information utilities.

Dow Jones news/retrieval service

In addition to publishing the Wall Street Journal and Barron's, Dow Jones offers a comprehensive on-line financially oriented service. Established in 1974, the Dow Jones News/Retrieval Service had well over 100 000 customers

Table 5.5 Database Inquiry Considerations

Access method
Number of databases on-line
Type of databases available
Search features
Hours of operation
Toll-free assistance
Initial subscriber fee
Connect charge per database
Monthly minimum fee
On-line document order

by the mid-1980s. Dow Jones News/Retrieval is a menu-based system that permits subscribers to easily move between each database in the service by typing a command preceded by two slashes (//). Figure 5.11 illustrates the basic structure of the Dow Jones News/Retrieval Service which is logically divded into four major groupings. By typing the command preceded by two slashes in each of the four groupings, subscribers can access the corresponding item in each grouping.

One of the more interesting features of Dow Jones News/Retrieval is its customer newsletter. By typing //INTRO, a subscriber can access a free on-line newsletter which contains pointers concerning the use of the News/Retrieval system and information about enhanced services available to users. To obtain additional information about any particular database one only has to enter the database access code followed by a space and the word HELP. In addition to being able to access Dow Jones News/Retrieval from several packet networks, one can also access this information service via MCI Mail, one of several electronic mail systems developed to send printed or electronic memos, letters, reports and other communications to users within the United States and abroad. Similarly, subscribers to the Dow Jones News/Retrieval Service can access the facilities of MCI Mail.

Other services

Although there are many additional information utilities that would warrant a description of their features and operation, space constraints unfortunately

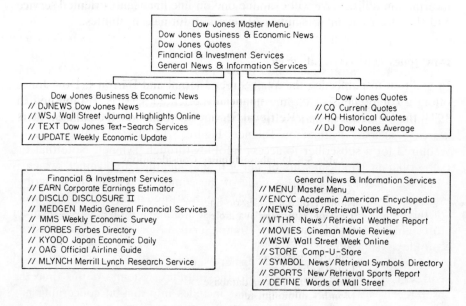

Figure 5.11 Dow Jones News/Retrieval

preclude the featuring of other systems. In concluding this chapter, we will examine several electronic mail systems which will serve as a representative example of the utilization and operation of a variety of electronic mail systems offered by packet networks, information utilities and firms specializing in electronic mail service.

CompuServe

CompuServe's subscriber base consists of over 300 000 members which makes it the largest information utility in the world. In addition to providing such features as Citizens Band radio simulation, access by special computer interest groups and other general interest features, since 1969 CompuServe has supplied a variety of business information services to corporations to include an electronic mail service. Today, CompuServe provides regular subscribers with an electronic mailbox for the transfer of information between subscribers while the firm also provides the capability for corporations to structure subnets that permit electronic communications between members of the corporation who are allowed access to CompuServe's InfoPlex™ electronic mail service.

InfoPlex®

InfoPlex is a special CompuServe electronic mail service that is designed for the corporate user. A business can set up a corporate subnet through the use of InfoPlex, permitting messages to be transferred between offices on a national or international basis. In comparison, the electronic mail facility available to CompuServe general subscribers lacks many of the more sophisticated features contained in InfoPlex, such as message broadcasting and an on-line directory of subscriber addresses.

Access to InfoPlex can be accomplished by dialing the nearest CompuServe telephone number in major cities or through a value-added communications carrier, such as Tymnet or Telenet. Figure 5.12 illustrates the sequence required for a subscriber to access InfoPlex through Tymnet. Note that the subscriber first indicates his or her terminal identifier to Tymnet, which is then followed by the address code of the computer system the subscriber wishes to be connected to. In the example illustrated in Figure 5.12, entering of the code CPS in response to the 'please log in:' message causes Tymnet to establish a connection to the CompuServe host computer that runs the InfoPlex system.

Once the subscriber enters his or her user id, password, address and code correctly, he or she is entered into the InfoPlex system. At this time the user receives a header message that includes information concerning any messages that have been transmitted to the user and are pending retrieval.

```
CONNECT

please type your terminal identifier A
-3271-215-
please log in: CPS

host: WELCOME TO COMPUSERVE 1134

User ID: 40802,7776
Password:
Address ? GIL
Code ?
InfoPlex 1E(104) -- Ready at 20:32 EDT 23-Sep-86 on T12QAl
    0 Messages pending
```

Figure 5.12 Accessing InfoPlex Via Tymnet

InfoPlex Utilization

Once access to the InfoPlex system is accomplished, users can enter commands preceded by the slash (/) character to check for messages, retrieve messages or create, store, send or save messages.

The key to the use of the InfoPlex system is its directory. By entering the command /DIR, members of an organization can obtain a listing of the broadcast codes and an alphabetical list of all address codes of persons currently allowed to access the InfoPlex system. Normally, each organization appoints a program administrator who coordinates the assignment of persons into the directory. This person is then responsible for coordinating the issuance of user ids, passwords and address codes. Usually, the address code of persons on an InfoPlex system used by an organization is the last name of an individual, with first and middle initials appended when differentiation between persons with the same last name is required.

If upon sign-on one is notified that there are messages pending, one can use the /SCA (scan) command to display a brief description of those messages or can enter one of the several different types of retrieval commands to type out all messages or a specified message in one's mailbox. Each InfoPlex command is abbreviated by entering its first three letters preceded by the slash character. Table 5.6 lists 10 of the more commonly used InfoPlex commands and their operational results, grouped according to their major category.

While InfoPlex is primarily used as an electronic mailbox-to-mailbox transmission system for a 'closed' user group consisting of the members of an organization provided with an address code and password, this system can also be used to send messages to MCI electronic mail users and Telex users. As an example of the former, entering the InfoPlex command

    /SEND > MCIMAIL:MCI ID

or

    /SEND > MCIMAIL:REGISTERED NAME

causes a previously composed InfoPlex message to be transmitted to an MCI Mail subscriber. The first example routes the message based upon an MCI user's unique identification number. In the second example, a previously created InfoPlex message is transmitted to an MCI user based upon the name the user registered with MCI. If the name is not unique, as is most likely in the case of JOHN SMITH, the message cannot be properly delivered and the InfoPlex user must then use the MCI ID, which is unique.

Many InfoPlex commands.have several options. Some examples of SEND command options include /RECEIPT and /RELEASE. The /RECEIPT option causes an automatic notice of receipt to be sent to the originator's mailbox once the transmitted message is retrieved. The /RELEASE option

Table 5.6 Major InfoPlex Commands

ADDRESS CODE	
/DIRectory	Lists the broadcast codes as well as an alphabetical list of all address codes for one's organization.
CREATING MESSAGES	
/COMpose	Opens workspace and enables one to create a message.
/USE file	Accesses a standard message placed into InfoPlex by the administrator.
CHECKING FOR MESSAGES	
/SCAn	Prints a brief list of the messages in one's mailbox.
RETRIEVING MESSAGES	
/RETrieve ALL	Causes all messages in one's mailbox to be displayed.
/RETrieve message-number	Causes only the message numbers entered to be displayed.
STORING MESSAGES	
/STOre address-code	Stores the message in one's workspace into the mailbox specified by the address-code.
/FORward message-number	Causes a message just received to be forwarded. InfoPlex will prompt the user for the address-code(s) of the intended recipient(s).
SAVING MESSAGES	
/SAVe message-number	Causes the specified message or a list of messages to be saved.
TRANSMITTING MESSAGES	
/SEND address-code	Sends a message from the user's work space to the specified address code. ·

permits the sender to compose a message which will be delivered to the specified address on the release date specified. Thus, the command /SEND/ RELEASE:(10/1/87) causes the composed message to be delivered on 10/1/87 to the specified address or addresses.

MCI Mail

When MCI Mail commenced operations on 27 September 1983, its initial enrollment consisted of approximately 55 000 subscribers. This subscription base resulted from an agreement negotiated with the Dow Jones News/Retrieval Service that enabled subscribers to that service to automatically become subscribers to MCI Mail.

When MCI Mail was established, the company opened 17 'postal centers' throughout the United States. These postal centers contain laser printers and serve as distribution sites for electronic messages that are reprinted on paper for delivery by courier or by the US Postal Service, depending upon the mode of delivery selected by the originator of the message. Currently a variety of personal computers, telex machines, word processors and electronic typewriters can be used to access MCI Mail.

Subscribers to MCI Mail are given a user name which is normally their first initial, followed by their last name and a password. Once they access the MCI computer system they can compose and edit messages, send and receive information, store data for a period of time and electronically scan advertisements and place orders for a variety of gifts, travel packages, investment aids and services if they should so desire.

Access

Telephone access to MCI Mail was available in several hundred cities in the United States and foreign locations as well as via a national toll-free '800' access phone number. To keep up to date on the availability of local access telephone numbers, subscribers can enter the command HELP PHONES once connected to MCI Mail. This command results in the display of an up-to-date listing of MCI Mail local access phone numbers.

MCI Mail is best categorized as a menu-drive electronic mail system. Once the subscriber dials an appropriate access number and enters his or her user name and password, the subscriber receives a sign-on message and one or more lines of information concerning the headlines for the day or other appropriate information concerning MCI Mail services. A typical sign-on sequence for MCI Mail is illustrated in Figure 5.13. Note that once the subscriber accesses MCI Mail and receives a listing of the current headlines, he or she is automatically informed of any messages in his or her in-box. Thus, a subscriber with one or more messages in his or her in-box might first read or scan such messages prior to composing and sending messages.

```
    CONNECT

    Port: 6.

    Please enter your user name: GHELD
    Password:
    Connection initiated. . . Opened.

    Welcome to MCI Mail!

    Today's Headlines at 7:00 am EST

    --UAW,GM Fail to Reach Agreement,
        12 Plants Expected To Close
    --State Department Presses Moscow
        For Return of Detained Seamen

    Avoid delay -- get answers to your
    MCI Mail questions instantly!
    Type HELP NEWS for details.

    MCI Mail Version 2.2

        Your INBOX has 1 message

    Press (RETURN) to continue
```

Figure 5.13 MCI Mail Sign-on

Command Summary

Once subscribers are successfully connected to MCI Mail, they obtain a main menu that enables them to select the action they would like to take on their MCI Mail messages. The main menu contains seven commands to include a help command which can actually be invoked at any time while using MCI Mail. Users may type HELP for additional information or HELP <topic> for information about a particular topic. Figure 5.14 illustrates the display of the main menu and the initial response of MCI Mail to a HELP PHONES command request.

In the main menu, SCAN provides the subscriber with a brief table of information about his or her mail to include a reference number, date of posting, whom the message is from if one is SCANning one's in-box, the subject of the message and its size in characters. If the subscriber enters the SCAN command, he or she will then have a second menu displayed on his or her terminal, which will specifically relate to the options one can select when using this command. Thus, a subscriber wishing to SCAN unread messages would enter the command INBOX after he or she entered the SCAN command. Figure 5.15 illustrates the main menu and the submenu resulting from a subscriber entering the SCAN command as well as the use of the INBOX command to scan an unread message that is currently in the subscriber's index.

```
Your may enter:

SCAN            for a summary of your mail
READ            to READ messages one by one
PRINT           to display messages nonstop
CREATE          to write an MCI Letter
DOWJONES        for Dow Jones News/Retrieval
ACCOUNT         to adjust terminal display
HELP            for assistance

Command (or MENU or EXIT): HELP PHONES

Thank you for accessing the MCI Mail
PHONES list.

* Customer Service: (800 424-6677)
* In Washington, call: (202) 833-8484

Following are MCI Mail local access
phone numbers:

Atlanta, GA. . . . . . . (404) 577-7363
```

Figure 5.14 MCI Mail Main Menu

```
You may enter:

SCAN            for a summary of your mail
READ            to READ messages one by one
PRINT           to display messages nonstop
CREATE          to write an MCI Letter
DOWJONES        for Dow Jones New/Retrieval
ACCOUNT         to adjust terminal display
HELP            for assistance

Command (or MENU or EXIT): SCAN

You may enter:

INBOX           to SCAN your unread messages
OUTBOX          to SCAN messages you sent
DESK            to SCAN messages read before
DRAFT           to SCAN your DRAFT message
ALL             to SCAN ALL your messages
HELP            for assistance

Command (or MENU or EXIT): INBOX

    1 message in INBOX

No.  Posted       From            Subject                     Size
 1   Sep 14 15:00  Gilbert Held    SAMPLE LETTER VIA MCI  385
                                   MA

Press ⟨RETURN⟩ to continue
```

Figure 5.15 Using the SCAN and INBOX Commands

Returning to the main menu illustrated in Figure 5.14, the READ command lets subscribers view messages in their entirety, one by one. The PRINT command causes messages to be displayed in their entirety; however, no pauses occur between messages. The CREATE command is the mechanism by which subscribers write their MCI Mail letters and causes a set of additional prompts to be displayed concerning to whom the letter is addressed, carbon copies, subject and text.

The ACCOUNT command provides the subscriber with a mechanism to read or change his or her terminal display settings for the current session or on a 'permanent' basis until the next time the subscriber wishes to change them. A list of the settings and possible adjustments resulting from the use of this command is contained in Table 5.7.

The last command on the main menu, disregarding the HELP command, is DOWJONES. The use of this command provides MCI Mail subscribers with access to the Dow Jones News/Retrieval® service. Charges for the use of this service are then billed at their standard rates to MCI Mail subscribers on their MCI Mail invoice.

Table 5.7 MCI Terminal Display Settings

Setting label	Adjustments
Terminal	PAPER causes continuous display without pausing.
	VIDEO causes a pause after each page is displayed until the subscriber presses the Return key.
LINE	Subscriber can adjust to match the length of his or her screen or paper.
PAGE	Subscriber can adjust to match the length of his or her screen.
TIME	Subscriber should substitute his or her own time zone for Eastern Time, resulting in a correct posting appearing on his or her mail.
LF PADDING	Subscribers can adjust the number of null characters sent to their terminal after a line feed to match the scrolling of their screen and printer.
CR PADDING	Subscribers can adjust the number of null characters sent to their terminal after a carriage return to match the scrolling of their screen and printer.

Creating Messages

Although MCI Mail offers subscribers a variety of services to include access to the Dow Jones News/Retrieval service as well as the ability to read electronic advertisements and other merchandise, the primary purpose of MCI Mail is the creation and transmission of messages. Once a subscriber is on-line, he or she can easily type and edit corrsepondence and then

```
Command (or MENU or EXIT): CREATE

**You have a DRAFT in process. You must delete it or send it before creating a new
one. Do you wish to delete it?

YES or NO: YES

TO:     GILBERT HELD
        235-8068     Gilbert Held          4-Degree Cons Macon, GA
TO:
CC:
Subject: SAMPLE LETTER VIA MCI MAIL
Text: (Enter text or transmit file. Type / on a line by itself to end.)

THIS ILLUSTRATES THE CREATION OF A LETTER VIA MCI MAIL THAT WILL BE
DELIVERED BY THE US POSTAL SERVICE. AFTER THE TEXT IS ENTERED IT IS
TERMINATED BY THE SLASH (/) CHARACTER AND RETURN. THEN ALL ONE DOES
IS TO ENTER THE COMMAND SEND FOR POSTAL DELIVERY. NOTE THAT ONE
COULD ALSO ENTER ENTER THE COMMAND 4Hour OR Onite TO OBTAIN 4 HOUR
DELIVERY OR OVERNIGHT DELIVERY OF THIS LETTER.
/

You may enter:

READ              to review your letter
READ PAPER        to review your letter for paper
EDIT              to correct your letter
SEND              U.S. Mail for paper; instant electronic delivery
SEND ONITE        OVERNIGHT courier for paper; PRIORITY electronic delivery
SEND 4HOUR        FOUR-HOUR courier for paper; PRIORITY electronic delivery
HELP              for assistance.

Command (or MENU or EXIT): SEND

One moment please; your message is being posted.

Your message was posted: Mon Sep 14, 1987 3:00 pm EST.
There is a copy in your OUTBOX.

Press ⟨RETURN⟩ to continue
```

Figure 5.16 Creating and Sending a Letter on MCI

arrange for it to be transmitted. Figure 5.16 illustrates the creation of a
sample letter by the use of the CREATE command from the main menu.
Note that in this particular example the subscriber sent a message to himself,
which obviated the necessity of entering an address.

In general, subscribers can send mail to other MCI Mail subscribers by
entering an addressee's name which will result in the name, company and
location of the addressee being displayed. Each time the prompt 'TO'
appears, another addressee's name can be entered if the subscriber wishes
to address individual copies of the message to more than one person. When
all TOs have been entered, pressing the return key will cause the prompt
'CC:' to be displayed. If one does not wish to send a carbon copy, pressing

the return key a second time causes the prompt 'Subject:' to be displayed. It should be noted that both CC and Subject are optional. In the correspondence creation example contained in Figure 5.16, after the subject was entered the prompt 'Text:' was displayed. This was followed by information telling the subscriber to enter text or transmit a file previously created off-line as well as specifying that the backslash character (/) should be entered on a line by itself to signify to the system that the text has ended. Thus, after the backslash was entered, MCI Mail displayed a menu of options for the subscriber to consider. While most of the commands listed in Figure 5.16 in response to the backslash entry are self-explanatory, the command READ PAPER probably requires some elaboration.

One of the options available to subscribers of MCI Mail which permits a degree of control over the appearance of their paper mail is the ability to register one's company or personal letterhead for a customized look. Another option is the ability to register one's signature, which then allows the subscriber to type /SIGNED/ in the leftmost position on a line by itself, resulting in the registered signature being printed in that position by the MCI Mail laser printer used for printing paper mail. Thus, subscribers would use the command READ PAPER to display the current draft showing the position of the letterhead, margins, page breaks, signatures and other relevant data.

As illustrated by the menu in the lower portion of Figure 5.16 displayed in response to the termination of text by the backslash character, subscribers can enter the EDIT command to make corrections to their letter or they can select one of three SEND commands to transmit their correspondence. Entering the command SEND by itself causes the previously entered text to be transmitted to the MCI Mail location nearest to the recipient where it is then printed and entered into the US Postal Service system for delivery by First Class Mail. If the correspondence is directed to an MCI subscriber as an instant mail letter, it will be transmitted immediately into the recipient's INBOX; however, the recipient must check his or her mailbox to determine that there is a letter awaiting retrieval. If the command SEND ONITE (for overnight delivery) is entered, any letter posted by 8 p.m. Eastern time on business days will be delivered by courier before noon on the next business day. If an Overnight Letter is posted on a weekend prior to midnight Sunday, it will be delivered by noon Monday if the recipient is located in one of MCI's four-hour delivery areas.

By entering the command SEND 4HOUR, any correspondence posted by 6 p.m. (recipient's local time) on a business day will be delivered by courier within 4 hours on the same business day. For correspondence posted after 6 p.m., it will be delivered prior to 10 a.m. on the following business day.

Normal MCI Mail letters delivered by the US Postal Service are mailed in envelopes that have a distinct shape and color. The MCI Mail envelope measures approximately 9 by $11\frac{1}{2}$ inches and contains two windows. The first window shows who the letter is from while the second window indicates the recipient and his or her address. Figure 5.17 illustrates the envelope of a typical MCI Mail letter, showing how information concerning the originator and recipient of the message is printed on a cover page in appropriate positions. When inserted into the envelope, this information is visible through the two windows. Unfortunately, the black and white reproduction of the envelope fails to illustrate its bold orange color, which is used to attract the recipient's attention. In Figure 5.17 the reader will find a copy of a letter sent by MCI Mail. Since this letter is printed in black and white on MCI's laser printer, its reproduction in this book accurately reflects what the recipient saw when he opened the MCI Mail envelope and removed the second page from the envelope which contained the message.

Electronic mail can be a most effective mechanism for communications within an organization since it eliminates the all too familiar 'telephone tag' syndrome where most calls to individuals never reach the desired party. In addition, for its visual impact, the ability to send a mailgram or cable can have a favorable impression upon the recipient. In spite of the numerous advantages of electronic mail, readers are cautioned to carefully examine the options and costs associated with the usage of electronic mail facilities

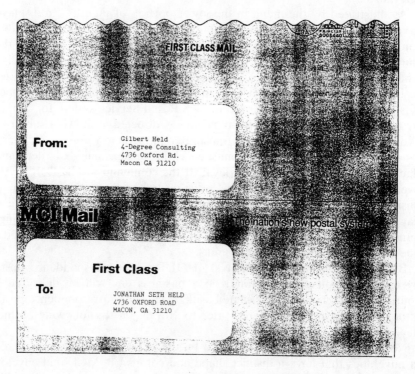

Figure 5.17 MCI Mail Envelope

MCI Mail   The nation s new postal system

September 18, 1987

JONATHAN SETH HELD
4736 OXFORD ROAD
MACON, GA 31210

THIS IS AN EXAMPLE OF THE TRANSMISSION OF A MCI MAIL LETTER. NOTE THAT
MCI WILL TRANSMIT THIS LETTER ELECTRONICALLY TO ONE OF "17 POSTAL
CENTERS" WHERE IT WILL BE PRINTED ON AN MCI LASER PRINTER AND THEN
PLACED INTO THE UNITED STATES POSTAL SERVICE MAIL FACILITY FOR
DELIVERY TO THE PARTY IT IS ADDRESSED TO. FOR A NOMINAL ANNUAL FEE
SUBSCRIBERS AN REGISTER A LETTERHEAD OR SIGNATURE TO CUSTOMIZE
THEIR CORRESPONDENCE.

Figure 5.18 MCI Mail Letter

Table 5.8 Electronic Mail Options to Consider

Membership charge
Start-up fee
Telephone access
    In-Wats availability and charges
    via packet network and charges
Connect time charges
    300 bps charges
    1200 bps charges
Message types and charges
    Electronic mailbox
    Cablegram
    Telex
    Mailgram
    Other
Editing features
Forms customization

Table 5.9 Electronic Mail Vendors

AT&T Mail	MCI Mail
AT&T	MCI Corp.
Somerset, NJ	Box 1001
	1900 M St. NW
Comet	Washington, DC 20036
Computer Corporation of America	
Fou Cambridge Center	OnTyme
Cambridge, MA 02142	Tymnet, Inc.
	2710 Orchard Parkway
Dailcom	San Jose, CA 95134
1109 Spring Street	
Silver Spring, MD 20910	Quick-Comm
	General Electric Information Service
EasyLink	401 N. Washington St.
Western Union	Rockville MD 20850
1 Lake Street	
Upper Saddle River, NJ 07458	Source Mail
	Source Telecomputing Corp.
InfoPlex	1616 Anderson Road,
CompuServe, Inc.	McLean, VA 22102
5000 Arlington Centre Blvd.	
1616 Anderson Road	Telemail
McLean, VA 22102	GTE Telenet
Columbus, OH 43220	8229 Boone Blvd.
	Vienna, VA 22180

offered by vendors of such services. Some vendors orient their facilities to large corporate clients and have a substantial subscription fee and a minimum monthly charge that can exceed several hundred dollars per month. In comparison, other vendors offer electronic mail as an optional portion of their total information utility service and only charge for the actual usage of their electronic mail facility. Table 5.8 lists the major items one should consider prior to utilizing an electronic mail service while Table 5.9 lists the major vendors offering electronic mail services when this book was prepared.

CHAPTER SIX

System/3X and 3270 Networking

In this chapter, we will first examine the methods used to connect IBM PCs and compatible personal computers to the IBM System 34, 36 or 38 series of minicomputers. Due to the extensive use of IBM 3270 and third-party equivalent networking devices used for communicating with mainframes, we will next focus our attention upon this area. After describing the elements of a 3270 Information Display System the methods by which members of the IBM PC series can be integrated into 3270 networks will be examined.

Although many older bisynchronous and more modern SDLC operating workstations are not an official part of 3270 networking products, their popularity of utilization with IBM mainframes has resulted in their inclusion in this chapter. After discussing the operation of products that enable PCs to operate as bisynchronous or SDLC workstations, we will conclude this chapter by discussing two alternatives to hardware products that permit IBM PCs to communicate with mainframes as 3270 devices or remote job-entry workstations.

6.1 SYSTEM/3X CONNECTIVITY

Due to the large base of installed IBM System 34, System 36 and System 38 minicomputers, many vendors developed communications products to enable members of the IBM PC series to communicate with these minicomputers. These products are basically combinations of hardware and software which enable IBM PCs to emulate an IBM 5251 local workstation, which is normally attached via a twinaxial cable to a System/3X minicomputer.

Local emulator

Two types of System/3X connectivity can be obtained by selecting appropriate vendor products – local and remote workstation emulation. Figure 6.1 illustrates an IBM PC functioning as a local 5251-11 terminal. To obtain this capability an adapter board must be installed in an IBM PC or compatible computer. This adapter board attaches directly to an IBM System/3X processor via a twinaxial cable connection. Depending upon the

238

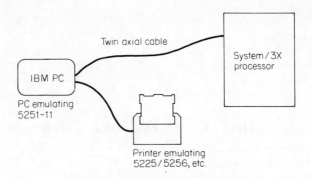

Figure 6.1 Local 5251 Emulation

When a local 5251 emulation capability is obtained, an IBM
PC is connected directly to a System/3X processor via a
twinaxial cable connection. Depending upon vendor hardware and software, the personal computer may function as
a 5251, 5291 or 5292 type terminal device

degree of vendor hardware and software features included with his or her
IBM 5251 emulation package, the PC user's printer may be supported as
an IBM System/3X matrix printer, such as a 4214, 5219, 5224, 5225 or 5256.
Other common features offered with IBM 5251 emulation packages include
hot key support, file transfer and format translation, record blocking and
security.

The IBM 5251 emulator hot key is actually a two-keystroke sequence
which permits the PC user to switch between PC DOS and multiple System/
3X sessions. Concerning file transfer, many 5251 emulation packages
translate System/3X formats such as EBCDIC, packed, binary, alphanumeric,
zoned and decimal to PC ASCII, DIF (Visical), WKS (Lotus 1-2-3), BASIC
and Binary formats. Similarly, PC formats to include those previously
mentioned as well as DOS print images may be converted to one or more
System/3X formats.

To enable faster file transfers, many vendors include a record-blocking
feature. Other vendors incorporate a variety of user ids, passwords and file
and record security features both to protect users and to enable them to
maintain control of their System/3X database resources.

Remote emulator

A remote emulator package for System/3X access enables an IBM PC or
compatible computer to function as a 5251 workstation via a dial-up or
leased line connection to the System/3X processor. Several types of 5251
emulation packages are currently marketed by vendors, with major

differences in the inclusion or exclusion of an autodial modem on the emulator adapter card and type of emulation supported.

Some vendors now include asynchronous or synchronous 2400 or synchronous 4800 bps modems on their 5251 remote adapter cards, resulting in the user saving desk space as well as an economic saving in comparison to purchasing an adapter card and stand-alone modem. Although most remote emulation packages turn the PC into a remote 5251 workstation as illustrated in the top portion of Figure 6.2, other emulation packages permit the PC to emulate an IBM 5294 remote controller. Then, other PCs at the remote location can be connected to the personal computer emulating the controller as illustrated in the lower portion of Figure 6.2.

When a 5251 remote emulation package is obtained, the IBM SNA/SDLC protocol is used for data transmission from the remote personal computer to the System/3X minicomputer. Although many vendors offer the same adapter boards due to Original Equipment Manufacturer (OEM) agreements between a few board manufacturers and a large number of retailers, software features can vary to a significant degree. This is due to a larger number of vendors supplying different types of software modules to retailers that package the software with the hardware as a system. Based upon this, most end-users should probably concentrate a higher percentage of the time they spend evaluating 5251 emulation packages on the software part of the package.

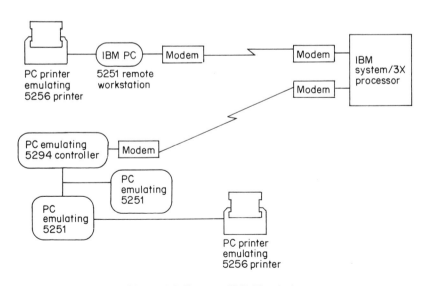

Figure 6.2 Remote 5251 Emulation

Some 5251 emulation boards include a built-in modem, reducing both the footprint of the system and its cost

6.2 THE IBM 3270 INFORMATION DISPLAY SYSTEM

The IBM 3270 Information Display System describes a collection of products ranging from display stations with keyboards and printers that communicate with mainframe computers through several types of cluster controllers as well as a member of the IBM PC series known as the 3270 PC.

First introduced in 1971, the IBM 3270 Information Display System was designed to extend the processing power of the mainframe computer to locations remote from the computer room. Controllers, which are called control units by IBM, were made available to economize on the number of lines required to link display stations to mainframe computers. Typically, a number of display stations are connected to a control unit on individual cables and the control unit, in turn, is connected to the mainframe via a single cable. Both local and remote control units are offered, with the key differences between the two pertaining to the method of attachment to the mainframe computer and the use of intermediate devices between the control unit and the mainframe.

Local control units are usually attached to a channel on the mainframe, whereas remote control units are connected to the mainframe's front-end processor, which is also known as a communications controller in the IBM environment. Since a local control unit is within a limited distance of the mainframe, no intermediate communications devices, such as modems, are required to connect a local control unit to the mainframe. In comparison, a remote control unit can be located in another building or in a different city and normally requires the utilization of intermediate communications devices, such as a pair of modems, for communications to occur between the control unit and the communications controller. The relationship of local and remote control units to display stations, mainframes and a communications controller is illustrated in Figure 6.3.

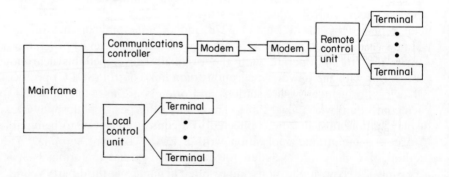

Figure 6.3 Relationship of 3270 Information Display Products

In a 3270 environment, the terminals are also known as display stations

Control unit operation

The control unit polls each connected display station to ascertain if the station has data stored in its transmit buffer. If the station has data in its buffer, it will transmit it to the control unit when it is polled. The control unit then formats the data with the display station's address, adds the control unit's address and other pertinent information and transmits it in a synchronous data format to the communications controller or to the I/O channel on the mainframe, depending upon the method used to connect the control unit to the mainframe.

3270 protocols

Two different protocols are supported by IBM to connect 3270 devices to a mainframe. The original protocol used with 3270 devices which is still widely used today is the byte-oriented bisynchronous protocol, often referred to as 3270 bisync or BSC. In the late 1970s, IBM introduced its Systems Network Architecture, which is basically an architecture that permits distributed systems to be interconnected based upon a series of conventions which includes a bit-oriented protocol for data transmission known as Synchronous Data Link Control, or SDLC. Thus, communications between an IBM mainframe and the control units attached to the communications controller are either BSC or SDLC, depending upon the type of control units obtained and the configuration of the communications controller which is controlled by software.

Types of control units

Control units currently marketed support up to 8, 16 or 32 attached devices, depending upon the model. The IBM 3276 control unit supports up to eight devices while the IBM 3274 control unit can support 16 or 32 attached devices. Older control units, such as the 3271, 3272, and 3275 have largely been replaced by the 3274 and 3276 and operate only bisynchronously, whereas certain models of the 3274 are 'soft' devices that can be programmed with a diskette to operate with the originally developed bisynchronous protocol or with the newer synchronous data link control (SDLC) protocol.

Devices to include display stations and printers are normally attached to each control unit via coaxial cable. Thus, under this design philosophy every display station must first be connected to a control unit prior to being able to access a mainframe application written for a 3270 type terminal. This method of connection excluded the utilization of dial-up terminals from accessing 3270 type applications and resulted in numerous third-party vendors marketing devices to permit lower-cost ASCII terminals to be attached to 3270 networks. In late 1986, IBM introduced a new controller known as the 3174 Subsystem Control Unit. This controller can be used to connect terminals via standard coaxial cable, shielded twisted-pair wire and telephone type twisted-pair wire. Other key features of this controller include an optional protocol converter which can support up to 24 asynchronous ports and the ability of this controller to be attached to IBM's Token-Ring Local Area Network.

Prior to discussing the methods by which personal computers can be connected to IBM control units, we will first review the classes of contemporary 3270 type terminals as the techniques developed to integrate personal computers into a 3270 network revolve around making the PC function as a particular 3270 type terminal. In addition, we will also examine the IBM 3270 PC, which was specifically developed to support multiple host computer sessions when connected to an IBM mainframe computer. By using the preceding as a foundation of knowledge concerning 3270 terminal and 3270 PC operations, we can then examine the techniques that permit conventional personal computers to communicate with mainframes as 3270 type devices.

Terminal displays

Currently, IBM 3270 terminals fall into three display classes – monochrome, color and gas plasma. Members of the monochrome display class include the 3278, 3178, 3180, 3191 and 3193 type terminals. The 3278 is a large, bulky terminal that easily covers a significant portion of one's desk and has basically been replaced by the 3178, 3180, 3191 and 3193 display stations which are lighter, more compact and less expensive versions of the 3278. The 3279 color display station was similarly replaced by the 3179 and 3194 which are lower cost and more compact color display terminals. The last class of display stations is the gas plasma display, consisting of the 3270 flat panel display.

The physical dimensions of a 3270 screen may vary by class and model within the class. As an example, the 3178 and 3278 Model 2 display stations have a screen size of 24 rows by 80 columns, while the 3278 Model 3 has a screen size of 32 rows by 80 columns and the 3278 Model 4 has a screen size of 43 rows by 80 columns.

Table 6.1 lists the family of terminals marketed for use with the IBM 3270 Information Display System during 1987. The reader should note that the 3179 and 3180 display stations can also be used with IBM System/36 and System/38 minicomputers. In addition, the 3193 and 3194 terminals which were introduced in 1986 can support the display of up to four host sessions when connected to the 3174 controller.

Each 3270 screen consists of fields that are defined by the application program connected to the display station. Attributes sent by the application program further define the characteristics of each field as indicated in Table 6.2. As a minimum, any technique used to enable a personal computer to

Table 6.1 IBM Display Stations

Model number	Display type	Screen (*inches*)
3178	monochrome	12
3179	color	14
3180	monochrome	15
3191	monochrome	12
3193	monochrome	15
3194	color	14

Table 6.2 3270 Terminal Field Characteristics

Field characteristic	Result
Highlighted	Field displayed at a brighter intensity than normal intensity field
Nondisplay	Field does not display any data typed into it
Protected	Field does not accept any input
Unprotected	Field accepts any data typed into it
Numeric-only	Field accepts only numbers as input
Autoskip	Field sends the cursor to the next unprotected field after it is filled with data
Underscoring	Causes characters to be underlined
Blinking	Causes characters in field to blink

function as a 3270 display station requires the PC to obtain the field attributes listed in Table 6.2.

3270 Keyboard functions

In comparison to the keyboard of a member of the IBM PC series, a 3270 display station contains approximately 40 additional keys, which, when pressed, perform functions unique to the 3270 terminal environment. A list of the more common 3270 keys which differ from the keys on an IBM PC keyboard is contained in Table 6.3.

Since most, if not all, of the 3270 keyboard functions may be required to successfully use a 3270 application program, the codes generated from pressing keys on a personal computer keyboard must be converted into appropriate codes that represent 3270 keyboard functions to enable a PC to be used as a 3270 terminal. Due to the lesser number of keys on a personal computer keyboard, a common approach to most emulation techniques is to use a two- or three-key sequence on the PC keyboard to represent many of the keys unique to a 3270 keyboard.

Table 6.3 Common 3270 Keys Differing from an IBM PC Keyboard

Key(s)	Function
CLEAR	Erases screen except for characters in message area, repositioning cursor to row 1, column 1.
PA1	Transmits a code to the application program which is interpreted as a break signal. Thus, in TSO or CMS the PA1 key would terminate the current command.
PA2	Transmits a code to the application program that is often interpreted as a request to redisplay the screen or to clear the screen and display additional information.
PFnn	Twenty-four program function keys on a 3270 terminal are defined by the application program in use.
TAB	Moves the cursor to the next unprotected field.
BACKTAB	Moves the cursor to the previous unprotected field.
RESET	Disables the insert mode.
ERASEEOF	Deletes everything from the cursor to the end of the input field.
NEWLINE	Advances the cursor to the first unprotected field on the next line.
FASTRIGHT	Moves the cursor to the right two characters at a time.
FASTLEFT	Moves the cursor to the left two characters at a time.
ERASE INPUT	Clears all the input fields on the screen.
HOME	Moves the cursor to the first unprotected field on the screen.

Emulation considerations

In addition to converting keys on an IBM PC keyboard to 3270 keyboard functions, 3270 emulation requires the PC's screen to function as a 3270 display screen. The 3270 display terminal operates by displaying an entire screen of data in one operation and then waits for the operator to signal that he or she is ready to proceed with the next screen of information. This operation mode is known as 'full-screen' operation and is exactly the opposite of TTY emulation where a terminal operates 'on a line-by-line' basis. A key advantage of full-screen editing is the ability of the operator to move the cursor to any position on the screen to edit or change data. Thus, to use an IBM PC as a 3270 display station, the transmission codes used to position the 3270 screen and effect field attributes must be converted to equivalent codes recognizable by the PC.

3270 PC

The IBM 3270 PC functions as both a 3270 type terminal and a personal computer. Although its system unit is identical to that of the PCXT, its functionality is obtained from a series of adapter cards that are installed into the system expansion slots in the system unit. Additional significant differences between the 3270 PC and other members of the PC series include its keyboard, display screen, operating system, method of mainframe connection and price.

The 3270 PC's keyboard has 39 additional keys in comparison to a conventional IBM PC keyboard, which are used to provide access to 3278 terminal functions. Incorporating these keys onto the 3270 PC keyboard eliminates the requirement for multiple key sequences used by many emulation programs to obtain equivalent 3278 terminal key representations. Some vendors, such as Digital Communications Associates, market a 3270 PC-compatible keyboard that can be used to eliminate the frequent annoyance of trying to remember which key sequence on a conventional PC keyboard is used by an emulation program to represent a particular 3278 terminal key. Figure 6.4 illustrates the Digital Communications Associates 3270 type keyboard which is marketed under the trademark IRMAkey/3270.

A variety of monitors to include the standard PC Monochrome Display as well as several types of color monitors work with the 3270 PC, the latter

Figure 6.4 IRMAkey/3270

Photograph courtesy of Digital Communications Associates Inc.

being required to display mainframe graphics. Several types of display adapters can be installed in the 3270 PC, with high-quality graphics of 1024 by 1024 pixels of resolution available for selection. In comparison, the standard color/graphics monitor adapter board offers a maximum resolution of 640 by 200 pixels, while the enhanced graphics adapter permits a resolution of 640 by 350 pixels. In addition, several adapter boards permit a 132-line graphics mode display option which permits the 3270 PC to function nearly equivalently to a conventional IBM 3279 graphics terminal.

Although the 3270 PC supports most conventional versions of DOS, its primary operating system is a proprietary control program that is designed to facilitate the connection and operation of the 3270 PC with a mainframe computer. Under the 3270 PC control program, one can be connected to up to four separate mainframe sessions at one time. Multiple sessions are managed by the 3270 PC employing a windowing display format, permitting the user to partition his or her screen into as many as seven windows. Up to four windows can be used for mainframe computer sessions while one window can be used for PC-DOS and the remaining two windows can be used as notepads. Another unique feature of the 3270 PC is its file-transfer software which operates in conjunction with special software that must be installed on the mainframe computer.

To transmit a file to the mainframe one can use the SEND command, specifying the physical storage location of the file on the 3270 PC and its name as well as the mainframe file name it should be stored under. Since IBM mainframes normally store data files in EBCDIC, the 3270 PC files are translated into EBCDIC for storage on the mainframe. Similarly, a RECEIVE command permits files on the mainframe to be converted into ASCII and downloaded onto the 3270 PC.

Designed to operate as a 3270 type terminal the 3270 PC must be interfaced via a coaxial connection to a control unit. Then, the control unit can be directly attached to the mainframe (channel attached) or connected to the communications controller which in turn is directly connected to the mainframe computer. This method of connection precludes using the 3270 PC in a dial-up mode to directly access a mainframe.

Although one could purchase a 3270 PC to obtain an interface into the world of 3270 networking, two major factors have contributed to the tremendous growth in third-party products that provide conventional PCs with similar networking capability. These factors are price and performance. From a cost perspective, it is often less expensive to obtain an IBM PC or compatible computer and through the use of third-party products obtain a hardware configuration that permits the personal computer to access a mainframe similar to a 3270 type terminal. With respect to performance, the variety of hardware and software products marketed by third-party vendors permits users to consider many alternative methods for attaching PCs to 3270 type networks, with varying levels of performance and cost associated with each method.

6.3 3270 CONNECTION METHODS

Although there are numerous methods by which non-3270 type terminal devices, including IBM PCs, can be attached to a 3270 network, such methods basically fall into four defined categories – protocol converters, terminal emulators, microcomputer/host software emulators and the utilization of specialized facilities offered by some packet networks. While each category has many advantages and disadvantages in comparison to the other categories, the actual method employed is normally based upon the existing network architecture of the organization to include control unit and PC locations and the requirements for linking PCs to the mainframe computers. Thus, the reader should note that the examples discussed in this chapter may not be applicable to all situations due to differences in the distribution of control units and terminals between user networks. Instead, the material presented in the remainder of this chapter should be used by the reader as a guide to the various approaches one can consider for connecting personal computers into a 3270 type network.

Protocol converters

As the name implies, a protocol converter converts dissimilar devices that communicate in two different protocols, enabling such devices to achieve communications compatibility. In an IBM 3270 networking environment, a protocol converter is normally designed to be interfaced between the communications control unit or front-end processor and a terminal device, or it can be installed directly into the system unit of a PC. The protocol converter is then either directly cabled to the front-end processor if the personal computer is located close to the mainframe or via a pair of modems if the PC is at a remote location. Another networking option commonly employed is to have personal computers transmit data via the PSTN or a value-added carrier to obtain access to a protocol converter, which in turn is then connected to the communications controller.

Most protocol converters are designed to appear to the front end as a 3270 type control unit on one side of the device while supporting asynchronous ASCII data input at the other end of the device. Figure 6.5 illustrates the use of protocol converters at both a local and remote location with respect to the corporate mainframe computer. Note that PCs can access the protocol converter via a direct RS-232 cable connection over the PSTN into a modem, which in turn is connected to the protocol converter or by using a packet network as a data transportation highway to the location where the protocol converter is installed.

Similar to software emulation programs, the protocol converter translates the 3270 screen formats into the character sequences recognized by the PC. In addition to performing this data-formatting conversion, the protocol converter performs several additional functions to include data link control

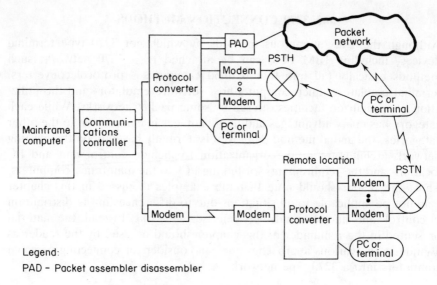

Figure 6.5 Employing Protocol Converters

conversion and transmission protocol conversion. Here the data link control conversion is simply the mapping of the communications line handling sequence of the PC to that of a 3270 type terminal. The transmission protocol processing is the conversion of the line-by-line data flow through the PC's communications buffer into data blocks with appropriate addressing and error detection that match the 3270 communications protocol supported by the communications controller.

Normally, the intelligence of the protocol converter is in the form of a ROM cartridge. PCs communicating with the protocol converter use a software program which works in conjunction with the ROM cartridge to obtain appropriate screen translations. Among the most popular type of personal computer software used for communicating with protocol converters are DEC VT100 terminal emulators due to the popularity of the terminal as well as the standardization of its screen codes by the American National Standards Institute.

Since a 3270 type control unit is designed to have terminals permanently connected to the device, a logical question that might arise is how protocol converters support access through value-added carriers or the PSTN. Whenever a user signs off a mainframe session, the protocol converter continues to respond to communications controller polls, making that device believe that terminals are inactive but attached to each protocol converter port. Then, after a user accesses the protocol converter via a value-added carrier or the PSTN the protocol converter transmits an appropriate code to the communications controller to indicate that an active terminal requiring servicing is there.

Control unit emulation

When the protocol converter emulates the operation of a control unit, the process is known as controller or control unit emulation. In our previous discussion of protocol converters we focused attention upon stand-alone devices. A second category of protocol converters is installed in the system unit of a PC and in effect converts the PC into a control unit.

One example of a protocol converter that is installed internally within the system unit of a PC and operates as a controller emulator is the Persyst DCP/88 hardware adapter which is used in conjunction with the firm's PC/3270 series software. This combination of hardware and softwre converts an IBM PC into a miniature 3274 control unit which is then capable of supporting up to four additional devices that can include three other PCs operating as 3278 type terminals and one high-speed printer operating at 600 lines per minute as illustrated in Figure 6.6. The multiple protocol communications controller illustrated in Figure 6.6 is another Persyst adapter board that is installed into a PC's system unit. This adapter enables a PC to emulate a 3278/9 terminal, supporting 3270 bisynchronous communications. In addition to permitting individual PCs to be connected to the company's DCP/88, the MPC can be installed in a PC to provide it with the capability to be connected from a remote location to a mainframe via the mainframe's communications controller as illustrated in Figure 6.7. The use of the Persyst

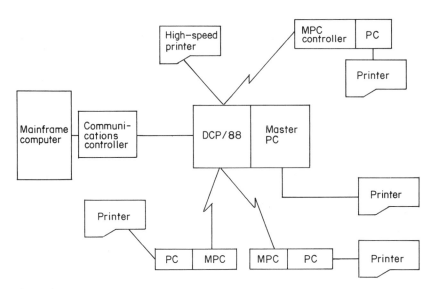

Legend:
    MPC – Multiple protocol communications controller which converts a PC into a
         3270 terminal, permitting configuration to be developed for specific applications

Figure 6.6 Persyst DCP/88 Converts a PC into a Control Unit

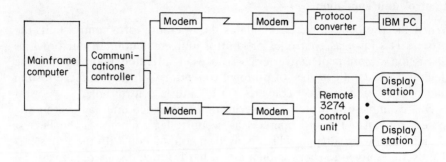

Figure 6.7 Remote Operations of Persyst MPC Board

The Persyst MPC board with PC/3270 software permits individual PCs to be connected to a mainframe using 3270 bisynchronous communications

MPC board illustrated in Figure 6.6 results in the device functioning as a terminal emulator since it connects a PC to a control unit which, in this particular instance, is the vendor's DCP/88 product. When the MPC board is used to connect a personal computer directly to the communications controller, it functions as a combined control unit and terminal emulator. This is because all terminals in a 3270 network must be connected via control units to the mainframe or to the communications controller. Thus, a single personal computer at a remote location must appear to the communications controller as a terminal connected to a control unit. Although a multiline protocol converter operating as a control unit emulator is an economical method to link a number of collocated PCs onto a common line to the mainframe, the economics of this approach may deteriorate under different network topologies. One example of a network topology that may be economically unsuitable for control-unit emulation is illustrated in Figure 6.8. Here a remote office has an existing 3274 control unit connected to several IBM- or plug-compatible display stations and one IBM PC. To utilize a protocol converter that functions as a control-unit emulator requires the installation of a separate communications line between the mainframe and the remote office as well as an additional pair of modems. In addition, another port on the communications controller is required to support the additional line, further increasing the cost of linking the PC to the corporate mainframe in this type of situation.

Terminal emulation

A terminal emulator permits the economical attachment of PCs to control units. Terminal emulation can be accomplished in several ways. First, one can obtain a protocol converter that functions as a terminal emulator. This type of device is connected between the personal computer and the control

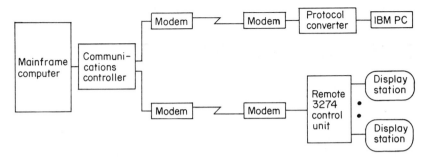

Figure 6.8 Controller Emulation may not be Cost Effective

When a controller emulator requires the installation of a separate line and an additional pair of modems there are probably other methods that are more cost effective to consider

unit, making the PC appear as a 3278 type terminal to the control unit. The protocol converter illustrated in Figure 6.9 is a stand-alone device which is connected to the personal computer on one end and cabled to the control unit on the other end.

A second and more popular type of terminal emulator is represented by a printed circuit board which is installed into one of the expansion slots of an IBM PC. The board provides the personal computer with a 3278/9 screen display, allowing the PC user to access mainframe full-screen applications. When appropriate diskette-based software is added, the PC user can transfer data to and from the mainframe.

Several third-party vendors have introduced terminal emulator products that permit a member of the IBM PC series to be connected via a coaxial cable to a local or remote control unit. These products consist of an adapter board which is inserted into the system unit of the PC and appropriate

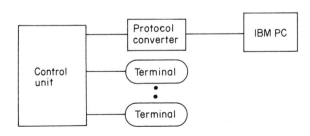

Figure 6.9 Protocol Converter Functioning as Terminal Emulator
When a protocol converter functions as a terminal emulator, PCs can be connected to both local and remote control units

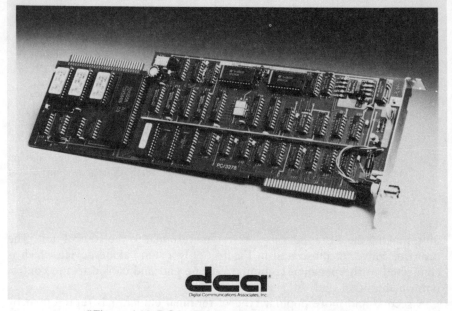

Figure 6.10 DCAs IRMA Decision Support Interface

Photograph courtesy of Digital Communications Associates, Inc.

software that permits the PC to function as a 3278/9 type terminal. In addition, some vendors offer file-transfer utilities that permit data files on the PC to be transmitted to mainframes operating IBM VM/CMS and MVS/ TSO operating systems.

A few of the more popular terminal emulator products include Digital Communications Association's IRMA decision support interface, CXI's 3270-PC Connection, Forte Data Systems' 3270/PC package and the previously referenced Persyst MPC adapter.

DCA's IRMA

IRMA™ is a printed circuit board that is installed into system expansion slots 1–5 of an IBM PC or PC XT or expansion slots 2–8 of an IBM PC AT in the personal computer's system unit. As illustrated in the lower right portion of the photograph shown in Figure 6.10, this adapter board provides a direct coaxial cable connection to an IBM 3274 or 3276 type control unit. This board provides the PC user with access to the mainframe by emulating a 3278 or 3279 type terminal and purchasers are provided with file-transfer software that permits the PC user to upload and download files between the PC and the mainframe. Another version of IRMA, called IRMA/2 is designed for use in the micro channel bus of members of the IBM PS/2 family of personal computers.

Software supplied by DCA with their IRMA terminal emulator adapter board includes file-transfer programs to access VM/CMS and MVS/TSO host computer environments. The file-transfer program for use with a VM/CMS host environment operates with the XEDIT editor while the second file-transfer program uses the EDIT function of TSO. Due to their reliance upon the use of editor facilities, file transfers using this software are relatively slow, since after one line of data is transmitted to the mainframe the program waits for the host's editor response prior to transmitting the next line of data. Due to this several third-party vendors have introduced specialized programs that operate on the mainframe and the PC and result in a significant increase in file-transfer throughput. Recognizing the slowness of their conventional file transfer, DCA was providing users without cost two high-speed file-transfer programs that operate on mainframes running VM/CMS, MVS/SP/TSO or MVS/XA/TSO operating-system environments. These programs used in conjunction with software operating on the personal computer can result in file-transfer operations approaching a 25 000–35 000 character per minute data transfer rate.

Conventional file transfer

Prior to performing a file transfer, the PC operator uses a DCA software program called E78 (if emulating an IBM 3278 terminal) which in conjunction with the IRMA adapter board permits full-screen access to the mainframe via a control unit. Assuming that the user's host environment is MVS/TSO, after log-on the PC operator would access TSO and receive a READY prompt. Next, by pressing at the same time the two shift keys on the PC's keyboard the E78 program is exited and the user's personal computer returns to DOS. At this time, entering the command FT78T initiates the DCA file-transfer program for use with a MVS/TSO host environment.

Figure 6.11 illustrates the ease of performing file-transfer operations with the software provided with the IRMA terminal emulator adapter board. The file-transfer operation illustrated in Figure 6.11 was from the personal

```
C)ft78t
IRMA File Transfer Version 1.25T
Confirm selections prior to transfer (Y/N): Y
Transfer direction (R/S): s
Transfer binary file (Y/N): n
Display copy to CON: (Y/N): n
Local filename: ftsample.txt
Data set name: test.data
Operands [none]:
Send to data set 'TEST.DATA' from local file 'FTSAMPLE.TXT'
Ok to continue (Y/N): Y

C)
```

Figure 6.11 File Transfer to an MVS/TSO Host

computer to the mainframe. Thus, the transfer direction entered was S for send. If data were to be downloaded from the mainframe to the personal computer the letter R for receive would have been entered in response to the 'Transfer direction' prompt.

When data is sent from the PC to the mainframe all ASCII characters are translated to EBCDIC. Similarly, when data transfer occurs in the opposite direction, the code conversion is from EBCDIC to ASCII.

IRMAlink

To provide higher-speed file-transfer capability between members of the IBM PC series and mainframes running under VM/CMS, MVS/SP/TSO and MVS/XA/TSO operating-system environments Digital Communications Associates developed several high-speed file-transfer software programs. Marketed under the name IRMAlink, these programs operate on both the mainframe and personal computer in conjunction with one another, eliminating the slowness of data transfers through EDIT or XEDIT. In addition, the utilization of a menu display on one's personal computer has simplified file-transfer operations to the entry of file names, transfer type information and the keying of a function key.

Figure 6.12 illustrates the completed IRMAlink FT/TSO menus for 10- and 12-function key PC systems. After logging onto the mainframe computer and entering the TSO 'Ready' mode the operator hits the IRMA hot key (Shift + Shift) to switch back to DOS. Then, entering the command FTTSO results in the execution of the FT/TSO file-transfer program and the display of the menu illustrated in Figure 6.12 less the file name, data set name and transfer type information. After entering those three items, the PC operator can press the F1 key, which results in the PC FTTSO program invoking the IRMAlink program on the mainframe which operate together to transfer the file.

With IRMA, an IBM PC can emulate several members of the 3270 terminal family to include the 3278 Model 2A (80 × 40 character screen), the 3278 Model 3 (80 × 32 character screen), the 3278 Model 4 (80 × 43 character screen), the 3279 Model 2 (80 × 24 character screen) and the 3279 Model 3 (80 × 32 character screen). Since screens on the standard PC series consist of 80 × 25 characters, IRMA provides a vertical scrolling capability for PC users to view the larger terminal screens it emulates. When emulating the 3279 color display terminal IRMA supports seven colors.

Since IRMA supports multiple LUs, once PC users log onto their mainframe they can direct printout to their parallel or serial printer as a mainframe addressable IBM 3287 printer while continuing to perform other operations on the mainframe. Due to the fact that most conventional 3278 terminals are not connectable to printers the productivity of IRMA users requiring immediate printout should normally exceed that of conventional 3270 terminal users who must either wait for the delivery of their print jobs

255

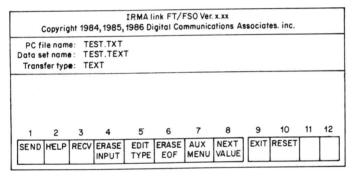

(a) Menu displayed on 10 function key PC

IRMA link FT/TSO Ver. x.xx
Copyright 1984, 1985, 1986 Digital Communications Associates. Inc.

PC file name: TEST.TXT
Data set name: TEST.TEXT
Transfer type: TEXT

Function Keys

1 SEND	2 HELP
3 RECV	4 ERS INP
5 EDIT TYPE	6 ERS EOF
7 AUX MENU	8 NXT VAL
9 EXIT	10 RESET

(b) Menu displayed on 12 function key PC

IRMA link FT/FSO Ver. x.xx
Copyright 1984, 1985, 1986 Digital Communications Associates. inc.

PC file name: TEST.TXT
Data set name: TEST.TEXT
Transfer type: TEXT

1	2	3	4	5	6	7	8	9	10	11	12
SEND	HELP	RECV	ERASE INPUT	EDIT TYPE	ERASE EOF	AUX MENU	NEXT VALUE	EXIT	RESET		

Figure 6.12 IRMAline FT/TSO File Transfer: (a) Menu displayed on 10 function key PC; (b) Menu displayed on 12 function key PC

by a member of the organization's production control staff or leave their terminal area and retrieve the print job from the data center or perhaps a remote printer located nearby.

Other valuable IRMA features include the capability to save up to nine screen images to memory for later recall or an infinite number of screens to a previously named file. Then, screens saved to a file or files can be retrieved and displayed or printed.

CXI and other products

The 3270-PC Connection from CXI Inc. is an add-in board and software which is installed in a personal computer to provide micro-to-mainframe communications by emulating an IBM 3270 PC. This product permits up to five interactive host applications to be windowed as well as one PC-DOS session and two notepads. Similar to IRMA, the 3270-PC Connection permits the use of one or more PC attached parallel or serial printers as mainframe-addressable IBM 3287 printers.

A similar product to CXI's 3270-PC Connection is Forte Data Systems' 3270/PC package, which also enables a member of the IBM PC series to emulate a 3270 PC. Since both of these products emulate a 3270 PC, the reader may be confused as to why a person would obtain a 3270 PC emulator instead of obtaining a 3270 PC. First, many persons have already obtained IBM PCs and the installation of an emulation package may permit one to obtain the same capability as a 3270 PC or perhaps some additional features without having to replace existing equipment. Another rationale for obtaining a 3270 PC emulator is economics. Usually the cost of a PC and a 3270 PC emulator can result in significant savings in comparison to obtaining an IBM 3270 PC.

To assist the reader in comparing different emulator adapter board products, Table 6.4 contains a list of selection features one may wish to consider during a procurement action. Although most entries are self-explanatory, three deserve additional elaboration.

The user-definable keyboard refers to the capability of the emulator to permit IBM PC keys or key sequences to be remapped. Although this may appear trivial at first, for installations using a number of different products to access their 3270 network this capability can reduce potential confusion of operations. As an example, some emulator products such as DCA's IRMA use the ALT-digit combination for the PF1–PF10 keys. Other

Table 6.4 3270 Emulation Adapter Selection Features

Emulator type
   Terminal emulated
   Controller emulated
Number of host sessions supported
Host printer sessions support
File transfer support
   TSO EDIT
   CMS EDIT
   CICS
   Other
User-definable keyboard
Interface data rate
Keyboard template available
PC memory requirement
Adapter board size
Hot key
Screen image saving to files
Screen image saving to memory

emulators might use the function keys for the first 10 PF keys. Thus, the ability to redefine the keyboard can enable an organization to use different vendor products in a common manner.

The adapter board size references the physical length of the board. Some half-size boards can be installed in the short slot behind the PC XT's disk drive, whereas a standard length board requires insertion into a fully available system expansion slot in the PC.

The number of host sessions supported refers to whether or not the emulator adapter can emulate a distributed-function terminal (DFT). The IBM 3278 and 3279 terminals are single host session display devices. In comparison, new IBM terminals include a DFT mode which enables up to four mainframe sessions to be executed from the remote terminal. Some adapter boards emulate a single-session terminal while other adapters emulate a DFT terminal, enabling multiple sessions to be controlled from a single PC.

Extending the connection

If personal computers are located at a distance from a control unit or a communications controller, coaxial cable cannot be used to connect the PC to the other device. Although one could use a protocol converter functioning as a control unit emulator and connect a PC via a dedicated communications link to the control unit, in certain situations PC activity in accessing the mainframe does not warrant the expenses associated with a dedicated circuit. Similarly, although one could employ a leased line to connect a PC to a communications controller, in many instances equipment that permits the PC to use the direct distance dial network may be more economically feasible than requiring the use of leased lines.

Figure 6.13 illustrates how personal computers can be interfaced to a control unit and a communications controller via the direct distance dial network or via the installation of a leased line between the PC and the device it is to be connected to, with the method employed normally governed by the anticipated activity of the PC. Thus, PCs with a low connect time would most likely be connected through the use of the direct distance dial network. At some point in time, the cost of numerous dialed calls during the month would equal the monthly cost of a leased line. At this point in time, it would be more economical to obtain a leased line to connect the PC to the communications controller or to the control unit.

For both types of communications facilities, a protocol converter is normally installed at the controller or control unit site and connected via coaxial cable to that device. These protocol converters have a serial RS-232-C interface, enabling them to be connected via a leased line or via the switched telephone network to an asynchronous ASCII device, such as a standard IBM PC. Since the protocol converter may not produce an ASCII code output compatible with an IBM PC, some third-party vendors offer a

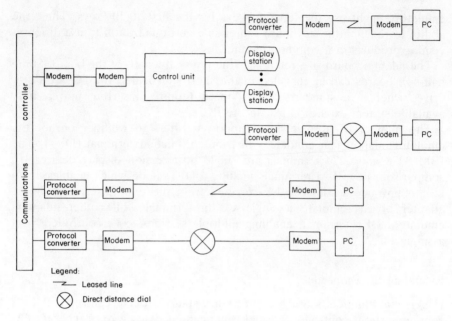

Figure 6.13 Remotely Connecting to Controllers

software program that provides the personal computer with asynchronous terminal emulation capability which, in turn, is compatible to the asynchronous terminal format supported by the protocol converter.

6.4 REMOTE JOB-ENTRY COMMUNICATIONS

In addition to making a personal computer appear to the mainframe as an interactive 3278 type terminal, there are other products that convert the PC into a remote job-entry (RJE) workstation. Products in this category result in the personal computer appearing as a 2780, 3780, 2770, 3770, or 3741 workstation and permit the PC user to communicate with the mainframe as a batch terminal. Two examples of batch terminal emulators available for use with IBM PCs are the AST-3780 from AST Research and the IRMAcom/3770 from DCA.

The AST-3780 is a hardware and software package that can be employed to enable an IBM PC to emulate common bisynchronous RJE workstations to include 2780, 3780, 2770 and 3741 devices. This package consists of an adapter board that is inserted into an expansion slot in the system unit of a PC and appropriate software that allows the PC to communicate as a bisynchronous workstation to IBM Honeywell and other mainframes that support such workstations. The components of the AST-3780 communications

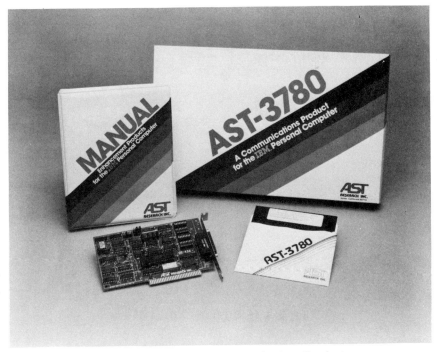

Figure 6.14 AST-3780 Communications Products

The AST-3780 Communications Product consists of an adapter board that is inserted into an expansion slot of a PC's system unit and appropriate software that enables the PC to operate as a bisynchronous workstation
Photograph courtesy of AST Research Inc.

product are illustrated in Figure 6.14. Included in the software are printer forms control functions that enable a printer attached to the PC to function as a workstation printer. Other software features included permit dynamic device selection between displays, printer and disk as well as the ability to perform text compression which is a feature of the 3780 protocol. In addition to connecting a PC to a mainframe, two PCs equipped with the AST-3780 package can communicate with one another. When connected to a mainframe, the AST-3780 package permits the PC user to interact with such mainframe packages as HASP, JES1, POWER and RES. Figure 6.15 illustrates two typical PC-equipped AST-3780 networking applications. In the top part of Figure 6.15, a PC equipped with the AST-3780 communications product functions as a remote batch workstation, connected via synchronous modems to a bisynchronous port on a mainframe computer or communications controller attached to a mainframe. In the lower part of Figure 6.15 two PCs, each with an AST-3780 Communications Product, communicate with one another similarly to the manner in which two conventional workstations would communicate with one another.

Connecting to the mainframe

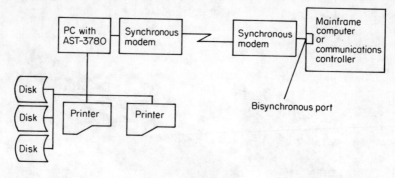

Bisynchronous port

PC to PC file transfers

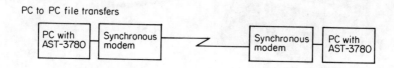

Figure 6.15 Using the AST-3780

6.5 HARDWARE ALTERNATIVES

Microcomputer/host software

Since both mainframe computers and PCs are programmable devices, hardware boxes and add-on boards may be eliminated in certain situations by using an appropriate communications software package. One such package being marketed is SIM3278 from SIMWARE of Nepean, Ontario. SIM3278/VM is a program package that can be installed on an IBM virtual mainframe (VM) and provides access to such VM applications as DMS, SPF, PROFS, XEDIT and STAIRS as well as such operating systems as OS/VS1, MVS, DOS/VSE running under CP. This program permits any ASCII terminal supported by SIM3278 to include IBM PCs to be connected to the mainframe computer via a direct cable, a leased line or via the dial-up telephone network. Once connected to a VM system, the PC user can connect to SIM3278/VM and the Control Program (CP) will initialize a logical 3270 screen which is associated with the user's terminal.

Some of the key features of SIM3278 are its multiple-session manager, on-line help facility and split-screen window-management facility. The product's multiple-session manager permits users to be logged-on to up to 12 user ids at one time, permitting the entry of a simple command to toggle the user from one session to another. As an example, users can easily switch from a CMS session to TSO or to another CMS session and so on, all without having to log-off or disconnect from the mainframe. Since the PC's keyboard differs from that of a 3278 terminal, it is often difficult to remember the PC keystrokes required to emulate a 3278 terminal function. To alleviate this problem a user of SIM3278 can type #HELP at any time to view a screen illustrating the PC keystrokes required to emulate 3278 functions. The vendor's split-screen window-management facility permits users to define up to four concurrent sessions to be displayed on their screen, providing a large portion of the power of a 3270 PC to a conventional PC or at the mainframe computer site. In such situations, one must only obtain the vendor's SIM3278/PC software for use on one's PC which is designed to operate in conjunction with the vendor's SIM3278 program that operates on the mainframe computer. Together, the two programs provide complete 3270 terminal emulation as well as file-transfer capability and printer support, representing a novel approach to linking PCs into a 3270 environment since it alleviates the procurement of specialized hardware.

Packet network facilities

Due to the extensive number of companies that have 3270 type networks, attaching PCs to those networks has become an all too familiar problem. While the previously discussed methods have been gainfully employed by many organizations, in certain instances those methods may not be economically viable to implement. For an example of a situation where the previously discussed 3270 interface strategies might be uneconomical, let us consider the following hypothetical situation.

Suppose an organization's mainframe computer is located in New York City and an existing 3270 network consists of leased lines from New York to regional offices located in Boston, Chicago, Dallas, Denver and Los Angeles. At each of the five regional offices let us further assume that a 3274 control unit is installed which services a number of conventional 3278/9 terminals located in each office. After the 3270 network was established, a large number of small area offices of the company obtained personal computers to perform local processing of data. In addition to their initial use, suppose each area office manager had a requirement for his or her personal computer to access a 3270 application program on the corporate mainframe. After studying the anticipated activity of the area offices, the corporate communications manager determined that each area office would require access to the mainframe for only approximately one hour per week. If the organization has 80 area offices and most of these offices are located at least 100 miles from a regional office, how can the personal computers be economically connected to the mainframe?

Based upon the preceding information, it would be very expensive to obtain hardware for each personal computer to make it function as a 3270 type terminal. In addition, although the one hour per week connect-time is

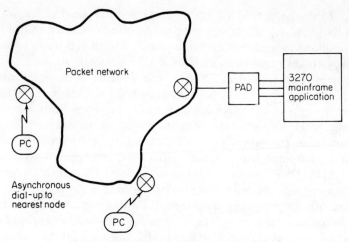

Figure 6.16 Packet Network 3270 Access

relatively low, when multiplied by 80 computers the cost of long-distance transmission over the switched telephone network would be considerable. Thus, from an economic perspective, the previously discussed hardware solutions and the microcomputer/host software method of integrating personal computers into a 3270 network might not be economically practical. To satisfy organizations with networking problems similar to this hypothetical example, several value-added carrier packet networks have implemented what is known as 3270 access.

Under the concept known as 3270 access, value-added carriers have implemented protocol conversion into the packet assembly/disassembly (PAD) computers they install at a company's mainframe location as illustrated in Figure 6.16. Under the 3270 access concept, both personal computers and conventional asynchronous terminals dial a packet network node and are then routed through the packet network to the PAD where the asynchronous data are converted into a synchronous, 3270 format. Since the packet network would have to develop a considerable amount of protocol conversion software to support the large number of different types of personal computers produced by various manufacturers, most packet networks support one or at most only a few asynchronous protocols which are then converted to emulate a 3270 type terminal by the PAD. As an example of this, Tymnet permits only VT-100 operating terminals and personal computers using VT–100 emulators to be converted into a 3270 protocol. This means that PC users must obtain a VT-100 emulator program for use on their PC if they desire to use Tymnet's 3270 access facility.

A significant extension to the 3270 access concept occurred in late 1986 with the introduction of X.25 communications adapter boards for use in the IBM PC and compatible computers. The installation of an X.25 board,

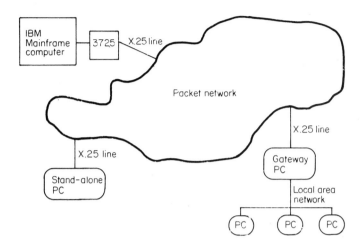

Figure 6.17 Expanding 3270 Access Methods

Through the installaion of an X.25 adapter board and appropriate software a PC can communicate with a mainframe directly via a packet network as well as serve as a gateway to the mainframe for other personal computers on a local area network.

marketed by Western Digital and Eicon Technology Corporation, and use of appropriate software enables a personal computer to directly access a mainframe computer via a packet network. As illustrated in the lower left portion of Figure 6.17, PCs equipped with an X.25 adapter board can communicate with a mainframe, such as an IBM 33XX or 43XX series computer without requiring the use of a PAD. In this instance it is assumed that an IBM 3725 communications controller has one or more X.25 lines connected to the packet network.

Taking the utilization of X.25 technology further, Eicon Technology Corporation developed an adapter board and software that can be used in a PC to obtain a local area network gateway to a remotely located mainframe via a packet network. This concept is illustrated in the lower right portion of Figure 6.17.

When an X.25 adapter is used in a personal computer, the packet network is no longer required to perform protocol conversion. Thus, although users still incur a data transportation charge based upon session duration and the quantity of characters of packets transported, the monthly cost associated with the use of a PAD is eliminated.

CHAPTER SEVEN

Local Area Networks

Although local area networks (LANs) are probably discussed more frequently in trade magazines, seminars and exhibitions than most other communications-related topics, until recently their level of utilization was far below their level of discussion. Now, this is rapidly changing due to the tremendous growth in the use of personal computers in business, factories and on college campuses.

One of the limiting factors of personal computers is the primary use of such devices as isolated workstations. This means that in most organizations it is difficult for personal computer users to share data and the use of peripheral devices, since such sharing normally requires physical activity to occur. Both the direct economical benefits of sharing data and the use of peripheral devices as well as productivity gains resulting from the integration of personal computers into a common network have contributed to an increasing demand for local area network products which is the focus of this chapter.

In this chapter, we will first examine the major benefits derived from the utilization of local area networks and their relationship to typical network applications. Next, we will look at the major areas of local area network technology and the effect these areas have upon the efficiency and operational capability of such networks. Here, our examination will focus upon network topology, transmission media and the major access methods employed in LANs. Using the previous material as a base, we will then briefly look at what is known as the IEEE 802 series of LAN standards and then examine several local area networks designed for utilization by personal computer systems.

7.1 UTILIZATION BENEFITS

In its simplest form a local area network can be considered as a cable that provides an electronic highway for the transportation of information to and from different devices connected to the network. By providing the capability to route data between different devices connected to a common network numerous benefits may accrue to individual personal computer users that may not be available to single user systems. Such benefits can include the ability for sharing peripherals, common access to data files and programs, equipment compatibility, dispersion of equipment and an increase in the probability of access to data.

Peripheral sharing

Even the largest organization cannot afford to purchase fully configured personal computer systems to include large-capacity disk drives, laser printers, plotters and other peripheral devices whose utilization may only be required a small portion of the time a PC system is in operation. Linking personal computers into a local area network makes each PC into a workstation on the net, with the capability to share access to other devices connected to the network. Thus, users of the LAN can obtain access to resources that would probably be too expensive to justify for individual computer systems.

Common access

Normally, most software sold for use on personal computers contains a license agreement commonly referred to as a 'shrink-wrapped' license due to its inclusion in the software package which is wrapped in a cellophane type covering. The typical terms of such licences state that the software is licensed for use on one computer system. This means that an office with 50 personal computers would theoretically require 50 spreadsheet programs, 50 database management programs and so on, if each PC user required access to a common set of programs. Because of the typical terms in a software license agreement, it would be illegal to place one version of a program in the network and have each personal computer user access it as required. However, recognizing the proliferation of local area networks, many software vendors have implemented multi-user versions of their products that are designed for operation on local area networks. In addition to being less costly than obtaining multiple copies of individual programs, these programs are normally rewritten to support concurrent operation. This means, as an example, that one user concurrently using a database program to access a common file already being modified by a second user would be temporarily denied the ability to change a record or field within a record until the second user completed his or her activity. Thus, in addition to providing common access to programs, a local area network may permit the sharing of data files as well as insuring the integrity of data on those files.

Equipment compatibility

Unfortunately, no known LAN can take a program written for one manufacturer's personal computer and convert it to operate on a personal computer manufactured by a different vendor when the two devices are incompatible. Thus, even though one might be able to transfer a BASIC language program written to operate on an IBM PC through a local area network to an Apple II computer connected to that network, the probability of the program operating on the Apple personal computer without modification would be minimal. What the LAN does provide is a common interface between different types of equipment produced by the same manufacturer or by different manufacturers which permits users to share common peripherals, including storage devices and printers. Thus, the LAN can free the organization to a degree from dependence upon any single vendor as well as provide a mechanism to integrate the utilization of peripheral devices that can be shared by many users. In addition, certain software products may enable a larger degree of equipment compatibility if they generate a standardized format data file. In such situations, an Apple II user would then be able to use a local area network to access a spreadsheet model previously created on an IBM PC. Assuming an Apple II version of the spreadsheet program is available, the Apple II user could then use that version of the program with the IBM PC model previously saved onto a common storage area of the network.

Distribution of hardware

Prior to the advent of personal computers, most large organizations centralized the physical location of terminals used to access the mainframe into 'terminal rooms'. Typically, such terminal rooms contained a number of cubicles, where a terminal and printer were located on a desk. Members of the organization would either contend for access to a terminal with other members of the organization or place their names on a chart to reserve a particular period of time.

In the early 1980s, the initial entry of personal computers into organizations was often financially disguised as the purchase of office equipment, calculators and the like by office managers attempting to bypass the firm's data-processing department. These desktop micros were usually placed in a convenient physical location near the user. As the utilization of personal computers proliferated, many organizations implemented policies concerning the acquisition and utilization of PCs. Since some users required a personal computer only to develop and exercise spreadsheet models while other users desired to prepare formal reports or access information utilities, the cost of providing individually tailored hardware systems for each user became prohibitive. This caused many organizations to revert to the 'terminal room' concept, locating groups of personal computers in a confined area.

Through the use of a local area network, it becomes economically feasible to distribute personal computers to the most convenient physical locations within a facility while retaining the shared use of expensive peripheral devices. Thus, the local area network can promote the placement of personal computers near the source of the end-user's physical workspace or application area.

Reliability of data access

One of the major advantages of implementing a local area network is the distributed processing environment it provides to users. This means users may be able to access applications independent of the operating status of any particualr personal computer. In addition, if applications are located on the network the failure of a mainframe computer will not lock out the user from access to his or her application.

Common gateway

When one personal computer is used as a common gateway to a mainframe computer other PCs on the network can obtain access through the gateway to the mainframe. Through the use of a gateway, a number of economical communications networking strategies can be considered to connect LANs to remotely located or collocated mainframes. As an example, one personal computer on the LAN could be connected via a leased line to a remotely located mainframe. If the transmission requirements of the personal computers on the LAN for access to the mainframe do not justify the use of leased lines alternative access methods to include asynchronous dial-up to the mainframe via the PSTN or a packet network could be considered. In addition, if the communications controller connected to the mainframe supports X.25, the installation of an X.25 adapter board in the gateway personal computer will permit access to the mainframe via a packet network without the use of a PAD.

7.2 LAN DISADVANTAGES

Although the benefits that can be obtained through the use of a LAN are considerable, as with most technologies there are certain problems and costs that must be considered prior to implementing the technology. Among the potential problem areas associated with LANs are cabling, software support, resources required to implement a LAN and the incompatibility of many hardware and software products.

LANs which use coaxial cable can be very expensive to install, especially if a new conduit must be constructed if an existing conduit is filled to its maximum capacity. Concerning software support, most local area networks contain hardware and software products from many vendors. This can require the user to contact the network hardware, network software and the application software vendors when an application is not working correctly.

The resources required to implement a local area network can be considerable with respect to both economics and effort. In addition to the user having to evaluate and select a system based upon a prior development of system requirements, most LANs with 20 or more stations will require a system administrator to control and coordinate usage. Finally, due to the rapid evolution of LAN products, it is quite common for certain hardware products to be incompatible with some LAN software products marketed by the same vendor. Although this incompatibility within a vendor's product line is the exception rather than the rule, such incompatibility becomes far more pronounced when hardware and software products are obtained from many vendors. Due to this, existing and potential LAN users must carefully evaluate products with respect to their compatibility.

7.3 TECHNOLOGICAL CHARACTERISTICS

Although a local area network by nature is a limited distance transmission system, the variety of vendor product offerings is anything but limited. Products currently marketed as well as expected offerings run the gamut with respect to their functionality, operation, application support and hardware and software requirements. In this section, we will examine the technological characteristics of local area networks to include their topologies, transmission media, the access method used to transmit data on the network and the hardware and software required to make the network operate. In addition, because of the communications connectivity offered by the IBM cabling system we will examine its features after discussing the different types of media used in local area networks.

Topology

The topology of a local area network means the structure or geometric layout of the cable used to interconnect stations on the net. Unlike conventional data communications networks that can be configured in a variety of ways by the addition of hardware and software, most local area networks are designed to operate based upon the interconnection of stations that follow a specific topology. The most common topologies used in LANs include the bus, the ring and the star as illustrated in Figure 7.1.

In a bus topology structure, a cable is usually laid out as one long branch onto which branches are used to interconnect each station on the net to the main data highway. Although this type of structure permits any station on the net to talk to another station, rules are required to govern the action necessary to recover from situations such as when two stations attempt to communicate at the same time. Later in this chapter, we will examine the relationship between the network topology, the method employed to access the network and the transmission medium employed in building the network.

In a ring topology, a single cable that forms the main data highway is shaped into a ring. Similar to the bus topology, branches are used to interconnect stations to one another via the ring. Thus, a ring topology can be considered to be a looped bus. Typically, the access method employed in a ring topology requires data to circulate around the ring, with a special set of rules governing when each station connection to the network can transmit data.

The third major local area network topology is the star structure illustrated in the lower portion of Figure 7.1. In a star network, each station on the net is connected to a network controller. Then, access from any one station on the net to another station can be accomplished through the network controller. Here the network controller can be viewed as functioning similarly to a telephone switchboard, since access from one station to another station on the net can occur only through the central device.

Some networks, from a topology perspective, are a mixture of topologies. As an example, the IBM Token-Ring Network can actually be considered to be a 'star-ring' topology, since up to eight personal computers are first connected to a common device known as a multistation access unit or MAU, which in turn is connected in a ring topology to other MAUs. Later in this chapter, we will examine the IBM Token-Ring Network in detail.

Although there is a close relationship between the topology of the network, its transmission media, and the method used to access the net, we can examine topology as a separate entity and make several generalized observations. First, in a star network the failure of the network controller will render the entire network inoperative. This results from the fact that

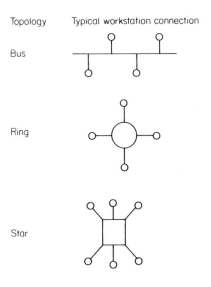

Figure 7.1 LAN Topology

The three most common geometric layouts of local area network cabling form a bus, ring or star structure.

all data flow on the network must pass through the network controller. On the positive side, the star topology is normally in existence within most buildings in the form of telephone wires that are routed to a switchboard. This means that a local area network that can use in-place twisted-pair telephone wires is normally simple to implement and usually very economical.

In a ring network, the failure of any node connected to the ring normally inhibits data flow around the ring. Due to the fact that data travels in a circular path on a ring network, any cable break has the same effect as the failure of the network controller in a star-structured network. Since each network station is connected to the next network station, it is usually easier to install the cable for a ring network. In comparison, if existing telephone wires are not available one would have to cable each station in a star network to the network controller, which could result in the installation of very long cable runs.

In a bus-structured network, data is normally transmitted from one station to all stations located on the network, with a destination address appended to each transmitted data block. As part of the access protocol only the station with the destination address in the transmitted data block will respond to the data. This transmission concept means that a break in the bus may affect only network stations on one side of the break that wish to communicate with stations on the other side of the break. Thus, unless a network station functioning as the primary network storage device becomes inoperative, a failure in a bus-structured network is usually less serious than if a failure occurs in a ring network.

Transmission medium

The transmission medium used in a local area network can range in scope from 'twisted-pair' wire, such as is used in conventional telephone lines, to coaxial cable, fiber-optic cable, and the atmosphere, which is used by some esoteric transmission schemes, including FM radio. Each transmission medium has a number of advantages and disadvantages associated with its use in comparison to other media. The primary differences between media concern their cost and ease of installation, the bandwidth of the cable, which may permit only one or several transmission sessions to occur simultaneously, the maximum speed of communications permitted, and the geographic scope of the network that the medium supports.

Twisted-pair wire

In addition to being inexpensive, twisted-pair wire is very easy to install. Normally, a screwdriver and perhaps a pocket knife are the only tools required for its installation. Anyone who has hooked up a pair of speakers to a stereo set normally has the ability to install this transmission medium. Although inexpensive and easy to install, twisted-pair wire is very susceptible to noise generated by fluorescent light ballasts and electrical machinery. This noise can affect the error rate of data transmitted on the network, although the utilization of lead-shielded twisted-pair cable can be employed to provide the cable with a high degree of immunity to line noise.

Since the bandwidth of twisted-pair cable is considerably less than coaxial or fiber-optic cable, normally only one signal is transmitted on this cable at any point in time. This signaling technique is known as baseband signaling and should be compared to the broadband signaling capability of coaxial and fiber-optic cable. Broadband signaling permits a cable to be subdivided by its frequency bandwidth into many individual subchannels, with each subchannel permitting an independent communications session to occur simultaneously with other sessions transpiring on other subchannels. Figure 7.2 illustrates the difference between baseband and broadband signaling. It should be noted that although a twisted-pair wire system can be used to transmit both voice and data, the data transmission is baseband since only one channel is normally used for data. In comparison, a broadband system on coaxial cable can be designed to carry voice and several subchannels of data as well as facsimile and video transmission. Another constraint of twisted-wire is the rate at which data can flow on the net and the distance it can flow. Although data rates up to 4 megabits (mbps) can be achieved, normally local area networks employing twisted-pair wiring operate at a lower data rate. In addition, twisted-pair systems normally cover a limited distance measured in terms of thousands of feet while a coaxial-based system may be limited in terms of miles.

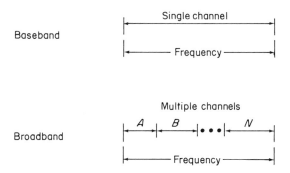

Figure 7.2 Baseband versus Broadband Signaling

In baseband signaling the entire frequency bandwidth is used for one channel. In comparison, in broadband signaling the channel is subdivided by frequency in many subchannels.

Coaxial cable

Coaxial cable consists of a central conducting copper wire covered by an insulator known as a dielectric. An overlapping woven copper mesh surrounds the dielectric and the mesh, in turn, is covered by a protective jacket which can consist of polyethylene or aluminium. Figure 7.3 illustrates the composition of a typical coaxial cable; however, it should be noted that over one hundred types of coaxial cable are currently marketed. The key differences between such cables involve the number of conductors contained in the cable, the dielectric employed and the type of protective jacket and material used to provide strength to the cable to allow it to be pulled through conduits without breaking.

Two basic types of coaxial cable are used in local area networks, with the type of cable based upon the transmission technique employed – baseband or broadband signaling. Both cable types are much more expensive than twisted-pair wire; however, the greater frequency bandwidth of coaxial cable permits higher data rates than one can obtain over twisted-pair wire.

Hardware interface

A coaxial cable with a polyethylene jacket is normally used for baseband signaling. Data is transmitted from stations on the network to the baseband cable in a digital format and the connection from each station to the cable is accomplished by the use of a simple coaxial T-connector. Figure 7.4 illustrates the hardware interface to a coaxial cable of a typical baseband local area network. Here the network adapter card is a hardware device that contains the logic to control network access and is inserted into one of the expansion slots in the system unit of an IBM PC. At the rear of the

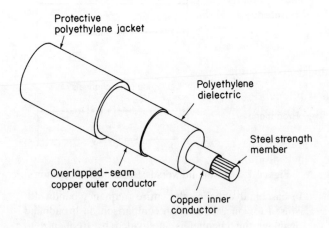

Protective polyethylene jacket

Polyethylene dielectric

Steel strength member

Overlapped–seam copper outer conductor

Copper inner conductor

Figure 7.3 Coaxial Cable

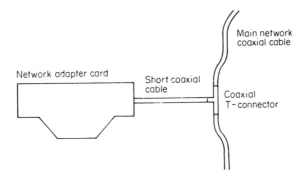

Figure 7.4 Hardware Interface to Coaxial Cable

The network adapter card is installed in the system
unit of the PC and connected to the main coaxial cable
of the network via a short coaxial cable interfaced to
a T-Connector.

computer's system unit a short section of coaxial cable is used to connect
the network adapter card to the baseband cable via a T-connector.

Since data on a baseband network travels in a digital form, those signals
can be easily regenerated by the use of a device known as a line driver or
data regenerator. The line driver or data regenerator is a low-cost device
that is constructed to look for a pulse rise and, upon detecting the occurrence
of the rise, to disregard the entire pulse and regenerate an entirely new
pulse. Thus, one can install low-cost line drives into a baseband coaxial
network to extend the distance over which transmission can occur on the
cable. Typically, a coaxial cable baseband system can cover an area of
several miles and may contain hundreds to thousands of stations on the
network.

Broadband coaxial cable

To obtain independent subchannels derived by frequency on coaxial cable
broadband transmission requires a method to translate the digital signals
from PCs and other workstations into appropriate frequencies. This
translation process is accomplished by the use of radio-frequency (RF)
modems which modulate the digital data into analog signals and convert or
demodulate received analog signals into digital signals. Since signals are
transmitted at one frequency and received at a different frequency, a 'head
end' or frequency translator is also required for broadband transmission on
coaxial cable. This device is also known as a remodulator as it simply
converts the signals from one subchannel to another subchannel.

The requirement for modems and frequency translators normally makes broadband transmission more expensive than baseband. Although the ability of broadband to support multiple channels provides it with an aggregate data transmission capacity that exceeds baseband, in general, baseband transmission permits a higher per-channel data flow. While this is an important consideration for mainframe-to-mainframe communications when massive amounts of data must be moved, for most personal computer file-transfer operations the speed of either baseband or broadband transmission should be sufficient. This fact may be better understood by comparing the typical transmission rates obtainable on baseband and broadband networks to drive a high-speed dot-matrix printer, and the differences between the time required to transmit data on the network and the time required to print the data.

Typical transmission speeds on baseband and broadband networks range from 2 to 10 mbps. In comparison, a high-speed dot-matrix printer operating at 120 cps would require approximately 200 seconds to print one second's worth of data transmitted at 2 mbps and 1000 seconds to print one second's worth of data transmitted at 10 mbps.

Fiber-optic cable

Fiber-optic cable is a transmission medium for light energy and as such provides a very high bandwidth, permitting data rates ranging up to billions of bits per second. The fiber-optic cable consists of a thin core of glass or plastic which is surrounded by a protective shield. Several shielded fibers in turn are bundled in a jacket with a central member of aluminum or steel employed for tensile strength.

Digital data represented by electrical energy must be converted into light energy for transmission on a fiber-optic cable. This is normally accomplished by a low-power laser or through the use of a light emitting diode and appropriate circuitry. At the receiver, light energy must be reconverted into electrical energy. Normally, a device known as a photo detector, as well as appropriate circuitry to regenerate the digital pulses and an amplifier, are used to convert the received light energy into its original digital format.

In addition to the high bandwidth of fiber-optic cables, they offer users several additional advantages in comparison to conventional transmission media. Since data travels in the form of light, it is immune to electrical interference, and building codes that may require expensive conduits to be installed for conventional cables are usually unnecessary. Similarly, fiber-optic cable can be installed through areas where the flow of electricity could be dangerous, since only light flows through such cables.

Since each fiber only provides a single, unidirectional transmission path, a minimum of two cables is required to connect all transmitters to all receivers on a network built using fiber-optic cable. Due to the higher cost of fiber-optic cable than coaxial or twisted-pair, the dual cable requirement of fiber cables makes them very expensive. In addition, it is very difficult to splice such cable, which usually means sophisticated equipment and skilled installers are required to implement a fiber-optic-based network. Similarly, once this type of network is installed, it is difficult to modify the network. Currently, the cost of the cable, difficulty of installation and modification make the utilization of fiber-optic-based local area networks impractical for many commercial applications. With the cost of the fiber-optic cable declining and improvements expected to simplify the installation and modification of networks using this type of cable, the next few years may witness a profound movement toward the utilization of this transmission medium.

IBM cabling system

The IBM Cabling System was introduced in 1984 as a mechanism to support the networking requirements of office environments. By defining standards for cables, connectors, faceplates, distribution panels and other facilities, IBM's cabling system is designed to support the interconnection of personal computers, conventional terminals, mainframe computers and office systems. In addition, this system permits devices to be moved from one location to another or added to a network through a simple connection to the cabling system's wall plates or surface mounts.

Cable Types

The IBM cabling system specifies seven different cabling categories. Depending upon the type of cable selected one can install the selected wiring indoors, outdoors, under a carpet or in ducts and other air spaces.

The IBM cabling system uses wire which conforms to the American Wire Gauge or AWG. AWG is a unit of measurement with respect to the wire diameter. As the wire diameter gets larger the AWG number decreases, in effect resulting in an inverse relationship between wire diameter and AWG. The IBM cabling system uses wire between 22 AWG (0.644 mm) and 26 AWG (0.405 mm). Since a larger diameter wire has less resistance to current flow than a smaller wire diameter a smaller AWG permits cabling distances to be extended in comparison to a higher AWG cable.

Type 1　The IBM Cabling System Type 1 cable contains two twisted pairs of 22 AWG conductors. Each pair is shielded with a foil wrapping and both pairs are surrounded by an outer braided shield. Type 1 cable provides the largest cable distance and is available in two different designs – plenum and nonplenum. Plenum cable can be installed without the use of a conduit while nonplenum cable requires a conduit.

Type 2　Type 2 cable is actually Type 1 cable with the addition of four pairs of 22 AWG conductors for telephone usage. Due to this, Type 1 cable is also referred to as data-grade twisted-pair cable while Type 2 cable is known as two data-grade and four voice-grade twisted pair. Due to its voice capability, Type 2 cable can support PBX interconnections. Like Type 1 cable, Type 2 cable supports plenum and nonplenum designs.

Type 3 Type 3 cable is conventional twisted pair, telephone wire. Both 22 AWG and 24 AWG conductors are supported by this cable type. One common use of Type 3 cable is to connect PCs to MAUs in a token-ring network.

Type 5 Type 5 is fiber-optic cable. Two 100/140 μm optical fibers are contained in a Type 5 cable. This cable is suitable for indoor, nonplenum installation or outdoor aerial installation. Due to the extended transmission distance obtainable with fiber-optic cable Type 5 cable is used in conjunction with the IBM 8219 token-ring network optical fiber repeater to interconnect two MAUs up to 6600 feet (2 kilometers) from one another.

Type 6 Type 6 cable contains two twisted pairs of 26 AWG conductors for data communications. It is available for nonplenum applications only and its smaller diameter than Type 1 cable makes it slightly more flexible.

Type 8 Type 8 cable is designed for installation under a carpet. This cable contains two individually shielded, parallel pairs of 26 AWG conductors.

Type 9 Type 9 cable is essentially a low-cost version of Type 1 cable. Like Type 1, Type 9 cable consists of two twisted pairs of data cable; however, 26 AWG conductors are used in place of the 22 AWG wire used in Type 1 cable. As a result of the use of a smaller-diameter cable, transmission distances on Type 9 cable are approximately two-thirds that obtainable through the use of Type 1 cable.

Connectors

The IBM cabling system includes connectors for terminating both data and voice conductors. The data connector has a uniquely design based upon the development of a latching mechanism which permits it to mate with another, identical connector.

Figure 7.5 illustrates the IBM cabling system data connector. Its design makes it self-shorting when disconnected from another connector. This provides a token-ring network with electrical continuity when a station is disconnected. Unfortunately, the data connector is very expensive in comparison to an RS-32 connector with the typical retail price of the data connector between $8 and $10, whereas RS-32 connectors cost approximately $3.

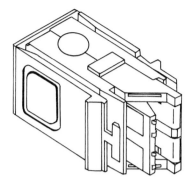

Figure 7.5 Cabling System Data Connector

Due to the high cost of data connectors and cable the acceptance of the IBM cabling system by end users has been slow to materialize. Since it provides a standard system of office interconnectivity its usage may significantly increase if it becomes more economical in comparison to the cost of conventional connectors and cable.

Access Method

If the topology of a local area network can be compared to a data highway, then the access method might be viewed as the set of rules that enable data from one workstation to successfully reach its destination via the data highway. Without such rules, it is quite possible for two messages sent to the same or a different address by two different workstations to collide, with the result that neither message reaches its destination.

Prior to discussing how access methods work, let us first examine the two basic types of devices that can be attached to a local area network to gain an appreciation for the work the access method must accomplish.

Listeners and Talkers

We can categorize the operating mode of each device as being a 'listener' or a 'talker'. Some devices, like printers, only receive data and thus operate only as a listener. Other devices, such as personal computers, can either transmit or receive data and are capable of operating in both modes. In a baseband signaling environment where only one channel exists or on an individual channel on a broadband system, if several talkers wish to communicate at the same time a collision will occur unless a scheme is employed that defines when each device can talk and, in the event of a collision, what events must transpire to avoid its recurrence.

For data to correctly reach its destination, each listener must have a unique address and its network equipment must be designed to respond to a message on the net only when it recognizes its address. Thus, the primary goals in the design of an access method are to minimize the potential for data collision and provide a mechanism for corrective action when data collides as well as to insure that an addressing scheme is employed to enable messages to reach their destination.

The three access methods primarily employed in PC based local area networks are carrier-sense multiple access/collision detection (CSMA/CD), carrier-sense multiple access/collision avoidance (CSMA/CA) and token passing. Each of these access methods is uniquely structured to address the previously mentioned collision and data destination problems.

CSMA/CD

Carrier-Sense Multiple Access with Collision Detection can be categorized as a 'listen' then 'send' access method. CSMA/CD is one of the earliest developed access techniques and is the technique used in Ethernet, which is the Xerox Corporation developed local area network whose technology has been licensed to many companies.

Under the CSMA/CD concept, when a station has data to send it first listens to determine if any other station on the network is talking. If the channel is busy, the station will wait until it becomes idle prior to transmitting data. Since it is possible for two stations to listen at the same time and discover an idle channel, it is also possible that the two stations could then transmit at the same time. When this situation arises, a collision will occur. Upon sensing that a collision has occurred, a delay scheme will be employed to prevent a repetition of the collision. Typically, each station will use either a randomly generated or predefined time-out period prior to attempting to retransmit the messages that previously collided. Since this access method requires hardware capable of detecting the occurrence of a collision, it is usually more expensive than the hardware required for other access methods.

The CSMA/CD access method is commonly used on baseband and broadband coaxial cable based networks. Although there are several versions of CSMA/CD marketed, by far the most common version is based upon licensed technology from Xerox Corporation, with over 50 vendors developing products based upon the vendor's Ethernet specifications. In an Ethernet network, data is packetized, with packets ranging in size from 64 to 1518 bytes. Figure 7.6 illustrates the Ethernet packet format. Ethernet uses 8-bit bytes for transmission, with each packet containing an 8-byte preamble for synchronization consisting of a sequence of 64 bits of alternating ones and zeros, followed by two 6-byte addresses, the first representing the packet's destination while the second address identifies the originator of the packet. The 16-bit type field specifies how the data is to be interpreted and is similar to the control field employed in the SDLC protocol. By appropriate coding in the type field the packet message will be denoted to contain supervisory data or information. The data field is byte oriented and is represented by '8*n*' in Figure 7.6 which means it comprises one 8-bit byte times *n* bytes. The cyclic redundancy check (CRC) covers the destination through the data field and provides the error-detection and correction mechanism to insure data reaches its destination correctly.

The CSMA/CD access technique is best suited for networks with intermittent transmission, since an increase in traffic volume causes a corresponding increase in the probability of the cable being occupied when a station wishes to talk. In addition, as traffic volume builds under CSMA/CD throughput may decline, since there will be longer waits to gain access to the net as well as additional time-outs required to resolve collisions that occur.

CSMA/CA   Carrier-sense multiple access with collision avoidance represents a modified version of the CSMA/CD access technique. Under the CSMA/CA access technique, each of the hardware devices attached to the talkers on the network estimates when a collision is likely to occur and avoids transmission during those times. Since this technique eliminates the requirement for collision-detection hardware, the cost of hardware to implement this access technique is usually less than CSMA/CD hardware. In addition, CSMA/CA eliminates vendors having to pay the licensing fees of Ethernet, which may be passed onto the end-user in the form of lower prices.

Token passing   In a token passing access method, each time the network is turned on a token is generated. Consisting of a unique bit pattern, the token travels the length of the network, either around a ring or along the

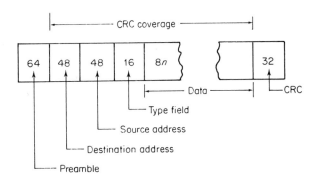

Figure 7.6 Ethernet Packet Format

On an Ethernet network data is packetized, with packets ranging in size from 64 to 1518 bytes

length of a bus. When a station on the network has data to transmit it must first seize a free token. The token is then transformed to indicate it is in use and is then appended to a packet of information being transmitted from one station to another. During the time the token is in use the other stations on the network remain idle, elminating the possibility of collisions occurring. Once the transmission is completed the token is converted back into its original form and becomes available for use by the next station on the network. Since a station on the network can only transmit when it has a free token, token passing eliminates the requirement for collision detection hardware. This means that the cost of a token passing network is usually less than an equivalent CSMA/CD network. Due to the dependence of the network upon the token, the loss of a station can bring the entire network down. To avoid this, several vendors have included special backup circuitry in their hardware, although this has reduced the difference in price between token passing and CSMA/CD networks.

Due to the variety of transmission media, network structures and access methods, there is no one best network for all users. Table 7.1 should be used by the reader to obtain a generalized comparison of the advantages and disadvantages of the technical characteristics of local area networks, using the transmission medium as a frame of reference. Table 7.2 compares the technical characteristics of seven popularly used local area networks.

Table 7.1 LAN Technical Characteristic Comparison

| Characteristic | Transmission medium | | |
	Twisted-pair wire	Baseband coaxial cable	Broadband coaxial cable
Topology	Bus, star or ring	Bus or ring	Bus or ring
Channels	Single channel	Single channel	Multichannel
Data rate	Up to 2 mbps	2–10 mbps	Up to 400 mbps
Maximum nodes on net	Usually < 255	Usually < 1024	Several thousand
Geographical coverage	In thousands of feet	In miles	In tens of miles
Major advantages	Low cost, may be able to use existing wiring	Low cost, simple to install	Supports voice, data, video applications simultaneously
Major disadvantages	Limited bandwidth, requires conduits, low immunity to noise	Low immunity to noise	High cost, difficult to install, requires RF modems and headend

Table 7.2 Technical Characteristic of Representative Networks

Vendor	Network	Transmission medium	Data rate (mbps)	Access method	Signal type
AST Research	PC Net	Twisted wire	0.8	CSMA/CD	Baseband
AT&T	StarLAN	Twisted wire	1.0	CSMA/CD	Baseband
IBM	Cluster	Coaxial cable	0.375	CSMA/CD	Baseband
IBM	PC network	Coaxial cable	2.0	CSMA/CD	Broadband
IBM	Token-ring	Twisted wire, fiber optic	4.0	Token	Baseband
Xerox	Ethernet	Coaxial cable	10.0	CSMA/CD	Baseband
3COM	Ethershare	Coaxial cable	10.0	CSMA/CD	Baseband

7.4 HARDWARE AND SOFTWARE REQUIREMENTS

Besides cable and connectors, the installation of a local area network requires a variety of hardware and software products. As a minimum, each PC on the network normally requires the installation of an interface card into its system unit. This interface card contains a number of ROM modules and specialized circuitry as well as a microprocessor that implements the access method or protocol used to communicate on the common cable. Figure 7.7 illustrates the network adapter card used in the IBM broadband local area network, more commonly referred to as PC Net, and the coaxial cable that attaches to the adapter.

In some local area networks, one personal computer must be reserved to process the network commands and functions. Since it services these commands and functions, it is normally called the network server. A combination of specialized software that overlays the normal disk operating system (DOS) on each personal computer connected to the network as well as software placed upon the server governs the operation of the network. To understand the role of the network server and the functions of LAN software, let us first review how a personal computer operates under a conventional version of DOS.

PC-DOS is a single-user operating system that is designed to provide access to peripherals attached to the system as well as control of those peripherals, the interpretation of commands to perform various funnctions on the system, management of disk storage and memory. Under DOS, your

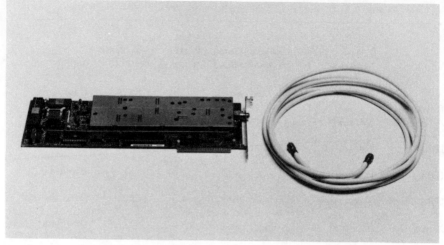

Figure 7.7 IBM Local Area Network Adapter Card

Photograph courtesy of IBM Corporation

keyboard is the standard input device and your display is the standard output device, with the control of the personal computer limited to one user.

As soon as a personal computer connected into a network is initialized, its network software routines are added to DOS, permitting the computer to interact with the rest of the network. Prior to the introduction of DOS version 3.1, this software was normally an overlay to DOS that served to filter commands. Thus, when a command was issued to perform a function on the PC the software overlay permitted the command to pass directly to DOS for execution. If a command is issued that references the network, the software overlay intercepts or filters the command from reaching DOS and in conjunction with the adapter board transmits the command onto the network. If the network is server based, the non-local commands must be sent to a server for processing. The left-hand portion of Figure 7.8 illustrates the hardware and software components required when LAN software is designed as an overlay to DOS.

Prior to the introduction of DOS 3.1, most LAN vendors either developed proprietary methods to lock files and records or ignored incorporating such features, in effect limiting their networks to simple file-swapping and printer-sharing applications. Since there was no Network Basic Input/Output System (NETBIOS), a proprietary network BIOS was developed and accessed via the vendor's LAN overlay software to send and receive data from the LAN adapter card. Here NETBIOS is the lowest level of software on a local area network, translating commands to send and receive data via the adapter

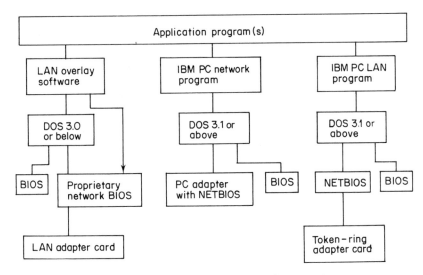

Figure 7.8 Potential PC LAN Hardware and
Software Relationships

card into the instructions in assembly language that actually perform the
requested functions.

With the introduction of the IBM PC Network in August 1984 IBM
released all three components required to implement an IBM local area
network using IBM equipment – the IBM PC Network Program, PC DOS
3.1 and the IBM PC Network Adapter. The IBM PC Network Program
was actually a tailored version of Microsoft Corporation's Microsoft Networks
(MS-NET) software which is essentially a program that overlays DOS and
permits workstations on a network to share their disks and peripheral
devices. DOS 3.1, also developed by Microsoft, added file and record-
locking capabilities to DOS, permitting multiple users to access and modify
data. Without file and record-locking capability in DOS custom software
was required to obtain these functions, since their absence would result in
the last person saving data onto a file overwriting changes made by other
persons to the file. Thus, DOS 3.1 provided networking and application
programmers with a set of standards they could use in developing network
software.

Included on the IBM PC Network Adapter card in ROM is an extensive
amount of programming instructions known as NETBIOS. The middle
portion of Figure 7.8 illustrates the hardware and software components of
an IBM PC LAN network.

When the IBM Token-Ring Network was introduced, NETBIOS was
removed from the adapter card and incorporated as a separate software
program which was activated from DOS. The right column of Figure 7.8

illustrates the hardware and software relationship for the IBM Token-Ring local area network. Here, the network operating system for the Token-Ring was renamed as the IBM PC LAN Program from its former name of the IBM PC Network Program.

Due to the standardization of file and record locking under DOS 3.1, any multi-user software program written for DOS 3.1 will execute on any LAN that supports this version of DOS. Although DOS 3.1 supports many networking functions, it is not a networking operating system. In fact, a variety of network operating systems support DOS 3.1 to include MS-NET, IBM's PC Network Program, IBM's Token-Ring Program and Novell's NetWare. This permits the user to select a third-party network operating system to use with IBM network hardware or the user can consider obtaining both third-party hardware and software to construct his or her local area network.

Servers

Some networks require the use of a dedicated server, typically a PC XT, PC AT or another fixed disk system, which means no local processing can be conducted on that device. In comparison, other networks operate with a nondedicated server, which means that local processing can be conducted concurrently with server operations.

Servers can be further categorized as disk servers or file servers. A disk server is the simplest form of server and is basically a fixed disk that can be partitioned into volumes. Each volume appears to every PC user on the network as a disk drive would appear to a single user system, e.g., a disk-drive letter designator. To the individual PC user the remote disk drive operates in the same manner as if it were attached to his or her computer. When the shared disk is partitioned volumes can be allocated as private or public. Typically, each personal computer on the network will be allocated at least one private volume and access and storage of data in that volume is limited to the assigned PC. Then a network user would be insulated from the possibility of other users using or changing the data files located on their private volume. In comparison, public volumes can be shared by a number of personal computers and require more sophisticated software to prevent one user from accessing a file or a record within a file when it is already being accessed by another user. To simplify software, some local area networks only permit read only public volumes while other networks permit read/write public volumes which incorporate several types of data access permissions.

One of the major problems associated with local area networks is the limited amount of true multi-user application software available for use on such networks. Even when the network software has a file or record lockout capability to permit only one user at a time to change a file or record the application software may not have this capability. This means conflicts can easily arise in the shared use of a single-user program, forcing users to place individual copies of each program in their private volumes.

In comparison to a disk server network where the fixed disk is partitioned, a file server provides access to the entire disk to each user. Here access to the fixed disk is by individual file names. Although a file server requires more sophisticated software than a disk server, it enables two or more users to share access to any file on the disk.

7.5 IEEE 802 STANDARDS

In 1985, the 802 Committee of the Institute of Electrical and Electronic Engineers completed a set of standards for local area networks. These standards govern the access method, transmission medium and other LAN characteristics. Since the completion of the standards they have been adopted by the American National Standards Institute, the National Bureau of Standards and most LAN vendors, including IBM and AT&T.

The IEEE 802 local area network standards define several types of LANs based upon different network access control methods and types of transmission media as illustrated in Figure 7.9. The logical link control, defined as the IEEE 802.2 standard, defines the exchange of data between devices attached to an LAN to include addressing formats.

At a lower layer, the IEEE standard defines three methods of access control. IEEE 802.3 describes a physical bus structure utilizing CSMA/CD as the access method, which is essentially similar to the Xerox Ethernet LAN. The IEEE 802.4 standard defines a physical bus employing token passing as the access method. This standard has been adopted by General Motors as the data link layer of their manufacturing automation protocol (MAP). IEEE 802.5 defines a physical ring network structure employing token passing as the access method, which is equivalent to the IBM Token-Ring Network.

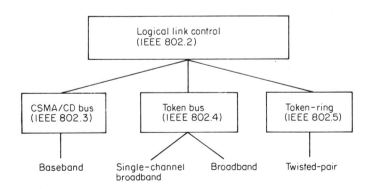

Figure 7.9 IEEE 802 LAN Standards

7.6 EXAMINING NETWORKS

Using the information previously presented in this chapter as a background in local area network operations and technology, we will now examine several such networks. Our examination is for illustrative purposes and should not be construed as an endorsement of any network product.

3COM EtherSeries

3COM's EtherSeries is a family of hardware and software products introduced in late 1982 as a microcomputer version of Ethernet. This local area network is a baseband, coaxial bus topology that employs the CSMA/CD access protocol and operates at a data rate of 10 mbps. Members of the EtherSeries include the EtherLink Interface adapter and a variety of servers as well as software products including EtherShare, EtherPrint and EtherMail.

The EtherLink adapter installs directly into an expansion slot in the system unit of a PC and provides the electrical and mechanical connection to the Ethernet cable. Unlike other Ethernet based networks, 3COM's adapter board contains a transceiver that permits its attachment to either RG-58 or RG-11 coaxial cable. The former cable is an optional and thinner version of the standard RG-11 Ethernet cable and represents a more economical method of interconnecting geographically localized networks where cable segments are under 300 meters. The thicker RG-11 cable supports cable segments up to 1000 feet in length and through the use of repeaters the maximum range of the network can be extended to 2.5 kilometers.

Several different types of network servers are supported by 3COM's EtherSeries. For networks with a limited number of workstations which in a typical environment is eight or less, a PC XT or AT can be used as the network server. For networks containing 9–30 workstations, the utilization of an Altos 850 microcomputer is recommended, while for networks with 30 or more workstations 3COM provides a Digital Equipment Corporation VAX minicomputer for the network server.

Both dedicated and non-dedicated servers are supported by the EtherShare software which partitions disk drives among network users on a shared, public, or private basis. For small networks the ability to have a non-dedicated server means that an installation with only a few workstations does not have to obtain a separate fixed disk-based PC that cannot be used for applications. This feature makes a limited size network more practical from an economic standpoint, since it doesn't require the procurement of a separate PC XT or another fixed disk PC to support the network. Of course, a user of the non-dedicated server will experience a degradation in response time to his or her activities in proportion to the overall network activity.

The EtherShare software permits a dedicated or non-dedicated server to have its fixed disk partitioned into logical units called volumes, ranging in size from 64K bytes to 32M bytes. Thus, a 100M byte drive, for example, could be logically subdivided into five individual 20M byte disk drives. The actual number of volumes that can be created depends upon the number of workstations in the network and the size of the fixed disk available for partition.

EtherShare permits each workstation to access up to four volumes, with each volume assigned as a drive specifier similar to the manner in which PC-DOS supports drive specifiers. Thus, if one workstation has two floppy diskettes those drives are A: and B:, the workstation can be linked to drives C:, D:, E:, and F:, which would represent shared fixed disk volumes. Similarly, if the workstation is a PC XT, its local diskette is A: and its local fixed disk is C:, while volumes D:, E:, F:, and G: can be assigned to the workstation as shared volumes. Figure 7.10 illustrates the volume assignments for a typical EtherSeries installation of four PCs, utilizing one PC as a non-dedicated server. Note that volumes C:, D:, E: and F: represent fixed disk partitions that can be assigned to all four PC users while volumes A: and B: represent local diskette drives that are not shared among users.

Under EtherShare volumes on the fixed disk can be public, private or shared. Access can be further restricted by assigning a password to each volume. If a public volume has no password it can only be accessed in a read-only mode, whereas, if it has a password assigned to it, workstations needing access to that volume must first supply the password.

A private volume can only be accessed by its creator when it has no password. If a password is assigned to a private volume, then any user on the network can access it for a read or write operation assuming they supply the appropriate password; however, access is limited to one user at a time.

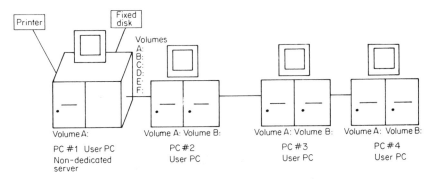

Volumes C:, D:, E: and F: represent fixed disk partitions that can be assigned to an individual work-station as a public, private or shared volume.

Figure 7.10 EtherSeries Volume Assignment

Volumes C:, D:, E: and F: represent fixed disk partitions that can be assigned to an individual workstation as a public, private or shared volume

Access to a shared volume for both read and write modes is available to all network users who know the password and the shared volume can be accessed simultaneously by more than one user. Due to the ability to permit multiple concurrent access, only application programs that are designed for concurrent access should be placed on a shared volume. Such application programs employ a file or record locking scheme that enables data to be changed in an orderly manner.

EtherShare contains a series of commands that can be employed by users to log into and out of servers, create or delete EtherShare volumes and network users, modify user access and volume parameters, display directories of users and perform other network-related activities. Network users can be given access to all commands or a subset of available commands, the latter enabling the network to be set up so that only the network manager or appropriate personnel have access to the full list of commands and the functions that result from issuing those commands.

In general EtherShare commands are self-explanatory and easy to use. As an example, a PC user would use the CREATE command to establish a new EtherShare volume and the LINK command to establish a connection between a standard DOS drive and a desired EtherShare volume.

EtherPrint

To enable printers to be shared, 3COM offers a software program known as EtherPrint for use on its network. EtherPrint contains a spooling feature that enables print requests to be temporarily stored on a disk until a printer is ready. In addition, EtherPrint produces page divider sheets which are used to separate one week's printout from another. Since data to be printed is spooled to a disk when the printer is busy, it frees the computer for other tasks. In comparison, other networks that provide shared access to printers without spooling capability will cause the PC requesting a printing operation to become inoperative until its print request is serviced.

EtherMail

An interactive electronic mail system known as EtherMail can be added to 3COM's EtherSeries local area network. Under EtherMail, messages are first directed to the file server, which functions as a post office. If multiple file servers are contained in the network the software will provide automatic addressing, eliminating the user from requiring to know which file server is responsible for a particular mail route. Once a message is placed on a server, it will be delivered whenever the destination user opens his or her mail folder. Since the file server and each PC must communicate with one another, EtherMail consists of two software modules, one which is placed on the server and the other which resides on each PC in the network. The

PC version contains an editor for controlling message composition as well as routines for the transmission and reception of messages.

Fox Research 10-NET

Fox Research's 10-NET is a baseband, twisted-pair wire, bus topology local area network that employs the Ethernet access protocol.

Under 10-NET up to 32 workstations can be linked together, with workstations consisting of a mixture of individual non-shared devices and superstations. The latter term is used by 10-NET to designate fixed disk systems whose resources to include printers and files are to be shared among other members of the network.

In addition to an adapter card that must be installed in the system unit of each PC connected to the network, 10-NET includes several software programs that provide the local area network with its functionality.

Once an adapter card is installed in each PC and the wiring of the network is completed, three programs must be run to initialize 10-NET: 10-NET, LOGIN, and MOUNT. The 10-NET program is used to bring a station and its devices up on the network and its initialization process varies, depending upon whether the station is a conventional workstation or a superstation. For both types of stations one must identify the station's ID and user name, while a superstation also requires the shared devices to be identified. Additional information required for a superstation includes specifying the number of active log-ins allowed, the number of files to be open at one time and the number of shared files to be open at any one time. By the careful trial-and-error utilization of different values for the preceding items one can tune 10-NET for optimum performance based upon the typical activities conducted on one's network.

The LOGIN program is used to identify workstations or superstations to other superstations on the network. The format of this command is:

    LOGIN   [user name][,password][,node ID][,node ID...]

Thus, a workstation with the user name GIL and the predefined password XYZ would be identified to superstations INVTRY and PAYROLL by entering:

    LOGIN GIL,XYZ,INVTRY,PAYROLL

Once the preceding connection is established the MOUNT program should be used to identify the superstation devices to include fixed disk, printer, communications port and so on that each workstation wishes to use via the network.

After the three preceding programs initialize the network, the user can select from a series of 12 additional programs that Fox Research actually refers to as commands to perform other functions on the network. Since 10-NET software operates as an extension of DOS, entering each command is equivalent to running a batch file which in turn causes a program to execute. Table 7.3 lists the 10-NET 'commands' and includes a brief overview of their operational result.

One of the more interesting aspects of 10-NET is its ability to provide conversational communications between network users in addition to its electronic mail capability. The former function is obtained through the use of the CHAT command while the latter is implemented through the use of the 10MAIL command.

To use CHAT, one can press CTRL plus F10 to bring up the CHAT menu. In addition to node-to-node communications between users, CHAT can also be used as a vehicle for printer spooling control as well as for controlling commands to be processed by the network server.

7.7 IBM LOCAL AREA NETWORKS

The original IBM Corporation product offering which permits PCs to be linked together is formally called a 'cluster'; however, this product can be viewed as a low-cost and limited-functioning local area network. Two newer IBM network products, the IBM PC Network and Token-Ring Network,

Table 7.3 10-NET Commands

Command	Operation
CHAT	Permits node-to-node communications between users
LOGIN	Connects a workstation or superstation to other superstations on the network
LOGOFF	Disconnects a station from a specific superstation
10MAIL	Sends and receives electronic mail
MOUNT	Establishes a connection between a local drive device and a remote superstation device
10NET	Brings a station and its devices up on the network
NETLOG	Reports on various uses of a 10NET superstation by station in the network
NETSTAT	Displays the current status of the network
NETSU	Sets or reports on security rules for a particular superstation
10NEWS	Provides information of general interest to the entire network community
UNMOUNT	Disconnects a previously mounted device located at a superstation from the station that has mounted it
10SPOOL	Causes data to be printed to be spooled to disk if the printer is busy
LOCATE	Lists files that match a search argument
LOCAL	Establishes individual calendars for network users
10CALMAS	Sets up a master calendar for controlling all individual calendars

provide users with a much more sophisticated networking capability although the increased sophistication requires a higher cost to obtain. In this section we will examine all three IBM networking products to obtain an understanding of the utilization and constraints associated with each product.

IBM Cluster

The IBM Cluster is a CSMA/CA access, bus topology local area network designed to operate on coaxial cable at a 375 kbps data rate. This product obtains its name from the fact that the hardware and software required permit the end-user to 'link' a number of IBM PCs together to form an interconnected work group or 'cluster'.

The IBM Cluster can be used with or without a disk server station contained on the network. Without a disk server, workstations on the network can send and receive messages and files; however, they cannot share storage on a common fixed disk.

When a fixed disk server is added to the network the other workstations can share the use of up to 20M bytes of storage. This storage limit results from the fact that only one server is supported by the Cluster. The fixed disk can be subdivided to public and private volumes. The public volumes are limited to a read only mode while the private volumes support read/write operations for each station in the cluster.

The IBM Cluster hardware consists of two different types of adapter cards. One adapter card is designed for attachment to the PCjr while the other type of adapter can be installed in the system unit of any other member of the IBM PC series. Due to the power constraints of the PCjr, that computer cannot contain a disk drive when it is used with the Cluster adapter. Since the Cluster Program will automatically download DOS from the disk server into a PCjr, this constraint does not represent a problem as the network permits the PCjr as well as other members of the Cluster to access programs and files from both public and private volumes.

The Cluster's software, marketed as the Cluster Program, contains a series of menu-driven programs to enable users to easily initialize the network. In addition to partitioning the fixed disk into public and private volumes the Cluster Program supports file transfers between stations within the Cluster and the transmission of messages to include broadcasts to all stations.

Although the Cluster supports up to 64 users, normally 6 to 10 workstations represents a more common configuration. Another constraint is the fact that the main coaxial cable must be less than 1000 meters in length and the connecting cable between each PC and the main cable cannot exceed 5 meters in length.

The absence of file and record locking capability, password protection and several commonly encountered functions on other local area networks to include printer sharing makes the IBM Cluster unsuitable for many organizations. For organizations that do not need such capability, this low-cost network may be a suitable alternative to more sophisticated and costly offerings from both IBM and other vendors.

IBM PC Network

The IBM PC Network was announced in August 1984, approximately 6 months after the IBM Cluster, and represents a more sophisticated local area networking capability than the vendor's initial product. The PC Network is a 2 mbps broadband coaxial cable system that employs the CSMA/CD access method.

Standard 75 ohm coaxial cable similar to standard CATV cable is used for the transmission medium of the network. Since this cable has a bandwidth of approximately 400 MHz of frequency and the actual data flows over a channel 6 MHz, it is possible to add voice, video and other information onto the PC Network cable.

The PC Network is designed to link all members of the PC series except the PCjr. Each PC connects to the common coaxial cable via a network adapter card that is manufactured for IBM by Sytek, Inc. Each adapter card contains two Intel microprocessors and associated circuitry that provide the card's intelligence. The Intel 80188 microprocessor operates the set of protocols known as LocalNet/PC. The LocalNet/PC protocols were originally developed by Sytek for that vendor's LocalNet 40 LAN, which was an expensive network designed for the minicomputer market. The second major chip on the adapter is an Intel 82586 chip that controls the CSMA/CD access method. Included on the adapter card is a modem that modulates and demodulates an analog carrier through frequency shift keying. Data is transmitted from a PC at 219 MHz and is received at 50.75 MHz. The former frequency is referred to as the forward direction frequency while the latter is known as the reverse direction frequency.

One of the problems associated with broadband transmission on coaxial cable is the fact that high frequencies tend to attenuate more than lower frequencies. This means that incorrect cable lengths and uneven signal attenuation, which is called cable tilt, can cause a broadband network to fall out of tune.

In most broadband networks, an RF generator is used to transmit signals through a range of high to low frequencies to a receiver to determine if a network is out of tune and, if so, by how much so that adjustments can be made to the network. IBM has eliminated the requirement to sweep and tune its network by employing fixed lengths of coaxial cable that are prebalanced with a built-in tilt compensation. Due to this design, connections are limited to certain combinations of 25, 50 100 and 200-foot coaxial cable segments that have built-in tilt compensation. An example of the constraints this can involve can be visualized by a requirement to connect two PCs 800 feet apart. The IBM *Technical Reference Manual* permits only four 200-foot segments to be used for this cabling requirement. While this may appear insignificant, it does preclude the use of eight 100-foot segments or three 200-foot segments and two 100-foot segments as well as other possible combinations, with the result that the planning and modification of a network requires careful consideration of the cable lengths.

In addition to the adapter card that is required for each PC on the network, a frequency translator or 'head-end' is required. Known as the Network Translator Unit, this device receives all signals transmitted on the network at 219 MHz and translates them to 50.75 MHz. The PC Network requires one Network Translator Unit which can support up to 72 PC workstations. Although the PC Network is capable of supporting 1000 or more devices, under the terms of the marketing agreement between Sytek and IBM it appears that installations requiring more than 72 interfaces will be referred to Sytek. In addition, customized equipment may be necessary to support such non-data services to include voice and video.

Hardware requirements

In addition to one PC Network adapter card required for each PC workstation, a minimum configured network requires one IBM PC Network Translator Unit (NTU) or head-end for the entire network and one or more cable kits to interconnect the various workstations to one another and the NTU. The NTU is provided with an eight-way splitter, which limits the number of workstations that can be interconnected to one another to eight in a minimum system as illustrated in Figure 7.11. Each PC in turn can be located up to 200 feet from the splitter. Thus, the maximum distance covered by a minimum system is 400 feet.

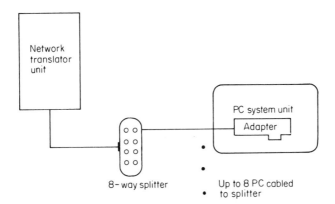

Figure 7.11 Minimum IBM PC Network

The minimum IBM PC Network supports the interconnection
of eight PCs through an eight-way splitter

294

To expand the PC Network to support a spanned distance in excess of 400 feet or to link more than eight PCs into the network requires the addition of one or more IBM Base Expander Kits and a combination of short-, medium- and long-distance cabling kits.

Figure 7.12 illustrates how access to the Network Translator Unit is expanded to additional PCs through the installation of one or more base expanders. First a T-connector is installed between the eight-way splitter and the NTU, permitting the first base expander to be connected to the network. The base expander in effect is another type of eight-way splitter to which one can connect a short (100-foot), medium (400-foot) or long (800-foot) distance kit. Since up to eight eight-way splitters can be connected to the base expander a maximum of 64 additional workstations can be added to the minimum network configuration, resulting in the capability of the PC Network to support a maximum of 72 workstations.

IBM PC Network Program

The IBM PC Network Program was introduced with the PC Network and is the network-operating system which enables users to share the use of printers, disks and communicate with other computers on the network. To

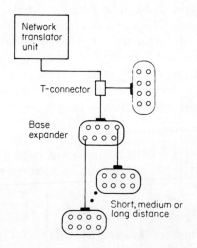

Figure 7.12 PC Network Expansion

Up to eight eight-way splitters can be connected to the base expander, with each splitter capable of supporting eight PCs. Thus, the PC Network can support up to 72 workstations

facilitate its use, network users can give instructions to the PC Network Program through the use of program menus or by issuing commands.

Computer and device names

Each computer attached to the network must be assigned a network name to identify it to the network. To distinguish network names from a directory and subdirectory they are prefixed with two backslashes (\\). Thus, \\GIL would reference the computer on the network assigned the name GIL, while \\GIL\DBASE would reference the directory DBASE on the computer named GIL.

Under the IBM PC Network Program, users can access shared devices once they know the network name of the computer with the shared device and the network name of the device they wish to use. Thus, if a letter-quality printer attached to the computer with the network name GIL was assigned the device name LTRPRINT, that printer could be accessed by any computer user attached to the network.

Hot key

Similarly to emulator products the PC Network Program has a 'hot key' capability which is actually a sequence of keys. By pressing the Ctrl-Alt-Break keys network users can toggle between the application they are executing and the PC Network Program.

DOS usage

Users on the PC Network can execute most DOS commands. In addition, many DOS commands that reference other PCs in the network can be issued. For example, the command:

```
COPY    PAY.DBF\\GIL\DBASE
```

results in the file PAY.DBF being copied from a default disk on one PC to the directory DBASE on another PC with the network name GIL.

PC configurations

Each personal computer using the PC Network Program can be configured in one of four ways – as a server, messenger, receiver or redirector. Table 7.4 compares the functional capabilities of each of the four PC configurations selectable with the PC Network Program. The key criterion in selecting the appropriate configuration is the hardware requirement for each configuration. As an example, a server requires one fixed disk, one diskette drive and at least 320K bytes of memory. In comparison, a redirector requires one diskette drive and 128K bytes of memory.

Table 7.4 PC Network Program PC Configurations

Function	Configuration			
	Server	Messenger	Receiver	Redirector
Send messages	Y	Y	Y	Y
Use network disks, directories and printers	Y	Y	Y	Y
Receive messages	Y	Y	Y	N
Save messages	Y	Y	Y	N
Use network hot key	Y	Y	N	N
Receive messages for other computers	Y	Y	N	N
Transfer messages to other computers	Y	Y	N	N
Share disks, directories and printers on local PC	Y	N	N	N

Network commands

Over 45 network commands are included in the PC Network Program. Similar to DOS commands, many network commands include optional parameters and switches. In addition, some network commands can be abbreviated. Table 7.5 lists 14 of the more common PC Network Program commands. As an example of the use of a parameter and switch in a network command, consider a network where it is desired to dedicate a PC XT as a server. Entering the command:

NET START SRV GIL/TS1:00

results in no time-slice increments being allocated to local applications on the server named GIL, in effect dedicating that computer as a pure server. This means that other users accessing the server will receive improved responses; however, the server will be incapable of operating application programs concurrently with the server function.

IBM Token-Ring network

Similar to the PC Network, every PC in a Token-Ring network must have an adapter card installed in an expansion slot in the system unit of a member of the IBM PC series. The original PC adapter card introduced with the Token-Ring product announcement in October 1985 has been supplemented by a second offering known as the Adapter II. Containing double the 8K byte buffer of the original adapter, the Adapter II is designed to provide increased performance for network servers since its additional memory enables the Adapter II to retrieve data from the network quicker than the original adapter.

Table 7.5 Common PC Network Commands

NET – starts PC LAN Program menus

NET CONTINUE – restarts PC LAN on computer after a NET PAUSE

NET ERROR – displays a list of network errors that have occurred on your computer

NET FILE – displays current users and current record locks for a file as well as closing a file that is opened by other computers or that has locked records

NET FORWARD – forward or stops forwarding messages sent to your computer or another computer

NET LOG – starts/stops placing messages you receive into a specified device or file or displays the status of logging

NET NAME – allows additional names for which you want to receive messages to be displayed

NET PAUSE – temporarily stops LAN functions on your computer

NET PRINT – permits you to send a file to a printer you are sharing with another network user or to a network printer you are using

NET SEND – permits you to send messages to other users or all users

NET SEPARATOR – permits you to control whether or not a separator page is printed at the beginning of your print file

NET SHARE – permits you to let other computers from using your devices or directories or stop them from doing so

NET START – begins the PC LAN

NET USE – permits you to specify a device or a directory on a network computer that you want to use or stop using or to list the network devices you're using

---

Topology

As previously mentioned, the Token-Ring network can actually be considered as a star–ring configuration since personal computers are connected to a multistation access unit (MAU) and MAUs are then connected to one another to form larger networks. Up to eight PCs can be connected to one MAU as illustrated in the left portion of Figure 7.13.

Two Token-Ring networks can be connected together by a bridge, so the two networks can logically function as one larger network. As illustrated in the middle of Figure 7.13, a PC AT can be used as a bridge. When used as a bridge, the PC AT has two Token-Ring Adapter II cards installed in its system unit. In addition, a special Token-Ring Network Bridge Program must be obtained and the PC AT must be dedicated to operating this program.

A variety of Token-Ring connectivity options are marketed by IBM which permits PCs on a Token-Ring network to be connected to IBM mainframes and System/36 minicomputers. The right portion of Figure 7.13 illustrates how a Token-Ring network can be connected to an IBM mainframe, such as a 43XX or 38XX computer system. In actuality, the MAU is cabled to the 3725 communications controller, with the communications controller requiring the installation of a Line Attachment Base (LAB) Type C and a

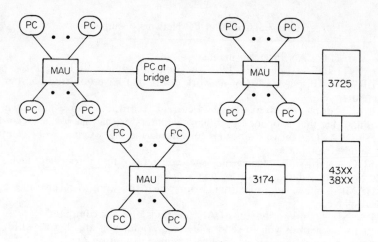

Figure 7.13 Token-Ring Connection Options

Token-ring Interface Coupler (TIC). Since up to four TICs can be installed in one LAB, up to four Token-Ring networks can be connected to one Type C LAB. Each personal computer on the Token-Ring network requiring access to the mainframe must operate the IBM PC 3270 Emulation Program Version 3.0, which results in the PC emulating a 3274 control unit with an attached 3278/9 display and 3287 printer.

In the lower portion of Figure 7.13, a Token-Ring network connection to an IBM mainframe through the use of an IBM 3174 controller is illustrated. Although six models of the 3174 controller were announced in early 1987, only three of these controllers offered Token-Ring support. Two of the three controllers were designed as remote devices, with an RS-232 connection to the 3725 communications controller. The third controller is designed to be channel attached to an IBM mainframe as illsutrated in the lower portion of Figure 7.13 and provides a gateway to the mainframe for a 'local' Token-Ring local area network.

Token and frame formats

Two types of transmission formats are supported on the Token-Ring network – token and frame. The token format as illustrated in the top of Figure 7.14 is the mechanism by which access to the ring is passed from one computer attached to the network to another device connected to the network.

Since the Token-Ring network was designed to support different types of transmission to include synchronous 3270 full-screen data transmission and asynchronous interactive transmission a priority mechanism was incorporated to account for the differences in transmission requirements between different devices. Using three bits enables priorities to range from 0 to 7. When the

Token format

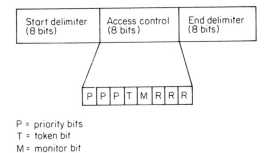

P = priority bits
T = token bit
M = monitor bit
R = reservation bits

Frame format

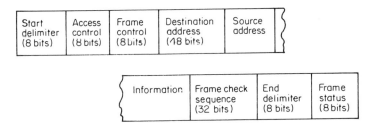

Figure 7.14 Token and Frame Formats

token bit is set to 1 it indicates that a frame is on the network. Thus, a personal computer on the network must first seize a free token. Then, it can convert the token into a frame for transmitting data on the network.

The monitor bit is used to prevent a token with a priority exceeding 0 or a frame from continuously circulating on the Token-Ring. This bit is transmitted as a 0 in all tokens and frames, except for a device on the network which functions as a monitor and thus obtains the capability to inspect and modify that bit. The reservation bits enable devices on the network to request the next token to be issued at the priority level of the device.

When a token is seized the device with data to transmit develops a frame as illustrated in the lower portion of Figure 7.14. The first two bytes of the frame format in effect are the first two bytes of the token format, with the token bit now set to 1. The frame control field informs a receiving device on the network of the type of frame and how it should be buffered. Frames can be either logical link control (LLC) or reference physical link functions according to the IEEE 802.5 media access control (MAC) standard.

The destination and source addresses are each six bytes in length and identify the intended receiver and the sender of the frame. The frame check sequence field is four bytes in length and contains CRC error-checking information which covers the frame control field through the information field.

The ending delimiter is a one-byte field that ends both a token and a frame. In fact, when a token is seized its end delimiter becomes the frame-end delimiter. Finally, the frame status field is used by a receiving device to indicate that it successfully copied information from a frame transmitted to it. By the receiver modifying this byte the sender receives information concerning the receiver's status.

Medium variations

Both low-cost unshielded twisted pair and IBM Cabling System Type 9 cable can be used to interconnect personal computers on the Token-Ring network. Table 7.6 compares the operational capability of the Token-Ring based upon the two types of medium that can be used. Since previously installed unshielded twisted pair may have many splices, the Token-Ring's 4 mbps signal can be significantly degraded when this medium is used unless one has prior knowledge about the condition of the wiring or uses new wiring.

Due to IBM's emphasis upon providing a variety of connectivity options for the Token-Ring network, this network can be considered to represent IBM's future networking strategies. In fact, although the Cluster and PC Network may still be supported for a while, it appears that those earlier products will shortly be replaced by the Token-Ring network.

Zero-slot LAN

In concluding this chapter, we will focus attention upon an alternative to conventional local area networks. Known as a zero-slot or a software-driven LAN, this networking product consists of one or more null modem cables which are used to interconnect two or more IBM PCs via their serial COM ports. Since this vendor's software drives the network via the computer's

Table 7.6 Operational Capability and Transmission Media

Operational capability	Unshielded twisted pair	IBM cabling system Type 9 cable
Capacity	72 devices	260 devices
Distance	about 300–600 feet	about 1000 feet
Speed	4 mbps	4 mbps
Attenuation	60 dB/km at 4 MHz (2 wiring closets maximum)	22 dB/1km at 4 MHz (8 wiring closets maximum)

COM ports, no network adapter cards are required to be inserted into the system expansion slots of the computers linked together, hence the term zero-slot LAN.

One of the more popular zero slot LANs is LANLink™ from The Software Link of Atlanta, GA. LANLink is a 'star' topology network where one computer is designated as a server, whose disks and printers are shared by up to 16 satellite computers. In addition, any satellite computer on a LANLink can operate as a server, which in turn can be used to service other satellite computers. This permits users to construct a star topology which branches into a tree or ring topology.

Since LANLink transfers data at a relatively low rate of 115.2 kbps, its support capability is limited to requirements for the interconnection of small numbers of personal computers. Although some features of more costly conventional LANs, such as electronic mail, are not included in LANLink, its software incorporates other features that are missing from most conventional LANs. One example of a software feature missing from many conventional LANs is LANLink's ability to redirect printer output on one server to another server.

With the cost of a zero-slot LAN one-fifth to one-tenth the cost of a conventional LAN, they deserve consideration from users who have a requirement to interconnect a small number of personal computers together.

CHAPTER EIGHT

Reviewing Networking Strategies

The objective of this chapter is to review the primary methods whereby IBM PCs and compatible personal computers can be integrated into a corporate data communications network. Using the information presented in previous chapters of this book as a foundation, the personal computer networking strategies discussed as separate entities will be appropriately grouped to provide the reader with an indication of the networking alternatives he or she should consider to satisfy organizational requirements.

Stand-alone workstation

The most elementary networking strategy is to use the personal computer as a stand-alone workstation, providing each device with an asynchronous communications adapter and a communications software program. This will permit the personal computer to be used for such functions as word processing and spreadsheet analysis, while providing the capability to transmit and receive information between personal computers and host processors on an as-required basis. Depending upon the type of network accessed and the communications software used, one may be able to communicate with a mainframe computer on a full-screen basis or access an information utility or mainframe on a line-by-line teletype basis. The typical stand-alone utilization of personal computers is illustrated in Figure 8.1

Currently, the stand-alone personal computer configuration is the most frequently employed for accessing a communications network. In this configuration, access to the corporate network is primarily via asynchronous dial-up communications. If a file-transfer capability is included in the emulator package, the company's host processor can be used as a store and forward mechanism for personal computer to personal computer file transfers. This permits the existing corporate communications network to be used to indirectly link personal computers together.

Although the stand-alone workstation is an economical method to link personal computers from a communications hardware and software perspective, one must have some type of 'Mail' system on one's host processor or develop a standard operating procedure to govern information transfer between PCs when the mainframe is used as a centralized repository.

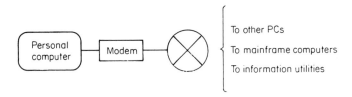

Figure 8.1 Using the PC as a Stand-alone Device

As a stand-alone workstation, each PC usually requires an asynchronous communications adapter and modem to access other PCs, mainframe computers and information utilities

This insures that the recipient can receive data from the originator. Since teletype emulation software does not emulate specific terminals, the personal computer may not be able to be used with certain host-processor application programs that are screen oriented and use specific command codes to control the terminal's display.

In Figure 8.2, the methods for obtaining line-by-line and full-screen access to a mainframe based upon the type of communications software operating in an IBM PC are illustrated. Assuming a TTY emulator is used, access to a mainframe is obtainable only on a line-by-line basis. If a full-screen terminal emulator communications program is obtained, such as a VT100 emulator, there are several methods whereby full-screen access to the mainframe can be established. First, a packet network could be used to obtain both a data transportation facility and a protocol conversion facility. If the packet network does not perform protocol conversion one could use either a stand-alone protocol converter attached to the organization's mainframe or a software program on the mainframe to operate in conjunction with the software operating on the personal computer.

Shared workstation

Although a stand-alone configuration precludes the sharing of such peripherals as hard disks, modems and printers when personal computers are located at a distinct geographical area, such peripherals can be shared if the computers are clustered with two or more devices at one location. When such situations arise, an elementary fallback switch can be employed to share the use of a common printer or modem between two personal computers as illustrated in Figure 8.3.

FBS – fallback switch

When peripherals such as a modem are shared among two or more PCs through the utilization of a fallback switch only one PC can access a shared peripheral at a time.

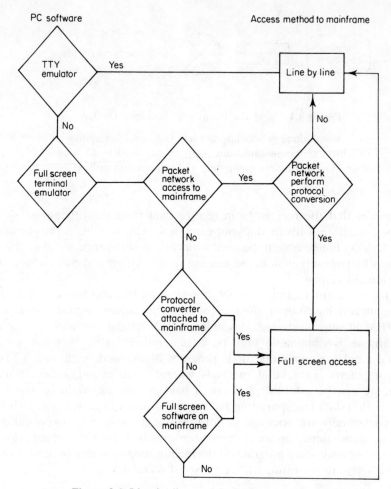

PC software   Access method to mainframe

Figure 8.2 Line-by-line and Full-screen Access

Using a combination of fallback switches that cost approximately $100 per unit two personal computers can share common peripherals, such as printers, plotters or modems, as illustrated in Figure 8.3. This configuration permits each personal computer to communicate similarly to a stand-alone device; however, the cost of peripherals is distributed among two or more systems. The advantages and disadvantages of stand-alone personal computers that share peripherals as illustrated are similar to individual stand-alone devices previously discussed. The only difference results in the sharing mechanism used. If each personal computer has an individual modem, then a shared peripheral stand-alone unit will function similarly to an individual stand-alone personal computer with respect to communications capability.

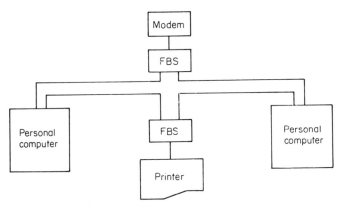

FBS – fallback switch

Figure 8.3 Sharing Peripherals when Clustered

When communications access is shared through the use of a fallback switch, only one personal computer can communicate at any one time. Obviously, this reduces the number of network entry points one has to provide for such computers to access the corporate network.

3270 access

A more sophisticated networking strategy is to use the PC as a 3270 type terminal replacement. Although the most common method to obtain 3270 access is by the addition of a synchronous communications adapter card into the system unit of a PC and the use of a 3270 type terminal software emulator, one can also use a protocol converter, install specialized software on one's mainframe computer or employ the services of a value-added carrier to obtain this transmission capability.

Figure 8.4 illustrates the primary methods whereby an IBM PC or compatible personal computer can gain access to a 3270 network on a full-screen basis. Since each of the access methods illustrated is dependent upon the prior installation of hardware and software products an organization's existing network structure normally has a large bearing upon the access method or methods selected.

Due to the variety of hardware and software offered to enable 3270 access, PCs can obtain such access as an individual terminal or through a connection to a cluster controller. For both methods, the primary advantage of 3270 access is the inherent ability of the personal computer to interface with the applications programs on a full-screen basis as well as the ability of the operator to use multiple keys on the personal computer to generate unique 3270 key codes that the application program uses in its operations.

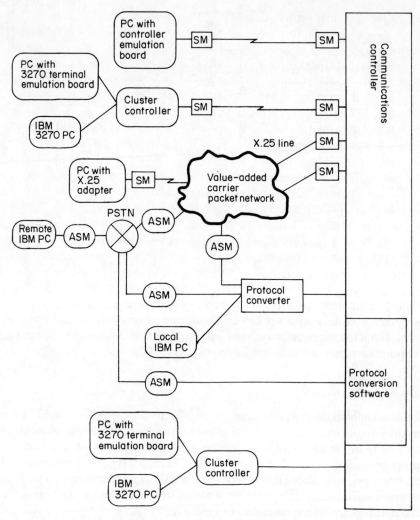

Figure 8.4 3270 Access Methods

Another advantage of 3270 access includes the ability to replace 3270 type terminal devices with a personal computer. This provides the user with local processing capability as well as the ability to transfer files. In comparison, a 3278 or 3279 terminal lacks both processing capability and file-transfer capability.

If 3270 access is accomplished via a combination of hardware and software, such as the installation of an adapter board in the system unit of an IBM

PC or the use of a protocol converter, one must also add an asynchronous communications adapter, modem, telephone line, and an interactive TTY emulator program if direct access to information utilities and other personal computers that transmit data asynchronously on a line-by-line basis is required. In comparison, if 3270 access is accomplished through a packet network that performs the data conversion, one can use the asynchronous communications adapter, modem, telephone line and emulator program to also access information utilities and other personal computers when 3270 access is not required, resulting in a degree of saving in hardware and software. This saving results from the fact that the packet network will perform the required protocol conversion, permitting the personal computer to use a common asynchronous communications adapter to access the organization's mainframe through the packet network as well as any required information utilities. Normally, the only software requirement for 3270 access through a packet network is for a specific terminal emulator, such as a VT 100 emulator program. Since some software emulator programs incorporate a simple line-by-line transmission option into the program, the program can also be used to access information utilities and other personal computers as well as the packet network for 3270 access. Then the personal computer user only has to obtain one communications program and asynchronous communications adapter to to obtain both 3270 access and the ability to access information utilities and other PCs.

Local area network

Another networking strategy being considered by many companies is the integration of personal computers into a local area network. When equipped with an appropriate hardware controller and software diskette, the personal computer becomes another network station on a local area network. This permits any personal computer on the network to communicate with any other network station to include peripheral devices, other personal computers and host processors as illustrated in Figure 8.5. Currently, the cost of linking personal computers into a local area network varies between $800 and $2000 per device. As an alternative to conventional LANs, users can consider the use of a zero slot LAN as previously described in Chapter 7. Doing so could reduce the cost of linking personal computers to approximately $150 per computer.

The primary advantage of a local area network is the capability to interconnect numerous devices via a common cable. This permits the sharing of peripherals among several network stations as well as the sharing of common information throughout the network. Since the cost per connection exceeds the cost of most dot-matrix printers, the economics of this networking strategy is, at best, marginally suitable for the sharing of low-cost personal-computer peripherals. Although a great deal of literature has been published concerning the electronic mail capability of some local area networks, unless

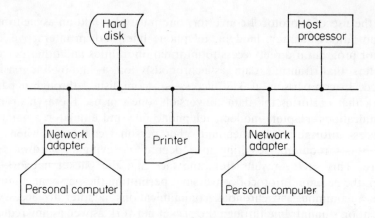

Figure 8.5 Using the Personal Computer as a Local Area Network Station

Although the local area network provides each PC on the network access to other workstations and devices a variety of software incompatibility problems, lack of a gateway and other constraints may preclude its efficient operation.

a gateway exists to enter the network from remote sites, the electronic mail capability of the network will remain localized. Since many vendor interface offerings are limited to only one type of personal computer, the use of a local area network may also be localized to a specific personal computer. Even if the local area network includes a gateway to enable the personal computers on the network to communicate with a host connected to the network, the personal computers may not be compatible with certain applications software programs. This is again due to the command codes of the personal computer differing from those codes used by the application program.

Summary

The governing factor for the most appropriate networking strategy is the communications application environment in which the personal computer is to be used. As indicated, there is no preferred networking strategy. What there is is an appropriate network strategy that can fulfil the communications application requirement of the personal computer in an economical and efficient manner.

To obtain an appreciation of how an organization's existing network structure and the applications requirement govern the selection of a networking strategy, consider the following examples. If one only desires to access an information network, the stand-alone strategy will suffice. If in addition to accessing an information network it is desired to replace an existing network terminal with a personal computer and the personal computer is to be located near a control unit, the use of an asynchronous communications adapter in one expansion slot and a terminal emulator board in a second expansion slot could satisfy this dual requirement. Here the asynchronous communications adapter could be connected to a modem to obtain access to an information network while the terminal emulator board could be connected to the control unit via coaxial cable to obtain access to the corporate mainframe.

As discussed, there is a large number of hardware and software products that can be used to enable personal computers to communicate on local area networks as well as with mainframes, information utilities and other personal computers. Prior to selecting a communications strategy the application or applications that the personal computer is to perform must be defined. Next, a review of the organization's existing data communications network must be performed, to determine both devices and software which might be available to use for personal computer communications support. Using this information as well as knowledge of the networking options presented in this book will then provide the reader with the ability to examine the variety of networking strategies that can be used to satisfy his or her current networking requirements.

Index